THE BOYHOOD CONSCIOUSNESS OF CHRIST

THE BOYHOOD CONSCIOUSNESS OF CHRIST

A Critical Examination
of Luke ii. 49

BY

REV. P. J. TEMPLE, S.T.L.

WIPF & STOCK · Eugene, Oregon

Wipf and Stock Publishers
199 W 8th Ave, Suite 3
Eugene, OR 97401

The Boyhood Consciousness of Christ
A Critical Examination of Luke ii.49
By
ISBN 13: 978-1-60608-503-5
Publication date 7/21/2009
Previously published by Macmillan Co., 1922

Nibil Obstat
   ARTHURUS J. SCANLAN, S.T.D.
             Censor Librorum
Imprimatur
  ✠ PATRITIUS J. HAYES, D.D.
       Archiepiscopus Neo-Eboraci

NEW YORK, June 2, 1922

PREFACE

EVER since Christianity presented itself for acceptance by mankind, questions of Christology have held a foremost place in religious research and discussion, and necessarily so, since the nature and personality of the Author of a religion claiming to be ecumenical and exclusive compel the attentive study of men interested in religious thought and life. The present generation has not been an exception in regard to the importance attached to these fundamental questions. Rather, in this respect it has set a new highwater mark. For while the fifth century is generally regarded as the golden age of christological controversy, yet, from the point of view of the number and variety of the scholars interested and of the individuality and diversity of the results reached, the last half century has had no parallel in the history of Christianity.

In these questions of Christology the ultimate determinant, the final test to which every student must come, is Christ's own mind as expressed in His words and in His manner of acting; everything that He says or does, either directly or indirectly to reveal His self-consciousness, is of the first importance; whatever be the method pursued in attempting a solution of a christological problem, one cannot evade the query, What did He say about Himself? Then, closely connected with the questions of His self-consciousness is that of its origin. When and how did it begin? Did He possess it from His earliest years? Or was there for Him, as for every normal child, a gradual unfolding of reason and of the consciousness of His relation to God? Or was it only in mature manhood, when on the threshold of His public career, that the consciousness of His mission and all that it implied flashed upon Him? Or was its coming rather like that of dawning day, at first dim, then steadily growing into fulness of light and culminating in the brilliant clarity of the noonday?

These important questions constitute one of the most popular of modern problems of the life of Christ. Speaking generally, in non-Catholic circles it is held that Jesus began His life "ignorant of His nature and destiny, an unthinking infant";[1] that at a certain point, by no means agreed upon, His consciousness dawned upon Him, and that it was subject to growth and development. And many pages of modern works are given over to the attempt to explain naturally the origin and to trace the development of Jesus' consciousness. The result has been a great diversity of opinion, as a glance at the chapter on the modern views will show. Failure to agree on so important a question affecting, as it does, our conception of Him for the first thirty years of His life, should arouse grave concern, and any effort to eliminate diversity and to establish the truth cannot be altogether unwelcome.

As in all questions of theological import, so regarding the present one, the final court of appeal is for the Catholic, the authority of the Church. But there is nothing to prevent him any more than another student from envisaging the consciousness of Christ as a scientific problem as well, to be treated according to the laws of historical criticism; and when so approached the solution is to be found along one path, the careful investigation of the historical evidence. But, unfortunately we are confronted by the fact that the historical data for the problem are meager, wherefore there is all the more necessity for exceptionally careful scrutiny. The canonical Gospels preserve only one saying of Christ outside His public ministry. The only occasion when Jesus breaks the silence of the first thirty years of His life is when in answer to His mother's question, why He had tarried in Jerusalem and caused the "parents" three days of anxiety and sorrow, He said in boyish accent: "Why did you seek me? Did you not know that in the (things) of My Father I must be?" (Τί ὅτι ἐζητεῖτέ με; οὐκ ᾔδειτε ὅτι ἐν τοῖς τοῦ Πατρός μου δεῖ εἶναί με; Luke ii. 49.) This saying of the twelfth year, in which His relation to God is expressed by the phrase, "My Father," is the all-important one for the problem of the origin and development of Jesus' consciousness. Views and theories must be based on it. In addition to the fact that it furnishes the saying in which a certain relationship to God is ex-

[1] Ramsay, The Education of Christ, 31.

pressed, the narrative of the "lost" Christ in the Temple deserves close attention for other reasons. It not only represents Him both in His words and in His actions as taking a certain attitude towards His "parents," but as with a few strokes of a brush, it also depicts an occurrence among the learned Rabbis of Jerusalem. These, too, deserve close attention because they reflect the consciousness of the twelve-year-old Christ. The present work is an attempt to examine critically all the elements of the Gospel incident, in particular the words of the Boy Jesus, to see if they constitute the solid basis for a theory of His consciousness.

Throughout the work a term is used which needs exact definition. Because of the variety of content given in the modern world to the title "Son of God" as applied to Christ, and to the corresponding term, Divine Sonship, I have decided for the sake of clearness to use the term, real Divine Sonship, in the sense of metaphysical Divine Sonship, that is, the identity of the ego in Jesus with the Second Person of the Blessed Trinity, the only-begotten Son of God, the eternal Word made flesh.

There remains the pleasing duty to express sincere thanks to all who have helped me; to Dr. Henry Schumacher, Professor of New Testament in the Catholic University, who supervised the work; to Dr. Franz Coeln, Professor of Sacred Scripture, and to Dr. Charles F. Aiken, Professor of Apologetics, for valuable suggestions; to Dr. Edwin Ryan of New York, for carefully reading and correcting the manuscript before it reached the printer; and to Mr. A. S. Freidus, Chief of the Jewish Division of the New York Public Library, through whose kind assistance much important literature was procured.

THE AUTHOR.

TABLE OF CONTENTS

SECTION I
EARLY PERIOD OF THE HISTORY OF THE QUESTION

CHAPTER
I. THE FATHERS ON LUKE ii. 49   PAGE
    1. The Greek Fathers 3
    2. The Latin Fathers 10
II. OTHER EVIDENCE OF THE VIEW OF THE EARLY CHURCH
    1. Further Evidence in the Fathers and Texts . . . 13
    2. The Apocryphal Gospels of the Childhood . . . 18
III. CONFLICTING HERETICAL OPINIONS 23

SECTION II
LATER PERIOD OF THE HISTORY OF THE QUESTION

IV. FROM THE FATHERS TO THE RISE OF MODERN RATIONALISM
    1. From the Eighth to the Twelfth Century 29
    2. From the Thirteenth to the Eighteenth Century . 32
V. THE MODERN VIEWS
    1. "Ordinary Israelitic Consciousness" 38
    2. "Special Ethical Sonship" 41
    3. "Mere Messianic Consciousness" 43
    4. "Real Divine Sonship" 45

SECTION III
PRELIMINARY QUESTIONS

VI. THE CORRECT TEXT OF LUKE ii. 49 53
VII. THE HISTORICAL TRUSTWORTHINESS OF LUKE ii. 49
    1. Luke's Early Chapters 60
    2. The Temple Episode 65
VIII. THE HISTORICAL BACKGROUND OF LUKE ii. 49
    1. Circumstances Leading to the Utterance of Jesus' First Recorded Saying 73
    2. Contemporary Jewish Conception of God's Relation to Man 81

TABLE OF CONTENTS

SECTION IV
CHRIST'S CONSCIOUSNESS AS EXPRESSED IN LUKE ii. 49

CHAPTER
IX. REAL DIVINE SONSHIP EXPRESSED IN THE FIRST RECORDED WORDS
    PAGE
  1. The Study of the Words "My Father" . . . 91
  2. The Other Words of the Text 98
  3. The Contrast with the Preceding Verse . . . 104

X. MESSIANIC CONSCIOUSNESS INCLUDED IN CHRIST'S FIRST SELF-INTERPRETATION 114

SECTION V
JESUS' FIRST RECORDED WORDS AND THE IMMEDIATE CONTEXT

XI. THE SCENE AMONG THE DOCTORS
  1. Word Scrutiny of Luke ii. 47, 48 (a) 121
  2. Explanation of Luke ii. 46 128

XII. THE "PARENTS" AND THE "SON"
  1. Their Attitude towards Each Other 135
  2. The Morality of the Temple Episode 143

XIII. THE CHRIST CHILD'S "WISDOM" AND "GRACE"
  1. Study of Luke ii. 40 and 52 151
  2. A Significant Silence in These Verses 161

SECTION VI
JESUS' FIRST RECORDED WORDS AND THE REMOTE CONTEXT

XIV. THE WHOLE LUCAN ACCOUNT OF CHRIST
  1. The Infancy Section 169
  2. The Beginning of the Ministry 171
  3. The Public Life 177
  4. The Acts of the Apostles 179

XV. THE WHOLE NEW TESTAMENT ACCOUNT OF CHRIST
  1. St. Matthew 182
  2. St. Mark 183
  3. St. John 185
  4. St. Paul 187
  5. Christ's Sonship in the New Testament 188

CONCLUSION 192

TABLE OF CONTENTS

BIBLIOGRAPHY
    I. List of works quoted 199
    II. Selected list on Christ's Consciousness in Boyhood 221
    III. Treatises on the Infancy and Boyhood of Christ . . 222

LIST OF ABBREVIATIONS FOR PERIODICALS AND COLLECTIONS . . 229

SCRIPTURAL INDEX 231

GENERAL INDEX 239

SECTION I
EARLY PERIOD OF THE HISTORY OF THE QUESTION

THE BOYHOOD CONSCIOUSNESS OF CHRIST

CHAPTER I

THE FATHERS ON LUKE ii. 49

1. THE GREEK FATHERS

THE earliest Father whose writings contain a reference to the episode of Christ's twelfth year is Irenaeus (†202). He complains against Marcion for discarding the early section of St. Luke's Gospel,[1] and mentions among the important things, with which Luke has made us acquainted in regard to Christ, "that at twelve years of age He was left behind at Jerusalem."[2]

There is another reference of Irenaeus' of more importance. He narrates that the Marcosians used a great number of apocryphal and spurious writings, which they forged for the purpose of showing that the Father of Jesus was unknown up to the time of Christ, and was not the Creator of the Universe. And "among other things they bring forward that false and wicked story which narrates that Our Lord, when He was a Boy learning His letters, on the teacher saying to Him, as is usual, 'Pronounce Alpha,' replied (as He was bid) 'Alpha.' But when again the teacher bade Him say, 'Beta,' the Lord replied, 'Do thou first tell Me what Alpha is, and then I will tell thee what Beta is.' This they expound as meaning that He alone knew the Unknown, which He revealed under its type, Alpha."[3] Mark that Irenaeus labels the story "false and wicked," but does not object to the view that at such an early age Christ did know and reveal His Father.

---

[1] Adv. Haer. III. 14, 4; cf. I. 27, 2.
[2] Id. Haer. III. 14, 3.
[3] Adv. Haer. I. 20, 1, English Transl., A-NF I. 344-345.

4 THE BOYHOOD CONSCIOUSNESS OF CHRIST

Irenaeus goes on to say that these heretics also colored some of the Gospel texts with their views; such as the answer Jesus gave to His mother when He was twelve years of age, and he adds, ὃν οὐκ ᾔδεισαν, φασί, Πατέρα κατήγγελλεν αὐτοῖς.[1] According to this statement we see that this very early sect understood that Christ's words announced His Father, — for them the God unknown and different from the creator of the universe. This contention of theirs, Irenaeus opposes; but he does not censure them for saying that Christ's words announced God to be His Father.

The three homilies (XVIII. XIX. and XX. in Luc.) of Origen (†254), that have reference to Luke ii. 49 (excepting a few fragments preserved in the original) have come down to us only in St. Jerome's Latin translation. He uses the text to refute the heretics who say that "the Law and the Prophets did not belong to the Father of Jesus Christ." He argues thus: "Certe Jesus in templo erat, quod a Solomone constructum erat, et confitetur templum illud patris sui esse quem nobis revelavit, cujus filium esse se dixit." If it is replied that one is a good and the other is a just God, Origen rejoins "quia igitur Salvator Creatoris est Filius, in commune Patrem Filiumque laudemus, cujus lex cujus et templum est."[2] It is clear from this how Origen understood Christ's Sonship: Father and Son are equal: "in commune . . ."

The same idea expressed above is contained in a Greek fragment generally attributed to him,[3] where in an argument against the contention of the Valentinians, that the Father of Christ was not the Creator or God of the Law or of the Temple, Origen writes that Jesus was in his own (ἦν ἐν ἰδίοις ὁ Χριστός) when He said, "Did you not know, etc." The Temple belonged to Jahweh, and in it Christ could not be said to be "in His own," unless He was really the Son of God; unless God the Creator was really the Father of Christ, ὁ πατὴρ τοῦ Χριστοῦ. Therefore Origen under-

---
[1] M.PG VII. 653.
[2] M.PG XIII. 1849 (also M.PL XXVI. 260).
[3] M.PG XIII. 1852 note. This has also been ascribed to St. Cyril of Alex. (v. g. by St. Thomas, Catena aurea, ad loc. Corderius attributes it to Cyril and Geometra, Catena LXV. Pat. Gr. 74). See M.PG LXXII. 509, note. We give it under Origen because it agrees with his thought and applies to the heretics against whom he was contending. Besides it is not at all like the style of Cyril, and it is not given by J. Sickenberger in Fragmente des Cyrill von Alex. zum Lukasevangelium, Leipzig (1909) (TU XXXI. B. Ht. I. p. 65 ff.).

stood Christ to express real Divine Sonship (we mean eternal, natural, Divine Sonship). Hence it was that this text supplied him with a powerful argument against those who denied that Jesus' Father was the God of the Old Law and of the Temple. So that he emphatically states (according to the Latin version) "taking the text simply (simpliciter sentientes), we are thus armed against all heretics who deny this. Behold, the Father is declared to be the God of the Temple (ecce Pater Deus templi asseritur) hence blush for shame all who accept the Gospel of St. Luke and who despise what is written therein." [1]

The great exegete goes on to give the typical sense, which was characteristic of the school of Alexandria. He expresses the opinion that what the "parents" did not understand in Christ's words was what was typified by the material temple; namely, every good and perfect man who is the possession of the Father and has Jesus within him.[2] Even in this allegorical interpretation he emphasizes the equality of Father and Son and attributes a Divine self-consciousness to Christ.

Titus of Bostra (✝374) is very clear and direct in his interpretation. He paraphrases Jesus' words thus: "Dost thou not know, mother, what has happened? Didst thou not conceive as a virgin (οὐ παρθένος οὖσα συνέλαβες)? Why do you name Joseph My Father?"[3] So he sees the words "My Father" in Jesus' reply, contrasted with "thy Father" in Mary's question, and evidently, referring to the contrast he goes on to say: καὶ εἰσάγει Πατέρα ἀντὶ πατρός, ἀντὶ τοῦ θρεψαμένου σωματικῶς τὸν ἀληθινόν. This explicit inference, "in place of His foster father, He brings forward the true Father," places it beyond doubt that Titus understood "Father" on Jesus' lips in the real sense of the word. He is of the opinion, strange to say, that Jesus did not say, οὐκ οἴδατε (in the plural), for they all did not know; but He addresses only the Mother who alone knew of the mystery of the Virgin Birth.[4]

[1] M.PG XIII. 1851-1852.
[2] M.PG XIII. 1852. Cf. Schola in Lucam, Supplem., M.PG XVII. 324.
[3] Titus von Bostra, edit. by J. Sickenberger, 152, given in TU (2d ser.) 6 (XXI).
[4] Id. What is ascribed to Titus of Bostra in Magna Bibliotheca Veterum Patrum (Colon. Agripp. 1618), and often quoted for him, does not belong to him. This is a Catena-like compilation and "cannot be of an earlier date than the sixth century" (Bardenhewer, Patrol. 271). The following is given under our text (Tom. IV. 343): "Deus et Dominus noster humana responsione, quam dare licebat repudiata,

6 THE BOYHOOD CONSCIOUSNESS OF CHRIST

In his catechetical lectures, St. Cyril of Jerusalem (✠386), takes up the different articles of the Creed; and in the seventh instruction treating of "The Father," he says: "Let us adore the Father of Christ, the Creator of the world, the God of Abraham, Isaac, and Jacob, and to whose honor the temple was built. For we shall not tolerate the heretics who sever the Old Testament from the New, but shall believe Christ's saying concerning the temple, "Did you not know that I must be in the (things) of My Father?" With this, Cyril joins the text, "Take these things hence and make not the house of My Father a house of traffic" (John ii. 16), and concludes that in these words Christ "most clearly confessed that the former Temple in Jerusalem was the house of His own Father" (τοῦ ἑαυτοῦ Πατρὸς).¹ This word "own" (ἑαυτοῦ) indicates that the author considered the relationship to God, expressed by Christ, to be special and peculiar; indeed the whole context of this entire section on "The Father" is evidence that he held the view of real Divine Sonship.

Didymus of Alexandria, (✠395) in quoting Luke ii. 49, has ἐν τῷ οἴκῳ for ἐν τοῖς (De Trinitate, III. 20).² He does not give any comment; but the view of real Divine Sonship is implied by the context; for treating here of Christ being subject to His parents, Didymus points out it was done freely and that thereby Christ did not lay aside His royal dignity but rather shows the sublimity of His Deity (δεικνύς τὸ ὑπέροχον τῆς θεότητος).

There is abundant evidence in the writings of St. Epiphanius (✠403) to show his interpretation of Luke ii. 49. Like St. Cyril of Jerusalem, he joins the text with the words "take these things hence and make not the house of My Father a house of traffic," to prove against heretics that the God of the Old Law is the Father of Jesus;³ like Irenaeus, he gives it as one of the passages into

---

divinam attulit minime obscure, per illam ostendens, se Deum esse carne obtectum. Nam cum Deipara Virgo Josephum qui vulgo parens illius habebatur, patrem illius appellasset ipse sermonem ita excepit, ut templi Dominum hic est Deum non autem Josephum patrem suum esse planum faceret. Quandoquidem cum in Dei templo, Nesciebatis, inquit, quod in his . . ." In the quotation, the contrast in Christ's words is pointed out and the view of real Divine Sonship is clearly interpreted.

¹ M.PG XXXIII. 612.
² M.PG XXXIX. 896.
³ Adv. Haer. Lib. II. Tom. 2, Haer. 63, M.PG XLII. 93.

which heretics read their doctrine that the Father of Christ was an unknown God.¹ Refuting the doctrine of the Ebionites, that "Christ" came upon the man Jesus only in His thirtieth year when the Holy Ghost descended upon Him in the form of a dove, Epiphanius brings forward many arguments from the infancy narrative to show that "Christ was God and Man immediately from His birth of the Virgin Mary." ² In this argument he appeals to what is narrated of the twelfth year about Christ sitting among the priests and elders, and to His reply to His Mother. Concerning the latter, he says it showed "that the Temple was erected to the name of God (that is His) Father," σημαίνων, ὅτι ὁ ναὸς εἰς ὄνομα Θεοῦ Πατρὸς ᾠκοδομήθη. "Hence" (he argues) "if from His very infancy He knew the Temple and the Father (εἰ τοίνυν ἀπὸ νηπίου οἶδε τὸν ναὸν καὶ τὸν Πατέρα) Jesus was not born as mere man (ψιλὸς ἄνθρωπος) nor (only) after His thirtieth year when the form of a dove descended upon Him did He call Himself Son and Christ, but straightway He teaches that in the (things) of His Father He must be" (εὐθὺς ἐν τοῖς τοῦ Πατρὸς αὐτοῦ δεῖν αὐτὸν εἶναι ἐδίδασκεν).³ Epiphanius, thus, infers from Christ's words that He was not born as mere man, and He called Himself Son (in the real sense since He was not mere man) and Christ, before his thirtieth year.

The same stand is taken in another part of his work. In this latter place Epiphanius employs Luke ii. 49 to refute the contention that the Holy Ghost came upon Jesus only at the time of His baptism. He writes that since Jesus performed no prodigies before the miracle of Cana, "lest occasion would be given to the other heresies which say that at the Jordan Christ came upon Him in the form of a dove, in His twelfth year, as Luke expressly points out, disputing with the priests and elders, He said to His mother, 'Did you not know . . . ,' so that there might be excluded the opinion of those who say that the Holy Ghost descended upon Him after the time of the baptism" (ἵνα πέσῃ ὁ λόγος τῶν λεγόντων, ὅτι ἀπὸ τοῦ χρόνου τοῦ βαπτίσματος κατέβη εἰς αὐτὸν τὸ Πνεῦμα τὸ ἅγιον).⁴ Here we have another indication

[1] Adv. Haer. Lib. I. Tom. 3, Haer. 34, n. 18, M.PG XLI. 620.
[2] Adv. Haer. Lib. I. Tom. 2, Haer. 30, n. 29, M.PG XLI. 456.
[3] Id. 457.
[4] Adv. Haer. Lib. II. Tom 1, Haer. 51, n. 20, M. PG XLI. 925.

8 THE BOYHOOD CONSCIOUSNESS OF CHRIST

that Epiphanius understood Christ's words to express real Divine Sonship.

The great defender of orthodoxy, St. Cyril of Alexandria (✠ 144), commenting on Luke ii. 49, explicitly states that "here for the first time He makes more open mention of His true Father and reveals His Divinity," 'Ενταῦθα οὖν πρώτως τοῦ ἀληθῶς Πατρὸς φανερώτερον μνημονεύει, καὶ παραγυμνοῖ τὴν ἑαυτοῦ θεότητα.[1] He goes on to bring out the meaning of the contrast between Jesus' reply and Mary's question. "His mother had said, 'Why hast thou done this to us?' He answered, 'Did you not know that I must be in the (things) of My Father?' showing He was more than human (τῶν ἀνθρωπίνων ἐπέκεινα μέτρων ἑαυτὸν ὄντα δεικνὺς) and teaching her that she had been made the handmaid of the dispensation in giving birth to Him but that He by nature and in truth was God and Son of the Heavenly Father" (φύσει δὲ καὶ ἀληθείᾳ θεὸς ἦν, καὶ Υἱὸς τοῦ ἐν οὐρανοῖς ὄντος Πατρὸς).[2]

There can be no question of this writer's position, which is also expressed in his work, De recta fide ad Reginas. When proving from St. Luke's Gospel that Christ is "the only Son and Lord," St. Cyril appeals to Luke ii. 49 as an argument for his purpose, for "Christ named the Father in heaven as His own Father," "Άθρει δὴ οὖν ὅπως ἴδιον ἑαυτοῦ Πατέρα τὸν ἐν τοῖς οὐρανοῖς ὀνομάζει.[3] In real critical style Cyril argues, "If He was only man and considered Himself no more than we are (νοούμενος καθ' ἡμᾶς) should He not have said, 'Did you not know that I must be in the (things) of the Father of all?' but He makes God His own Father (ἀλλ' ἴδιον αὐτοῦ ποιεῖται), for He alone was divinely born of God according to nature, and having become man He retained His own Father by nature, God."[4] This writer, therefore, not only favors the view that Christ expressed His real Divine Sonship and Divinity in Luke ii. 49, but more than this, he appeals to this text as an excellent argument in favor of his opinion.

Cyril's great opponent, Theodoret of Cyprus (✠458), seems to hold that, in the first recorded words, the Boy Jesus rebuked His

---

[1] In his explanation of St. Luke's Gospel, ad loc. M.PG LXXII. 509.
[2] M.PG LXXII. 509.
[3] M.PG LXXVI. 1320.
[4] Id.

mother "as her Lord."[1] In a work on the Incarnation, towards the end of a summary of the incidents of the Childhood account, he writes, Christ "attends at the temple, puts to shame the Judaic dullness, and this when only twelve years old. Having remained behind He is found and blamed by His mother. He defends Himself and quietly reveals His Divinity (ἠρέμα πως παραγυμνοῖ τὴν θεότητα); 'Do you not know,' says He, 'that I must be in the (things) of My Father,' showing that He is not alone what He appeared to the eyes to be, but He is also God (hidden in what was seen) who proceeded from the Father before all time and from all eternity" (δεικνὺς ὡς οὐ μόνον ἐστὶ τὸ ὁρώμενον, ἀλλὰ καὶ θεὸς ἐν τῷ ὁρωμένῳ κρυπτόμενος, ὑπέρχρονος καὶ προαιώνιος ἐκ τοῦ Πατρὸς προελθών).[2] From these explicit expressions, "reveals His Divinity," "showing He is not alone what He appeared to the eyes to be, but is also God," there cannot be any doubt that Theodoret infers from Christ's words strict Divinity and real Divine Sonship.[3]

To the question, then, what view the Greek Fathers hold concerning the self-consciousness of Christ as expressed in Luke ii. 49, it is to be answered that they are unanimous in understanding them as a declaration of real Divine Sonship. More than this, they nearly all employ these words to defend or demonstrate His true Divinity. Origen and Cyril of Jerusalem make use of the first recorded words to refute the heretics who contended that Jesus' Father was not the God of the Old Law. Besides using them for this purpose, Epiphanius also wields them against the Ebionites, who said that "Christ" came upon Jesus at the baptism. By these words, Cyril of Alexandria proves Christ's Divine self-consciousness, pointing out that if He thought Himself no more than we are, He would have used different words; and both he and Theodoret explicitly state that in these words Christ revealed His Divinity.

[1] M.PG LXXXIII. 144.
[2] M.PG LXXXIV. 73. This is found almost verbatim in a work on the Incarnation ascribed to St. Cyril of Alex., M.PG LXXV. 1462; but the latter part of St. Cyril's work has been shown to be spurious and to belong to Theodoret. Cf. Bardenhewer, Patrol., 363. Here Christ's words are given differently.
[3] Tischendorf (Oct. Maj. I. 439) mentions a reference to Theodoret as 5, 1063; I have not been able to verify it. A spurious work "Dialogus contra Macedonianos" (I. 19), attributed both to Theodoret and Athanasius, quotes Lk. ii. 49, without any comment (M.PG XXVIII. 1324). The text is given, ἐν τῷ οἴκῳ ... Likely, this is the reference cited by Tischendorf.

10 THE BOYHOOD CONSCIOUSNESS OF CHRIST

2. THE LATIN FATHERS

In the twenty-sixth chapter of his work, Adversus Praxeam, when showing the agreement of Matthew and Luke with John in respect to the distinct personality of the Father and the Son, Tertullian (✠250) mentions that Christ, by the first recorded words, testified from His very boyhood that He was the Son of God: "His itaque rebus quodcumque sunt, spiritu Dei et sermone et virtute, collatis in virginem, quod de ea nascitur, Filius Dei est. Hoc se et in istis Evangeliis ipse testatur statim a puero; Non scitis, inquit, quod in Patris mei me esse oportet?"[1] From a context of the Virgin Birth, and from the object of this chapter, it is clear that Tertullian understood this Divine Sonship, to which Jesus testifies from His boyhood, in the real sense.

Juvencus, who, in the year 330 or thereabouts, wrote a kind of Gospel harmony in hexameter verse, renders Luke ii. 49 as follows:

> Ille autem; Quid me tantum, quid quaeritis? inquit,
> An nondum sentis, genetrix, quod iure paternis
> Sedibus et domibus natum inhabitare necesse est?[2]

Note that Juvencus uses the word "natum" which would not suit moral Sonship but which points to real Divine Sonship as his view.

St. Ambrose (✠397) sees in Jesus' words a reference to both the Divine and the human element of Christ and implies the interpretation of real Divine Sonship. After quoting the text he adds: "There are two generations in Christ, one paternal and the other maternal; the paternal is the more divine (Paterna illa divinior); the maternal that which descended to our labor and usage, and so those things which are performed above nature, above age, above custom, are to be ascribed not to human powers but to the divine powers . . . Here the mother is censured because she demands what is human" (hic mater arguitur quia adhuc quae humana sunt exigat).[3] Ambrose goes on to point out that even at twelve years of age Christ has disciples, for the mother learns from her Son: "Sed cum hic duodecim describatur annorum, illic discipulos

---

[1] M. PL II. 189.
[2] Corp. Script. Lat. (edit. J. Huemer), XXIV. 18.
[3] Corp. Script. Lat. (edit. Schenkl), XXXII. 75.

habere doceatur, vides matrem didicisse de filio, ut exigeret a validiore ministerium quae stupebat in iuniore miraculum." [1]

In a homily (II. De concordia Evangelistarum Matthaei et Lucae in generationibus Domini, chap. 10), Augustine (✠430) writes concerning Jesus first recorded saying: "Hoc propterea dixit, quia Filius Dei erat in templo Dei. Templum enim illud non erat Joseph, sed Dei." [2] After this explicit interpretation of Divine Sonship, further on (after again quoting the text) he says He does not wish to be their Son in such a way as He would not be understood to be the Son of God: "Non enim sic se volebat esse filium eorum, ut non intelligeretur Filius Dei; Filius enim Dei, semper Filius Dei creans illos ipsos. Filius autem hominis ex tempore, natus de virgine sine semine maritali, parentem tamen habebat utrumque." It is plain he here has in mind real Divine Sonship. In chapter 12 he points out that Christ did not deny Joseph the name of father ("Non sic indicat Patrem Deum, ut neget patrem Joseph") nor did He mean to say "you are not My parents. But they are his earthly parents, He the Eternal Father" (Vos non estis parentes mei. Sed parentes illi temporaliter, pater ille sempiterne.) [3]

Augustine again brings out the force of the contrast in Christ's words in another work, De Nuptiis et Concupiscentia. He gives the mother's question and thus introduces Christ's words: "At ille ut ostenderet habere se praeter illos patrem, qui eum genuit praeter matrem, respondit sic." [4] This certainly is a clear and emphatic interpretation of real Divine Sonship: that Christ uttered this reply to Mary to point out that besides the parents He had a Father who begot Him without a Mother.

In a letter (Epist. XVI. 2) to the bishops of Sicily, Leo the Great (✠461) says that Christ's earliest recorded saying signifies "He was the Son of Him to Whom also belonged the Temple" (significans ejus se esse filium cujus esset et templum). [5] This indicates that Leo understands real Divine Sonship.

[1] Erasmus, Biblia Critica, VI. 265 (cf. also Albertus Magnus, Comment. ad loc; Opera omnia, VII. 256) interchanges "miraculum" and "ministerium" to suit the sense.
[2] M.PL XXXVIII. 342-343.
[3] M.PL XXXVIII. 343.
[4] Corp. Script. Lat. (edit. Vrba and Zycha), XLII. 225.
[5] M.PL LIV. 697.

The conclusion from this patristic study is, that the Fathers are unanimous in the view that Jesus at twelve years of age revealed His real Divine Sonship; the Latin Fathers are clear and explicit on the point, and the Greeks go beyond this, nearly all using the text, Luke ii. 49, to defend or demonstrate Christ's true Divinity.

It is to be noticed that those who understand ἐν τοῖς as "house," e.g., Origen, Juvencus, take the side of the common opinion. And these Fathers quoted above represented different times, different countries (Alexandria, Jerusalem, North Africa, Rome, etc.), different schools, indeed hostile camps, e.g., Cyril of Alexandria and Theodoret. Moreover, they use quite different ways to express their views, thereby proving their independence and indicating that they are voicing tradition.

The Fathers' explicit inferences of real Divine Sonship from Christ's words become all the more remarkable in the light of the fact, that but few of them had occasion to give more than passing notice to the Gospel text. On account of this, we need not expect to find brought out by them everything that is therein implied. Yet at least three of them indicate that in Christ's words is conveyed a contrast to the words His mother had just uttered; Titus of Bostra sees "My Father" opposed to "thy Father"; and Cyril of Alexandria and Augustine bring out the force of the contrast between the heavenly Fathcrhood and the earthly parentage.

CHAPTER II

OTHER EVIDENCE OF THE VIEW OF THE EARLY CHURCH

1. FURTHER EVIDENCE IN THE FATHERS AND TEXTS

BESIDES the direct statements of the Fathers on Luke ii. 49, given in the previous chapter, other evidence can be furnished which would imply the view expressly taken by those already mentioned. How the Boy Christ's expression of Divine Sonship was understood, would be implied by assertions of Christ's Divine Sonship and preëxistence. Such assertions can be found even in the Apostolic and Sub-apostolic Fathers, linking up the first Father who directly refers to this text (Irenaeus) to the time contemporary with the Gospel writers.

The Didache (65–80) gives instruction "to baptize in the name of the Father and of the Son and of the Holy Ghost" (VII.).[1] I Ep. Clement (96) refers to Christ as "the Son" and says that "concerning the Son, the Master said thus: 'Thou art My Son, I today have begotten Thee'" (XXXVI.).[2] Christ is called "Our God" and "Son of God" by Ignatius (98–117) in the same breath as he speaks of His Virgin Birth of the Holy Ghost (Ephes. XVIII.; Smyr. I. 1).[3] He also mentions "in the Son and Father and in the Spirit" (Mag. XIII.),[4] and says that Christ "was with the Father before the world" (Mag. VI.).[5] The Ep. Barnabas (70–132) speaks of the Son of God coming in the flesh (e.g. V.), and narrates that Christ "manifested Himself to be the Son of God" (V.), that He "said He was the Son of God" (VII.).[6] The Pastor of Hermas (90–155) states that "the Son of God is older than all His creatures,

[1] Lightfoot, Apostolic Fathers, 220.
[2] Lightfoot, Apostolic Fathers, 73. Clement refers to Christ's preëxistence, XVI.
[3] Lightfoot, Apostolic Fathers, 141, 156; cf. Ephes. VII.
[4] Id. 146.
[5] Id. 144; cf. also VII.
[6] Id. 273, 276. Christ's preëxistence stated, v.g. VI. 12.

14   THE BOYHOOD CONSCIOUSNESS OF CHRIST

so that He became the Father's adviser in His creation" (III. Sim. IX. 12).¹ Jesus is called God's "Beloved Son" in Epistle to Diognetus (about 150). This work mentions a great and unutterable scheme conceived in God's mind which "He communicated to His Son alone" (VIII.).² St. Justin Martyr (155–160) says that the "Word of God is His Son" and mentions texts which "were written" to prove "that Jesus the Christ is the Son of God" (1 Apol. LXIII.).³ He frequently uses the words "the Son," "the Father," and his meaning is clear. Thus he says "and His Son, who alone is properly called son, the Word who was with Him and was begotten before the works" (II. Apol. VI.).⁴

That real Divine Sonship was expressed in the first recorded words of Jesus would be implied by the Fathers, who refer to the Child Christ as "God." Many Fathers said that the Magi offered incense to the Christ Child "as to God": Irenaeus,⁵ Origen,⁶ Juvencus,⁷ Ambrose,⁸ Jerome,⁹ Gregory of Nazianzus,¹⁰ Chrysostom,¹¹ Gregory the Great.¹² Ephraim writes "God as a Babe,"¹³ and Augustine states "from the time He began to be man, from this time He is also God."¹⁴

The Fathers, interpreting the scene of the Boy Christ among the Doctors, Luke ii. 46–48, maintained it to have been miraculous, thereby implying the view presented in the previous chapter.¹⁵

More direct is the evidence from the statements of the Fathers on the question of the increase of Christ's knowledge and their

---

[1] Id. 469. This writer frequently uses "Son," "Son of God."
[2] Id. 507.
[3] A-NF I. 184.
[4] A-NF I. 190.
[5] Adv. Haer. III. 9, 2, M.PG VII. 871.
[6] Contra Celsum I. 60, M.PG LX. 772.
[7] Harmon. line 250, Corp. Script. Lat. XXIV. 16.
[8] Exposit. Luc. in Luc. ii, M.PL XIV. 1569.
[9] Exposit. Matt. ii, M.PL XXX. 557.
[10] Oration XIX. 12, M.PG XXXV. 1057; Oration XXXVIII. 17, M.PG XXXVI. 352.
[11] Θεὸν ἐν σαρκὶ προσκυνούμενον. In Matt. Hom. VII. 4, M.PG LVII. 77.
[12] Thus vero in Dei sacrificium ponebatur. Hom. in Evang. I 10, 6, M.PL LXXVI. 1112.
[13] Hymn I. in Nativ. N.P-NF (2d ser.) XIII. 223.
[14] Ex quo homo coepit, ex illo est et Deus. De Trin. XIII. 17, M.PL XLII. 1031.
[15] As a rule the Fathers refer to Christ as "disputing," and give the interpretation that the scene was miraculous. See below, p. 132–3. Chrysostom says that when Christ was twelve years old "He manifested Himself" (ἐξέφηνεν ἑαυτόν), in Matt. Hom. X. 2, M.PG LVII. 186.

explanations of Luke ii. 52, "and Jesus advanced in wisdom . . . ." As to how "Jesus advanced in wisdom" the Fathers are divided, some of them holding that the text merely has reference to external manifestation of wisdom,[1] while others claim it means that Christ increased "according to human nature."[2] But all insist that according to His divine Nature He knew no increase. For instance, Athanasius writes, "it was only His human nature that advanced; Wisdom Himself did not advance, rather He advanced in Himself" (αὐτὸς ἐν ἑαυτῷ προέκοπτε).[3]

We have such assertions as that of Clement of Alexandria, who says of Christ, "for Him to make any additions to His knowledge is absurd, since He is God,"[4] and that of John of Damascus, who states that those who assert there was an increase of wisdom and grace in Christ "deny that He enjoyed the Hypostatic Union from the first moment of His existence."[5]

That Christ had no development, but was perfect from the beginning, is stated by some of the Fathers. Clement of Alexandria asks, "Will they not own, though reluctant, that the Perfect Word born of the Perfect Father was begotten in Perfection, according to economic fore-ordination?"[6] Explaining that "wisdom and age" were only gradually evidenced, Gregory of Nazianzus asks, "How could He become more perfect Who from the beginning was perfect?" (τοῦ ἀπ' ἀρχῆς τελείου).[7] That Christ was a perfect man already in the womb (perfectus vir in ventro femineo)[8] was stated by Jerome. And he also states that His infancy was not prejudicial to His Divine wisdom, "infantiam humani corporis divinae non praejudicasse sapientiae."[9] Cyril of Alexandria says that "a wonderful wisdom might easily have appeared (ἐκφῆναι)

[1] V. g. Cyril of Alex. In Luc., M.PG LXXII. 507–8; Nilus, Epist. I. 288, M.PG LXXIX. 188.
[2] Ambrose, De Incarnat. VII. 72, M.PL LXV. 231: Proculus, Epist. XIV. M.PG LXV. 869; Gregory of Nyssa, M.PG XLV. 735. For other references see Schulte, Die Entwickelung der Lehre vom menschl. Wissen Christi.
[3] Oratio III. Contra Ar., M.PG XXVI. 433. See also Epist. to Epict., M.PG XXVI. 1060. Also Theodoret, De Incarnat., M.PG LXXXIV. 72; Vigilius, Contra Eutych. V. 12–13, M.PL LXII. 143–144, etc.
[4] Paedag. I. 6, M.PG VIII. 279.
[5] De Fide orthod. III. 22, M.PG XCIV. 1080.
[6] Loc. cit.
[7] Oratio XLIII. in Laud. Basil. M.PG XXXVI. 548.
[8] In Jerem. vi. 22, Corp. Script. Lat. (edit. Rieter), LIX. 398.
[9] In Isaiam iii. 7, M.PL XXIV. 110.

16   THE BOYHOOD CONSCIOUSNESS OF CHRIST

in the Babe," [1] but that it would be incongruous to the laws of "the economy." And Augustine holds that ignorance and mental weakness were not in the Infant Jesus, ". . . quam plane ignorantiam nullo modo crediderim fuisse in infante illo, in quo Verbum caro factum est, ut habitaret in nobis, nec illam ipsius animi infirmitatem in Christo parvulo fuerim suspicatus, quam videmus in parvulis." [2]

These Fathers, attributing no ignorance and no mental development to the Christ Child, would imply the interpretation of real Divine Sonship in the first recorded words.

This interpretation is also implied by other evidence in connection with words in the context of Luke ii. 49. In Luke ii. 33, according to the correct text, Joseph is mentioned as ὁ πατὴρ αὐτοῦ; in both Luke ii. 41 and 43, Mary and Joseph are called οἱ γονεῖς αὐτοῦ, and in the question which drew forth Christ's first words, Mary refers to Joseph as ὁ πατήρ σου, Luke ii. 48. There is widespread evidence of a distaste for the names "parents" and "father" in these verses.

Frequently do we find the Fathers explaining why Mary referred to Joseph as "Thy Father." Thus Origen, giving Luke ii. 48 as an example, says that the word "father" is "granted" to Joseph in Scripture on account of His faithful ministry, "Pro fideli ministerio, patris ei vocabulum Scriptura concessit." [3] Epiphanius often repeats that Joseph was not father, but was only in the place (ἐν τάξει) of a father.[4] The reason why Mary ca led Joseph father was, according to St. Cyril of Alexandria, to avoid the suspicion of the Jews.[5] Likewise, St. John Chrysostom assigns the reason why the Virgin Birth was concealed, not only by Mary but even afterward by the Apostles, "that the Virgin should be preserved and delivered from all suspicion." [6]

Both Augustine and Jerome explain the use of the words

[1] Quod unus est Christus, 760, M.PG LXXV. 1352.
[2] De Peccatorum Meritiis et Remissione, II. 48, Corp. Script. Lat. LX. 119. Commenting on Jerem. i. 6, "I do not know to speak, because I am a youth," Origen (Hom. I. 8, in Jerem. M.PG XIII. 265) seems to attribute this passage to the Logos before He assumed human nature. Hence He would not be an exception to the Fathers given above.
[3] In Levit. Hom. XIII. M.PG XIII. 539.
[4] Twice in Adv. Haer. I. II. xxx. 29 M.PG XLI. 456-7; again, M.PG XLII. 686.
[5] Explan. in Luc. Evang. ad loc., M.PG LXXII. 508.
[6] In Matt. Hom. III. N.P-NF (1st ser.) X. 15.

"parents" and 'father.' Augustine says, because of their conjugal fidelity Mary and Joseph are called "parents," and Joseph is Christ's father, being the husband of Mary but the "father in purpose only."[1] St. Jerome states, that to preserve the reputation of Mary, Joseph was regarded by all as father;[2] and he mentions the fact of Joseph being called father by Mary, who had conceived of the Holy Ghost, as an example of things referred to in Scripture according to the opinion of the time and not according to reality (non juxta quod rei veritas continebat).[3] So, too, Sophronius explains that Joseph was only thought to be father, and it was Mary who "had not known man" who says "thy father."[4]

And instead of quoting Mary's words correctly: "Thy father and I," many early writers betraying their reverence for the Virgin Mother invert the order giving "I and Thy father"; this is done by Origen,[5] Jerome,[6] Epiphanius,[7] Sophronius,[8] and Chrysostom.[9]

This tendency to dislike the name father as applied to Joseph, to dislike to include him under the name of parents is also evidenced in the manuscripts of the Greek texts and the versions.[10]

First as to the Greek texts in Luke ii. 33 (for ὁ πατὴρ αὐτοῦ καὶ ἡ μήτηρ [Tisch. adds αὐτοῦ] we find 'Ιωσὴφ (or ὁ 'Ιωσὴφ) καὶ μήτηρ αὐτοῦ in AEGH KMSUVΓΔΛΠ al pler go cop (dz recent) syr (harcl text); and in Luke ii. 43 (instead of γονεῖς) we find 'Ιωσὴφ καὶ ἡ μήτηρ αὐτοῦ in ACXΓΔΠ unc⁸ al pler go syr (harcl text) aeth.

The same thing is to be noticed in some of the Old Latin versions. For "pater ejus et mater" of ii. 33, we find "Joseph et mater

[1] De Nuptiis et Concup. I. XIII. Corp. Script. Lat. XLII. 225. Cf. Concord. Evang. Matt. Luc. serm. LI, M.PL XXXVIII. 342 ff.
[2] Perpet. Virgin. of B. Mary, N.P-NF (2d ser.) VI. 33 ff.
[3] In Jerem. proph. V. Corp. Script. Lat. (edit. Reiter), LIX. 345.
[4] In S. apost. Pet. et Paul, IX, M.PG LXXXVII. 3364.
[5] Loc. cit.
[6] In the last place cited. In the other place Jerome quotes the text correctly.
[7] In the three places cited.
[8] Loc. cit.
[9] Twice, cf. Tischendorf, Oct. Maj. ad loc. It is also done in later works: Dial. Maced. (Tischendorf, op. cit.), Pseudo-Augustinus (Lib. Quaest. LXI. 3), Alcuin (Adv. Fel. VII), Photius (Ad Amphil. CLVIII), and others.
[10] Vogels, "Die Eltern Jesu," BZ XI (1913) 33 ff., has collected the texts. Here we only indicate the changes, and refer to this article for the authorities for the preferred reading.

ejus" in a b c d f ff² g l q r; aur δ. The word "parentes" of ii. 41, is changed into, "Joseph et Maria," by a b c ff² g l q r. And "pater tuus et ego" of ii. 48, is left out in a b ff² g l r (aur. reverses the order, "ego et pater tuus," and e has the reading, "propinqui tui et ego").

As to the Syriac versions, the Curetonian drops out "Thy father and I" in ii. 48, the Sinaiticus has "kinsfolk" for "parents" in ii. 41, 43. The Peschitto inserts "Joseph" instead of "father" in ii. 33, "kinsfold" instead of "parents" in ii. 41, "Joseph and His mother" instead of "parents" in ii. 43.

All these changes could not have been caused through error, or through the "love of amplification."[1] Most scholars agree that these changes were deliberately made on account of a dislike to name Joseph as father. How early this evidence appears, is seen from the fact that the changes are found not only in the Greek manuscripts but also in the Old Latin and Syriac versions. This objection to the name father when applied to Joseph, and to having him included under the word "parents," is evidence of first rate importance, to the early belief in the Virgin Birth and is indirect evidence as to how the Early Church viewed the words "My Father" on Christ's lips. It was for them the expression of real Divine Sonship.

2. THE APOCRYPHAL GOSPELS OF THE CHILDHOOD

We shall have occasion to mention the Protevangelium of James, the Gospel of Pseudo-Matthew, the Childhood Gospel of Thomas, and the Arabic Gospel of the Childhood. The Protevangelium of James "is very old"[2]; some scholars date the writing in the early decades of the second century, but most scholars place it "in the second half of the century."[3] The Gospel of Pseudo-Matthew is a recension of the Protevangelium and its date lies between the fourth and the sixth century.[4] Of the Childhood Gospel of Thomas there are three forms, two in Greek and

---
[1] Plummer (Comment. on St. Luke, 75) says: "the love of amplification or of definiteness might suffice."
[2] Hoffman, Apocrypha, Sch–HEnc I. 106.
[3] Findlay, Gospels (Apocryphal), HDG I. 681.
[4] Cf. Reid, Cath. Enc. I. 607. Findlay, HDG I. 682.

OTHER EARLY CHURCH EVIDENCE 19

one in Latin. Irenaeus' citation from it (Adv. Haer. I. 20, 1) would suggest it is a gnostic production of the second century;[1] but the forms in which it has come down to us bear but slight evidence of this influence. The date of the recension by an orthodox hand is placed about the third century.[2] The Arabic Gospel of the Childhood is a translation of a lost Syriac original.[3] Its date is comparatively late, though probably before the Mohammedan era.[4]

These Apocryphal writings may contain authentic material in the additions to the narratives of the Gospels, but in this respect their value remains problematic, and consequently slight. The chief and great value of the Apocryphal Gospels is that they reflect the views of the times in which they were written and extensively read. Nearly all the Apocrypha were written with a deliberate dogmatic purpose and even those which were not, are "doctrinally significant."[5] The Childhood Gospels, as we have them, were written in the interests of orthodoxy, and their value is enhanced because of their remarkable popularity, especially in the East.[6] The Protevangelium was translated into Syriac, Coptic and Arabic; the Arabic Gospel of the Childhood enjoyed a wide circulation not only in the Churches of the East, but also in Mohammedan circles.[7]

What do we find in these accounts of Christ's Childhood? They most explicitly and emphatically testify to the Virgin Birth of Christ.[8] They attribute wonderful innate miraculous power to the Child Jesus, — having His "every word accomplished,"[9] and ascribe great preternatural knowledge to Him. The Pseudo-Matthew, the Gospel of Thomas, and the Arabic Gospel mention

[1] Cf. Hoffman, Sch–HEnc I. 106. Tasker puts it 160–180 A.D. (HDB Extra vol. 433, Apocryphal Gospels).
[2] Some place the present form before the third century (cf. Bardenhewer, Patrol. 74. Hoffman, loc. cit.). Some place it after the third century (cf. Findlay DHG I. 683, Michel Textes et Documents, Évang. Apoc. I. XXXII).
[3] Cf. Batiffol, Évang. Apoc. VDB II. 2116. Hoffman, op. cit. 106, Reid, Cath. Enc. I. 607, Tasker, HDB Extra vol. 433.
[4] Cf. Reid, Cath. Enc. I. 607, Tasker, HDB Extra vol. 433.
[5] Findlay, HDG I. 673.
[6] Cf. Findlay, HDG I. 674.
[7] In the Koran Jesus is represented as working miracles in His Childhood.
[8] E.g. Protevang. XIX (A–NF VIII. 365), Ps. Matthew, XIII (A–NF VIII. 374).
[9] Gosp. of Thomas (both Greek forms), IV (A–NF VIII. 395, 398).

three occasions on which the Child Jesus was taken to school, but on each occasion it was He who was the Master, giving evidence of preternatural knowledge. They witness to Christ's real Divinity as a child; they have this stated by others,[1] but what is more significant for our purpose, they represent Him as testifying to His Divinity and Divine Sonship. For instance, the Gospel of Thomas (first Greek form), III.: "I am here from above — as He that sent Me on your account has commanded Me"[2]; (second Greek form), VI. "I am before the ages"[3]; (Latin form), VI. "and before all I was Lord . . . and My Father hath appointed this . . ."[4]; in Pseudo-Matthew, XXI. "that one of thy branches be carried away by My angels, and planted in the paradise of My Father."[5] According to the Arabic Gospel, I., Jesus says from the cradle, "I am Jesus, the Son of God, the Logos whom thou hast brought forth as the angel Gabriel announced to thee; and My Father has sent Me for the salvation of the world."[6] So that if the Apocryphal Gospels of the Childhood reflect the views of the times in which they were circulated (and in regard to doctrine they certainly do), then in these early centuries it was held that Christ as a Child was conscious of His mission, Divinity and Divine Sonship. They certainly do not reflect any tradition of a growth or development of His Self-consciousness, or that at a certain stage of His life He awoke to the consciousness of His Divine Sonship. They vividly depict Him as wielding miraculous power and fully conscious of His Nature and Personality, and this as a Child. The Apocryphal Gospels with which we are dealing are concerned with Christ only before His twelfth year and do not go beyond that. Two of them, the Gospel of Thomas (first Greek form XIX.) and the Arabic Gospel (L.–LIII.) end their accounts by narrating the Temple episode. In describing the Gospel incident of the twelfth year,

---

[1] E.g. Ps. Matthew, XXIV: "Unless this were the God of our Gods, our Gods would not have fallen on their faces before Him" (A–NF VIII. 377); Gosp. of Thomas, VII. "Assuredly He was born before the creation of the world" (A–NF VIII. 396); Arabic Gospel, X. "A god has come here in secret who is God indeed" (A–NF VIII. 406); etc.

[2] A–NF VIII. 396.
[3] A–NF VIII. 399.
[4] A–NF VIII. 401.
[5] A–NF VIII. 277; cf. Chs. XX. XXX.
[6] A–NF VIII. 405.

the Gospel of Thomas represents Christ before the Doctors as "shutting the mouths of the elders and teachers of the people, explaining the main points of the Law and the parables of the Prophets."[1] It gives His words in answer to His mother;[2] and it represents the Scribes and Pharisees as then addressing Mary thus: "Blessed art thou among women, for such glory, and such virtue and wisdom, we have neither seen nor heard ever."[3] From the context one can easily see that the writer of this Childhood Gospel of Thomas understood Christ's reference to His Father in Luke ii. 49 in the real sense. Indeed this work represents Christ as previously divinely self-conscious, v.g. VIII., "I am here from above."

The Arabic Gospel of the Childhood is of comparatively late date, but nevertheless important because it is a translation of a Syriac original; because of its wide circulation, and the great emphasis it places on the Child Jesus' Divinity and Divine self-consciousness. As we mentioned, this work represents the Child Jesus shortly after birth as proclaiming His Divinity and mission; it represents the twelve-year-old Christ before the doctors discoursing on the natural sciences and on questions of Scripture: "Things which the understanding of no creature attains to."[4] It likewise gives Christ's answer to His mother thus: "Why do you seek Me? Do you not know that I must be in My Father's house?"[5] There is no question (as is clear from the whole context of the work) that this writer understands the words "My Father" on the Boy's lips as expressing real Divine Sonship.

Since the Apocryphal Gospels of the Childhood cast sidelights on what people thought of Christ in the early centuries, they certainly afford widespread evidence for the view that Christ as a Child was fully conscious of His Divinity, for the view that in His first recorded words He expressed true Divine Sonship. If there is any one doctrine emphasized in these Apocrypha, it is the doctrine of a Child born of a Virgin, possessing Divine powers and Divine knowledge, and this doctrine implies that the words "My

[1] A-NF VII. 398.
[2] Text given by Michel, Textes et Documents, Évang. Apoc. I. 188.
[3] A-NF VIII. 398.
[4] A-NF VIII. 415.
[5] For Arabic Text, see Thilo, Codex. Apoc. N.T. 128.

22 THE BOYHOOD CONSCIOUSNESS OF CHRIST

Father," in which the Boy Jesus referred to God, were taken literally.

Now in regard to doctrine, these Apocrypha are orthodox. They could not become so remarkably popular if they contained fundamental doctrines opposed to the opinions of the time. As Findlay says, "The Childhood Gospels stand in the main current of ecclesiastical doctrine in their view of the Person of Christ."[1] So that we have early and widespread evidence that the view of the Early Church was that Christ did not undergo any development in His Divine self-consciousness, that as a Child He was conscious of His Divinity and Divine Sonship, and hence that His words, given in Luke ii. 49, express real Divine Sonship.

The objection that the Apocryphal Gospels were rejected and condemned by the Fathers does not touch what we have said. The latter, it is true, recorded their antipathy for the "false and wicked stories"[2] and "ludicrous miracles"[3] recounted in these writings, but they do not object to the doctrine which shines through almost every page of these writings, the Child Jesus' Divinity and Divine self-consciousness. If this was false and opposed to the received tradition, it would be the first thing the Fathers would attack and condemn.

[1] HDG I. 674.
[2] Irenaeus, Adv. Haer. I. 20, 1, M.PG VII. 653.
[3] Epiphanius, Adv. Haer. II. 1, Haer. LI. 20; cf. Cyril of Jerusalem, Cat. IV. 36.

CHAPTER III

CONFLICTING HERETICAL OPINIONS

THERE is no evidence, in the early centuries of the Christian era, of any explicit denials of the view that Jesus, in the first recorded words, expressed real Divine Sonship. A denial, however, is implied in the various heresies of that period which denied the Divinity of Christ and taught that Jesus, a mere man up to his thirtieth year, was at baptism indued with a higher personality.[1]

Cerinthus, a contemporary of St. John, held that Jesus was a mere man born of Mary and Joseph, and professed the view that "after His baptism, Christ descended upon Him in the form of a dove from the Supreme Ruler, and that then He proclaimed the unknown Father and performed miracles." [2]

Likewise, maintaining Jesus to be the son of Joseph, Carpocrates (beginning of second century) thought that "a power descended upon Him from the Father, that by means of it, he might escape from the creators of the world." [3] We do not know what Carpocrates' view was, as to when this power came on Jesus; he may have held it was at the baptism.

According to Irenaeus,[4] the opinion of the Ebionites in respect to the Lord are similar to those of Cerinthus and Carpocrates. Epiphanius[5] says they held that Christ came upon Jesus, the mere man, at His baptism, when the Holy Ghost, in the form of a dove, descended upon Him. The Christology of the Elkesaites resembled

---

[1] Cf. Bornemann, Die Taufe Christi, 41–49; Brandt, Die jüdischen Baptismen, Zatl W XVIII (1910) 90 ff.; de Pressensé, The Early Years of Christianity, Book I. 1–193; Duchesne, Early History of the Church, 112 ff.

[2] Irenaeus, Adv. Haer. I. 26, I (A–NF I. 352), also Hippolytus, Refutation of all Her. X. XVII.

[3] Irenaeus, Adv. Haer. I. 25, I (A–NF I. 350).

[4] Adv. Haer. I. 26, 2 (A–NF I. 352).

[5] Adv. Haer. I. II. Haer. XXX. 29 (M.PG XLI. 465). Thus in the Gospel used by the Ebionites (Epiphanius, Haer. XXX. 13, M.PG XLI. 429) in the account of the baptism there are three voices from heaven, one addressed to Christ Himself, "I have this day begotten Thee."

24   THE BOYHOOD CONSCIOUSNESS OF CHRIST

that of the Ebionites and Cerinthus: Jesus, the son of Joseph and Mary, became Divine after baptism, by union with the Aeon Christ.[1]

The work, Libellus adversus omnes Haereses, which most probably belongs to Victorinus of Pettau, states that a certain Marcus and a Colarbasus, composing a novel heresy out of the Greek alphabet, said that "Jesus Christ descended, that is, that the dove came down on Jesus."[2] For this meaningless expression, "denique Jesum Christum descendisse," there has been recommended the reading, "in Jesum Christum descendisse," i.e., that Christ descended on Jesus,[3] thus conforming in view to the heresies previously mentioned.

According to Clement of Alexandria,[4] the followers of Basilides (about 120–140) kept the anniversary of the baptism of Jesus "as a festival, spending the night before in readings." From this, it would seem to have been their view that, it was only at the baptism that Nous, the first emanation of the Supreme Father, took upon him in Jesus the semblance of humanity.[5] We know from Tertullian[6] that the Valentinians (Valentinus died about 160) held that upon Christ the natural Son of the Demiurge (born through the Virgin, not of her) "Jesus descended in the sacrament of baptism, in the likeness of a dove." Irenaeus tells us that the Ophites, holding that Jesus, born of a Virgin, was more righteous than other men, said, "Christ, united to Sophia, descended into him, and thus Jesus Christ was produced."[7] That these heretics had in mind the baptism, is plain from the fact that Irenaeus goes on to state that "they strove to establish the descent and ascent of Christ, by the fact that neither before His baptism, nor after His resurrection from the dead, do His disciples state that He did any mighty works."[8]

Marcion (born 110) mutilated for his purpose the Gospel

---

[1] Cf. Bardenhewer, Patrol. 190. Duchesne, Early History of the Church, 96.
[2] A-NF III. 653. Cf. Irenaeus, Adv. Haer. I. 21, 3 (A-NF I. 346).
[3] Cf. A-NF III. 653, note 2.
[4] Strom. I. xxi. 45 (M.PG VII. 888).
[5] Irenaeus, Adv. Haer. I. 24; 3, 4.
[6] Against the Valent., XXVII. (A-NF III. 516). Cf. Arendzen, art. Gnosticism, Cath. Enc. VI. 595.
[7] Adv. Haer. I. 30, 12 (A-NF I. 357).
[8] Adv. Haer. I. 30, 14 (A-NF I. 357).

CONFLICTING HERETICAL OPINIONS 25

according to St. Luke, and professed the view that "Jesus, being derived from that Father who is above the God that made the world, and coming into Judea in the time of Pontius Pilate, was manifested in the form of a man to those who were in Judea."[1] Rejecting the Gospel narratives of Christ's baptism and temptation, commencing his account of the God-Manifest with Luke iv. 14, Marcion does not attach any importance to the baptism account; yet his view implies a rejection of the Fathers' interpretation of Luke ii. 49.

We know from many sources the position of Theodotus of Byzantium (about 190). Hippolytus[2] says he appropriated his notions of Christ "from the school of the Gnostics, and of Cerinthus and Ebion," and he describes his view thus: Jesus was a mere man yet was born of a virgin. He "at His baptism in the Jordan received Christ, who came from above and descended (upon Him) in the form of a dove. And this was the reason, according to Theodotus, why (miraculous) powers did not operate within him prior to the manifestation in him of that Spirit which descended (and) which proclaims Him to be the Christ." In the very next chapter (XXIV.), there is described the view of another Theodotus, a banker. He developed the Melchisedecian heresy, and holding views similar to the adherents of the other Theodotus, asserted "that Jesus is a (mere) man, and that, in conformity with the same account (already given), Christ descended upon him."[3]

According to an anonymous fragment "Against the heresy of Artemon,"[4] Theodotus' heresy was adopted by Artemon (or Artemas, about 230). Whether the view in regard to Christ's baptism was taken up, however, is not certain. A somewhat similar situation is presented in the case of Paul of Samosata, Bishop of Antioch (260–270). We are told in Malchion's letter[5] that he swaggered "with the abominable heresy of Artemas."

---

[1] Irenaeus, Adv. Haer. I. 27, 2 (A–NF 352). Cf. Tertullian, Adv. Marc. IV. vii. (A–NF III. 351).
[2] Refutation of all Her. VII. xxiii. (A–NF V. 114–115).
[3] A–NF V. 115.
[4] Also called "The little Labyrinth" (Theodoret, Haer. Fab. II. 5). It is preserved by Eusebius (Hist. Eccles. V. 28), and it is attributed to Caius and to Hippolytus.
[5] Fragment preserved by Eusebius, Hist. Eccles. VII. xxx. 4 and 5 (A–NF VI. 170–171).

26   THE BOYHOOD CONSCIOUSNESS OF CHRIST

Paul held that the Son or Logos (merely the impersonal wisdom of God) dwelt in the man Christ as we live in houses. The time when the Son or Logos first came to the man Jesus was, he thought, not at the baptism, but at His very birth. This opinion seems to have been held also by Beryllus, bishop of Bostra (about 240), who, denying Christ's preëxistence, said that "He did not possess Divinity, but that the divine paternity only took up its abode in Him." [1]

All these early views, implying a denial of the Fathers' interpretation of Luke ii. 49, were heretical. They were condemned by synods; they were refuted by orthodox writers.[2] The fact that the Church looked upon these views as heretical intimates that the contrary view was regarded as orthodox. It is an indirect indication that the view of the early Church concerning Luke ii. 49, was the one expressed by the Fathers in their comments on the passage.

---

[1] Eusebius, Hist. Eccles. VI. xxxiii. Lucianus, presbyter of Antioch, is said by Theodoret (Eccles. Hist. I. 3) to be the successor of Paul of Samosata. Another man affected by Antiochean influence was Theodore of Mopsuesetia (428). In the words of the II. Conc. Constantinople (553) which condemned Theodore, he held that Christ "as a mere man was baptized in the name of the Father, and of the Son, and of the Holy Ghost and obtained by this baptism the grace of the Holy Spirit, and became worthy of Sonship" (n. XII.). Another man many centuries later, Faustus Socinus (1539–1604), had many affinities with Paul of Samosata. To him, Christ was a deified man but not God, and he taught that Christ in His baptism was endowed with miraculous power.

[2] Against the "falsely called Gnostics," Irenaeus, among other arguments, triumphantly appeals to the annunciation of the angels to the shepherds that "there is born in the house of David, a Saviour who is Christ the Lord," Luke ii. 11, (Adv. Haer. III. 10, 3), and he refutes the contention that "Christ" or the "so-called Superior Saviour descended upon Jesus at His baptism (Adv. Haer. III. 17, 18). St. John Chrysostom refutes the contentions of Marcion and Paul of Samosata, pointing to the fact that the Magi worshipped the Child Jesus. "Let Marcion be ashamed, beholding God worshipped in the flesh; let Paul be ashamed, beholding Him worshipped as not being merely a man" (in Matt. Hom. VII. 5; cf. In. Phil. Hom. VII; Irenaeus Adv. Haer. III. 9, 2). Against the Ebionites' view that "Christ" came to the man Jesus at His baptism, Epiphanius not only appeals to the facts of Christ's Childhood, but in a special way appeals to Christ's words given in Luke ii. 49.

SECTION II
LATER PERIOD OF THE HISTORY OF THE QUESTION

CHAPTER IV

FROM THE FATHERS TO THE RISE OF MODERN RATIONALISM

1. FROM THE EIGHTH TO THE TWELFTH CENTURY

THE commentators who immediately followed the Fathers are unanimous in inferring real Divine Sonship from Jesus' earliest recorded words, Luke ii. 49, and nearly all of them see a contrast between these words and the words of the Virgin Mother in the preceding verse.[1]

Bede (✝735) explicitly points out the force of the contrast in Christ's words and the question of Mary. He writes: "He (Christ) did not refuse to have Joseph as His parent, but simply and clearly insinuated to us, as well as to them, who is His real Father (simpliciter et aperte qui sit verus sibi pater, nobis pariter et illis insinuat)."[2] Again he says, "Not because they sought Him as their Son does He blame them, but He draws their attention to what He owes Him, of Whom He is the eternal Son (sed quid ei potius cui aeternus est filius debeat, cogit oculos mentis attollere)."[3]

Bede in a sermon goes further in his deduction from Christ's first words. Jesus' words are an indication of Divine majesty; "Divinae majestatis indicium fuit, de qua alibi dicit: Omnia quaecumque habet Pater mea sunt; atque ideo rectissime templum non minus ad se quam ad Patrem pertinere testatur."[4] Evidently he gives ἐν τοῖς a wider interpretation than any of the Fathers, seeming to understand by it all the things (omnia quaecumque) of the Father, and among others, the Temple which He testified also

---

[1] This is done by works of uncertain date of this period. Catenae Graecorum Patrum (edit. A. Cramer II. 27) has, "My Father is not Joseph but God, who is Lord of the temple." An ancient treatise on Luke says, that Jesus' earliest words were to "remove the suspicion caused by Mary's words" and to show "that His Father is God and not Joseph" (M.PG CVI. 1189).
[2] In Lucae evang. I., M.PL XCII. 348.
[3] Id. 350.
[4] Homil. XII. in Dominica prima past Epiph., M.PL XCIV. 65.

belonged to Him. Also besides "Temple" he mentions "majesty and glory," for he adds, "Quia in his quae Patris mei sunt oportet me esse; quia nimirum quorum una est majestas et gloria, horum etiam una sedes ac domus est; nec solum materialis Dei domus, sed etiam domus intellectualis." Thus this scholar branches off into the symbolical interpretation, and says finally (expressing in an emphatic way an interpretation of Divinity) that Christ's words are a declaration of His eternal power and majesty, "declaratio est consempiternae Deo Patri potestatis et gloriae." [1]

The contrast in Jesus' words and Mary's reference to Joseph as "father," is recognized by Alcuin (✠804), for he says the purpose of the words was to point out that His Father is God rather than Joseph ("ut ostenderet Patrem suum esse Deum magis quam Joseph").[2]

Photius (✠891) interprets ἐν τοῖς symbolically, "the illustrious people who are called the temple and house of the Father." He continues (interpreting real Divine Sonship) "and while the Son clearly proclaimed His own Father" (τὸν ἴδιον Πατέρα σαφῶς ἀνακηρύξαντος τοῦ Υἱοῦ) clearly also were revealed the thoughts of those who said He was not the son of a carpenter nor born of any earthly man but of Him Who begot Him before all time." [3] In another work, after quoting Luke ii. 49 Photius asks, "What is clearer than this, or more efficacious for closing the mouths of the impious?" and goes on to give a paraphrase of Christ's own words thus: Πατὴρ ἐμὸς ἀληθῶς, ᾧπερ ἀνιέρωται τὸ ἱερόν. Τὰ δὲ τοῦ Πατρὸς πάντα ἐστὶν ἐμά. Οὐκοῦν οὐκ ἔδει ζητεῖν ἀλλαχοῦ, ἐξὸν εὑρίσκειν ἐν τοῖς τοῦ Πατρός.[4] So that this writer sees in Christ's saying not only a declaration that God is His true Father, but also a declaration that all the things of the Father are His.

The opposition in Jesus' words, "My Father" and "Thy father" used in reference to Joseph, is brought out by Haymo of Halberstadt (✠895) in his comments: "quis verus pater ejus sit ipse manifestat," again, "utramque suam naturam Dominus nobis commendat." Besides he says, "the Temple, the prophets, and the frequent meditation on Divine Scripture belong to His

[1] Id. 66.
[2] Adv. Felicem, IV. 1, 12, M.PL CI. 137.
[3] Ad. Amphilochium, CLVII., M.PG CI. 832.
[4] Contra Manichaeos, IV. 16, M.PG CII. B. 213.

THE RISE OF MODERN RATIONALISM 31

Father," and "beautifully in these His works He demonstrated that He was the Son of God," — pulchre in his suis operibus Filium Dei se demonstravit.[1] Simeon Metaphrastes (✟970) has a number of remarks on Luke ii. 49; the following are a selection. "Mary had spoken of Joseph as father; Christ, as it were, correcting what was said spoke of One who was real Father" (ὁ Χριστὸς ὥσπερ τὸ ῥηθὲν διορθούμενος περὶ τοῦ ὄντως λέγει Πατρός). "He showed He was by nature God, since a son has the same nature as his father" (οὕτω δείκνυσιν ἑαυτὸν ὄντα φύσει Θεόν, εἴγει τῆς αὐτῆς φύσεως ὁ παῖς τῷ τεκόντι). "He shows that the Father's house, evidently the Temple, and besides, all the things of the Father, are His. He points out it is rather they who are to be blamed for not knowing these things, and for not saying or thinking the truth of things. Here for the first time He makes more open mention of His true Father and reveals His Divinity" (ἐνταῦθα πρώτως τοῦ ἀληθῶς Πατρὸς φανερώτερον μνημονεύει καὶ παραγυμνοῖ αὐτοῦ τὴν θεότητα).[2] In one statement after another, this writer most explicitly gives expression to his interpretation of Divinity and brings out the significance of the contrast in Christ's words and the words of Mary.

Another commentator, who infers Christ's Divine Sonship from this contrast, is Theophylact (✟1107). He writes, "Since Mary had called Joseph 'father' He replied, 'He is not my true father, otherwise I would be in his house; but God is My Father'" (οὐκ αὐτός ἐστιν ὁ ἀληθής μου πατήρ, ἢ γὰρ ἂν ἐν τῷ οἴκῳ αὐτοῦ ἤμην, ἀλλ' ὁ Θεός ἐστί μου πατήρ.)[3]

Euthymius Zigabenus (✟1118) thus points out the contrast: "His mother had spoken of His adopted father; He manifested to her Him Who was Father by nature" (αὐτὸς δὲ ταύτῃ τὸν φύσει Πατέρα αὐτοῦ ἐγνώρισε).[4]

A reflection of Bede's exegesis is given by Zacharias Chrysopolitanus (✟1155). After quoting the text, he writes: "Non quod eum quasi filium quaerent vituperat, sed cogit eos attollere mentis oculos ad quaerendum quid debeat aeterno Patri, ostendens

[1] Homil. XVII., M.PL CXVIII. 124.
[2] Vita sanctorum, etc., M.PG CXV. 548.
[3] Ennaratio in evang. Lucae, M.PG CXXIII. 733.
[4] Commentar. in Lucam, M.PG CXXIX. B. 897.

et templum et omnia quae Patris sunt, non minus ad se quam ad Patrem pertinere, quorum una est majestas."[1] The position of the writers of this period, on Luke ii. 49, is epitomized in the above quotation: the interpreting real Divine Sonship from the contrast with the preceding verse, the taking a wide view of ἐν τοῖς, "Temple and all the things of the Father, of which one is majesty."[2]

2. FROM THE THIRTEENTH CENTURY TO THE EIGHTEENTH

A. The Medieval Theologians

John Scotus Erigena (ninth century), a forerunner of the Scholasticism of the Middle Ages, held that as Christ was the Wisdom of the Father to Whom nothing was hid, and as He had accepted a stainless human nature (incontaminatam humanitatem), He never suffered the ignorance inflicted as a punishment on fallen man; but from His very conception He knew Himself and all things and could speak and teach (confestim, ut conceptus et natus est, et seipsum et omnia intellexit, ac loqui et docere potuit).[3] This doctrine presupposes the view of real Divine Sonship as expressed by Christ in His first recorded words.

The first writer of a Summa Theologiae incorporating Aristotelian philosophy, Alexander of Hales (✠1245), maintains that Christ did not assume ignorance, did not learn anything from angels, but enjoyed a threefold knowledge: the Beatific Vision, uncreated knowledge, and the knowledge of experience. In a certain kind of the latter knowledge, Christ made advance; the rest He had from the beginning.[4]

[1] In unum ex quatuor, I. 2, M.PL CLXXXVI. 88.
[2] There are other writers of the twelfth century who refer to the Lucan text. Bruno, in his commentary on St. Luke, interprets it symbolically: "An nesciebatis quia in his quae Patris mei sunt, et inter eos qui Patris mei voluntaten faciunt, oportet me esse" (M.PL CLXV. 365). Identical words are found in Anselm's Homil. VII. in Evang. secundum Luc. (Opera. edit. Gerberon, p. 172). Aelredus has a treatise, De Jesu Puero Duodenni; but concerning the Boy's words, he merely says, "jam hic coelestium mysteriorum in quibus per triduum fuerat observatus incipit reserare secretum" (M.PL CLXXXIV. 855). Isaac of Stella, in his second sermon for the Sunday within the Octave of the Epiphany, has this in reference to the passage: "excepta tamen hac unitate naturae, et naturali unitate Patris et Filii, a qua non recessit, nec Pater, nec Filius: etiam in sua mineratione non recessit Filius a Patre dum in ejus semper mansit obedientia et voluntate" (M.PL CXCIV. 1777).
[3] De Divisione Naturae, IV. 10, M.PL CXXII. 777.
[4] Summa Theologiae, pars III. quest. XIII. 43–45.

THE RISE OF MODERN RATIONALISM 33

That Christ had a manifold knowledge (cognitionem multiplicem) was held by Albert the Great (✠1280). His division is much the same as the previous writer, but he explains Christ's advance in knowledge as according to manifestation (secundum ostensionem).¹ Albert's pupil, St. Thomas of Aquin (✠1274), who laid down the lasting lines of Catholic theology, has a treatise on "The Perfection of the Child conceived" in which he states that "Christ, in the first instant of His conception, had the fulness of sanctifying grace, the fulness of known truth, free will and the beatific vision."² In his treatise on Christ's knowledge St. Thomas says, that as man Christ had a threefold knowledge, the Beatific Vision, infused knowledge, and acquired knowledge; in the last alone He made progress.³

These views of the perfection of Christ's knowledge from the beginning, imply the interpretation of real Divine Sonship from the words of the Boy Jesus recorded by St. Luke. And other writers of this period express much the same views, for they were incorporated in systematized Catholic theology. Thus Dionysius the Carthusian (✠1471) taught, that from the first moment of His conception Christ was a perfect man, that he was perfect "not by reason of His age, but on account of the fulness of grace, the eminent degree of virtues and the perfection of wisdom," and that Christ made no advance in these excepting in regard to the exercise of them (sed quantum ad exercitium).⁴

B. *Commentators of this Period*

It may be said in general, that the commentators who lived between the thirteenth and the nineteenth centuries follow in the footsteps of the previous writers interpreting Luke ii. 49, in the sense of real Divine Sonship, and recognizing a contrast between these words and the words of Mary. Concerning the interpreta-

---

[1] In Lib. III. Sent. dist. XIII. art. XI. XII. Opera (edit. Jammy, Lugduni 1651) XV. 140-141.
[2] Summa Theologica, pars III. quest. XXXIV. (transl. III. 2, pp. 96-104).
[3] Summa Theologica, pars III. quest. IX.-XII. (transl. III. 1, pp. 145-184). For other references to Christ's knowledge see Abelard, Sic et Non, LXXII, M.PL CLXXVIII. 1444-7; John Duns Scotus, Lib. III. Sent. dist. XIV. quest. II.-IV. Opera (edit. Weddingi, Parisiis, 1894) XIV. pp. 488 ff., etc.
[4] Comment. in Ps. I. art. IX. Opera V. 409.

34   THE BOYHOOD CONSCIOUSNESS OF CHRIST

tion of Divinity and Divine Sonship, it is sometimes stated explicitly and emphatically, yet more often implied. As to the contrast, we often find statements which point out the force of the contrast such as: Christ as it were corrected His mother who had called Joseph Father; He opposed the Person and claims of His true Father, God, to those of the earthly parents; He states He is more closely connected with God than with them, and hence they should not wonder if He neglects or dismisses them for God.

Thus Bonaventure (☦1274) paraphrases Christ's words: "Unde non debetis mirari si vos dimisi propter Patrem aeternum."[1] And as a supplement to this is the paraphrase of Albert the Great (already mentioned): " Patris veri substantialis et aeterni, cui plus debeo quam vobis."[2] Both of these ideas are found in Ludolphus of Saxony (☦1335), who besides says of the relationship of the words of the Son and the Mother: " quasi corrigendo verbum matris."[3] The line of thought of these writers is implied in Nicholas of Lyra's (☦1340) comment on passage: " magis enim afficiebatur ad patrem naturalem et aeternum quam ad matrem naturalem et patrem putativum."[4]

The early Reformers made no change in the exegesis of Jesus' first words. Thus Luther (☦1546) says of them: "Als sollt er sagen: Ich bin ja eur Sohn; aber doch also dass ich mehr jenes Sonn bin, der im Himmel ist."[5] The same idea is expressed by Melanchthon (☦1560),[6] Hofmeister (☦1562),[7] Calovius (☦1686),[8] and J. C. Michaelis (wrote 1735).[9] As to Catholic writers Maldonatus (☦1583) explicitly states that Christ opposed the Person of God His Father to the person of Joseph: " Personam vero Dei Patris personae hominis patris opponit . . . docet se alium

---

[1] Comment. in Luc. ad loc. Opera omnia, VII. 68.
[2] In Evang. Luc. ad loc. Opera omnia, XXII. 2551.
[3] Vita Christi, 38 (b).
[4] Biblia latina cum postillis, IV. ad loc.
[5] Luthers Werke (deutsche), I. 153. There is no doubt that Luther understands real Sonship from what he adds: Offenbaret sich also umb unsertwillen, dass wir ihn recht sollen kennen und einbilden lernen, dass er nit allein ein wahrer Mensch, sonder auch wahrer Gott sei.
[6] Sermon for Sunday I after Epiph. Opera omnia, XXIV. 368, he says: Discernit patrem suum a Joseph.
[7] "Vides iam quis verus hujus pueri pater." In Evang. Luc. ad loc. 213.
[8] "Partim ad Patrem verum propriumque revocat corrigens dictum Matris," Biblia illustrata, ad loc.
[9] Christ signifies, "se quidem aeternum patris filium carne humana indutum" Exercitatio theol.-philol. ad Luc. ii. 49, in Miscell. Gronig. I. 274.

THE RISE OF MODERN RATIONALISM 35

veriorem cui magis obedire debeat patrem habere."[1] So does Toletus (✠1600): "Opponit autem parentibus Patrem aeternum."[2] Lucas (✠1619) too, interprets: " quod non illum sed alium praestantiorem ac sublimiorem Deum, inquam agnoscat Patrem."[3] The opposition of Christ's words to those of His mother is referred to by Cornelius Jansenius Yprensis (✠1638): " Negotia Patris negotiis humanis societati videlicet parentum opponit ";[4] and by Sylveira (✠1687): " Recurrit ad praeceptum Patris naturalis quo obligabatur."[5]

There is no question then that these writers understand there is a contrast between Jesus' reply and the question of Mary, and that the contrast was equivalent to an assertion of Divine Paternity. Indeed some of the writers of this period argue in favor of the true Divine Sonship from the fact that Christ said "My Father" and not "our Father." This is done by Stella (✠1571),[6] Cajetan (✠1530)[7] and Cartwright (✠1603)[8] and Sylveira (already mentioned).

What is characteristic of this period, is the view of the writers as to what is signified by ἐν τοῖς. As we saw, the writers of the previous period, speaking generally, understood "the Temple and all things (of the Father)." Making a further development of this matter, the commentators, with whom we are now dealing, selected and emphasized from these "things" the Father's Will or works, or (on the part of Christ) Jesus' mission, office, function, Messiahship. Hugo de S. Caro (✠1263) may be referring to Christ's mission when he explains ἐν τοῖς as "in locis et templo et in operibus."[9] Certainly, Bonaventure (✠1274) holds that Christ referred to His mission, saying that Luke ii. 49 agrees with John vi. 38.[10] That the Boy Christ mentioned He was doing the

---

[1] Comment. in quat. Evang. ad loc. II. 123.
[2] Commentarii. ad loc. p. 217.
[3] Comment. ad loc. Given in Migne, Cursus S. S. XXII. 465.
[4] Tetrateuchus sive Comment. ad loc. II. 78.
[5] Comment. in Textum Evang. ad loc. I. 352.
[6] De Observantia in S. J. C. Evang. I. 151.
[7] Comment. ad loc. III. 189.
[8] Comment. in totam Historiam Evang., 110.
[9] Postilla super IV. Evang. ad loc. Hugo well serves as a connecting link between the writers of this period and those of the previous one, reflecting the views of the latter.
[10] Comment. in Luc. ad loc. Opera omnia, VII. 68.

works of His Father, is expressed by Ludolphus (✠1335),[1] Cajetan (✠1535),[2] and Faber Stapulensis (✠1536).[3]

By this time the view was widely adopted that the word to be supplied in Christ's saying was "business"; and this word is suggestive of and almost synonymous with mission.[4] We have a clear interpretation of mission in Erasmus (✠1536): "Did ye not remember in your myndes that I muste nedes bee aboute my Fathers business, as often as He calleth me to the office and function appoyncted unto me?"[5] There is a reference to this view in Melanchthon (✠1560): "Ita Christus erat vocatus ut fungeret ministerio in isto populo, et scivit, se ejus rei specimen edere debere, etiam in illa sua aetate tenere."[6] Calvin is many times explicit on the matter. For instance: Principium quoque finem designat, cur in mundum missus fuerit, nempe ut munus impleat sibi a patre coelesti injunctum.[7]

Another step taken by the interpreters of Luke ii. 49 was to say that this business or mission referred to by Christ was the salvation of the world. Salmeron (✠1585) does this: versari in negotiis Patris Mei, et in procuranda salute hominum.[8] So does Toletus (✠1600): Opera quae ... ut Redemptor, faciebat, appellasse ea quae patris sunt.[9] The passage is explained in a Messianic sense by Lucas (✠1619): In negotiis quae Pater Meus Deus mihi injunxit, mandavit, ut Christo suo, ab ipso misso ad hominum redemptionem ad salutem procurandum.[10] A somewhat different signification is given by Piscator (✠1625): In

[1] He gives as a paraphrase of Christ's words: "in templo, doctrina et in operibus quibus manifestetur pater meus" (Vita Christi, 38).
[2] Comment. ad loc. III. 189.
[3] He has in his paraphrase: "in domo patris mei esse ut illa facerem opera quae patris mei sunt" (Comment. in quat. Evang. ad loc.).
[4] This was only for a time. Very soon the controversy between the rival claims of "house" and "business" arose to be continued to the present day. Many commentators, such as Grotius, Hammond, Polus, devoted their remarks on the Lucan text entirely to this controverted question.
[5] Paraphrase of the Gospels, ad loc. fol. xxxix. In his Annotationes, Erasmus also writes (referring to our text): "Christus suum negotium quod totum e coelo pendebat purem esse voluit ab humanis affectibus" (p. 169).
[6] Sermon for Sunday I after Epiph. Opera omnia, XXIV. 368.
[7] Comment. in Harm. Evang. Opera omnia, XLV. 106; cf. also Sermon XXXIX. Opera omnia, XLVI. 476; Maldonatus, Comment. ad loc.; Beza, J. C. D. N. Nov. Test. ad loc. 86; Aretius, Comment. D. N. J. C. Nov. Test. ad loc. 304.
[8] Comment. in Evang. Histor. ad loc.
[9] Commentarii. p. 218.
[10] Comment. ad loc. Given in Migne, Cursus S. S., XXII. 465.

negotiis quae Pater Meus mihi mandavit ad expediendum puta ad docendum qui sim, et cujus rei gratia a patre missus sim in mundum.[1] This view is also expressed by Sylveira (negotiis mei Patris, seu saluti generis humani ad quam veni),[2] and by Cornelius à Lapide (me negotia saluti generis humani ad quem a Patre coelesti missus sum inchoando tractare).[3]

Other writers who see in Christ's words a reference to His Messianic mission are, Tirinus (✝1636): Patris sui negotia vocat opera theandrica seu divino-humana Messiae propria,[4] and Cornelius Jansenius Yprensis (✝1638): cogitandum vobis erat officii illius mei causa in quo a vobis non dependio, me mansisse Jerosolymis.[5] Along the same lines is the interpretation of Natalis Alexander (✝1722);[6] while J. G. Michaelis (1736) states that Christ showed He was not ignorant of His priestly office, "se immutabili Patris consilio pontificem maximum constitutum ut pro hominibus ea perageret, quae apud Patrem suum coelestem peragenda esse non ignorat."[7]

Concerning this period, therefore, it may be said that its characteristic feature is the fact that its commentators saw in Christ's words a reference to His mission, called by the later ones the salvation of the world. But, be it noted, none of the writers states that Messiahship alone was expressed by the Lord.

[1] Comment. in Nov. Test. ad loc. 222; cf. also Corderius' own comments in Catena, LXV. Patr. Graec., 75.
[2] Comment. in Textum Evang. ad loc. I. 352.
[3] Comment. in S. Script. VIII. 534.
[4] In univers. S. Script. Comment. ad loc. IV. 199.
[5] Tetrateuchus sive Comment . . . ad loc. II. 78.
[6] Exposit. litteralis et moralis S. Evang. ad loc. II. 137.
[7] Loc. cit. This writer has a special section to show that Christ here gave a prelude of His priestly office (op. cit. 276–282). Many of the writers of this period, e. g. J. G. Michaelis, see The Boy Christ fulfilling the prophecy of Malach. iii. 1.

CHAPTER V

THE MODERN VIEWS

BEFORE the rise of modern rationalism, there was practically only one view professed in regard to Christ's reference to His Father in Luke ii. 49, — the view of real Divine Sonship. Now there arises a variety of views; and among a certain class of scholars there is a definite break with the past. The reason for the great departure and the wide divergency of opinion is to be found in the a priori rejection of miracles. This rejection led some to deny the genuineness and historicity of the early chapters of St. Luke, and the account of the Boy Christ; it led others to explain the account and the first recorded words in a natural sense; it occasioned the theory of a gradual growth or development in Christ's view of Himself.

On account of these factors, the rejection of the miraculous, the explaining Christ's first words naturally, the attempting to trace a gradual development of His self-consciousness, there is among modern scholars almost every shade of opinion in regard to the degree of relationship to God that the Boy Christ expressed in His words. They may, however, be classified under four main headings.

1. "ORDINARY ISRAELITIC CONSCIOUSNESS"

The most extreme view of Christ's first self-interpretation, is the view of ordinary Israelitic Consciousness. Certain scholars claim that Jesus' words could be said by any ordinary Jewish boy; that they contain no hint that the speaker considers Himself the Messiah; that they express no special relationship with God; that the sense in which God was called "Father" is the sense in which any ordinary Israelite of that day spoke of God as "Father."

The first to attempt to trace a development in the self-con-

THE MODERN VIEWS

sciousness of Jesus and thus to introduce this modern problem was Karl Hase (Life of Christ, 1829). He held that in His childhood Christ had no Messianic consciousness.[1] Being uncertain whether Christ became fully aware of His mission before His Public Life, he says that the first words indicate "an unpausing development" showing "the same sense of the nearness of God in a purely human and childish form which is the idea of His life."[2] Gess contends that in no "exceptional sense" Jesus said "the God of Israel" is His Father.[3]

Explicitly denying to the twelve-year-old Boy any consciousness of Divine Sonship or Messiahship, Schenkel sees in His words "an early presentiment . . . of His destined devotion to the concerns of the Divine Kingdom, of His duty to subordinate earthly duties to His eternal calling."[4] Even "this presentiment or foreboding of His destiny"[5] is rejected by B. Weiss, who views Luke ii. 49, as an "expression of a genuine Israelitic consciousness, containing nothing contrary to the 'usus loquendi' of the Old Testament." The same stand, in different words, is taken by Oscar Holtzmann[6] and by H. Holtzmann.[7] This mode of explaining Christ's words as a predilection for things spiritual — the word "Father" having only a religious sense — is also adopted by Feine,[8] M. J. Weber,[9] and Kent.[10] Daab gives a slight reference to Luke ii. 49,[11] and then goes on to indicate Christ's religious development.[12] Much the same thing is done by Stapfer.[13]

[1] Life of J., 66. Schweitzer says about this author "Hase created the modern historicco-psycholgical picture of Jesus." (Quest of the Historical J., 61.)
[2] Idem, 51. In a later work, Geschichte Jesu (1876), 224, he admits that there is expressed in Jesus' words, "sein ganzes Verhältniss zur Gottheit," yet insists it is only the saying of a pious child.
[3] Christi Person und Werk, 271.
[4] Das Charakterbild J. 36, Eng. transl., 59.
[5] Life of Christ, I. 279; cf. Comment. in New Test., R. 24–25.
[6] Leben Jesu, 76, transl., 100.
[7] Hand-Comment. I. 151.
[8] Theologie des n. T., 104, 114. In another work casting doubts on the genuineness of our passage, this writer says it denotes that Christ felt Himself a special man with a special relation to God. (Eine Vorkanonische Überlieferung d. Luk., 25.)
[9] La methode d'education . . . , 12.
[10] The Life and Teachings of J., 54.
[11] Jesus von Naz., 48.
[12] Id., 48–50.
[13] J. C. before His Ministry, 39–127.

With the exception of a few extremists [1] who hold that Christ never announced that He was the Messiah, and with the exception of a few [2] who hold that it was only toward the end of the Public Ministry that profession of Messiahship was made by Jesus, the bulk of negative scholars date the dawn of Christ's Messianic consciousness at His baptism.[3]

Placing the birth of His messianic consciousness at the baptism, not a few of these scholars such as Martin,[4] Neumann,[5] Bousset,[6] reject Luke ii. 49 as unhistorical. Others such as Dickey,[7] and H. Miller,[8] declare that the text may not be historical, "but it is certainly in keeping with any inference that may be fairly drawn from His later development." Others, in fact the majority of these scholars, take for granted the unhistorical character of the Temple episode and deliberately overlook Christ's first words when treating of His self-consciousness; such as Harnack,[9] Wernle,[10] Guinebert,[11] Bacon,[12] Weinel,[13] Schweitzer.[14] This is also done in some special treatises on Christ's self-consciousness, such as those of Baldensperger,[15] E. Schürer,[16] H. Holtzmann,[17] Spaeth,[18]

---

[1] Wellhausen, Israelitische und jüd. Geschichte (1885), 342, Einleitung in die drei ersten Evang. (1905), 92. Wrede, Das Messias Geheimnis in den Evang. (1901). Martineau, The Seat of Authority in Religion (1905), 357. Cf. Cairns, The Self-assertion of Jesus, Contemp. Rev. LXXXV (1904) 362. Nat. Schmidt, The Prophet of Naz. (1905), 261. Merx, Die vier kannonischen Evang. (1905-1911).

[2] Such as Schenkel, op. cit., P. W. Schmidt, Jesus in Modern Criticism, 38-42. For the wider view on Christ's Messianic consciousness see Faut, Christologie seit Schleiermacher, 78-81.

[3] Cf. R. Mackintosh, The dawn of the Messianic Consciousness, Exp. T. XVI (1905) 157-158 and 211-215; also Dickey, The Significance of the Baptism of J. BW XXXVII (1911), 359-368.

[4] Life of Jesus, 76, 84.

[5] This writer says the text was formulated by a later hand, but "in any case, the term Father is used here in a purely religious sense." Jesus, 47-48.

[6] Jesus, 1, 8.

[7] Significance of the Bapt. of J., BW XXXVII (1911) 366.

[8] Our knowledge of Christ, 51, 56, 57. Cf. Life of Jesus, in the Light . . ., BW XLIII (1914) 75 ff.

[9] What is Christianity? 36, 149.

[10] The Beginning of Christianity, 46.

[11] Manuel d'hist. anc. du Chrét., 179.

[12] Christianity, Old and New, 156, 161.

[13] Jesus in the Nineteenth Cent., 151.

[14] Quest. of the Historical J., 370, 384.

[15] Das Selbstbewusstsein Jesu im Lichte der messianischen Hoffnungen seiner Zeit.

[16] Das messianische Selbstbewusstsein J. C.; cf. p. 13.

[17] Das messianische Bewusstsein J.

[18] Die Entwickelung J., 6.

O. Holtzmann,[1] von Sodon,[2] Völter.[3] Also a number of moderns, when considering Jesus' earliest recorded sayings, hesitate and are not willing to express an opinion,[4] and others according to their interpretations see very little self-consciousness therein expressed.[5]

2. "A SPECIAL ETHICAL SONSHIP"

Somewhat different from the view just described is that held by another class of modern scholars, who say: Christ's first words would not be used by an ordinary Jewish boy; they indicate that the Boy Christ had an exceptional self-consciousness, expressing a very special relationship to God, a conception of personal sonship without parallel in previous history. But this sonship was only religious, moral, ethical, an intense feeling of love and devotion; it was not real Divine Sonship, nor did it denote messianic consciousness, which arose later.

In the first place there are two scholars belonging to this class, O. Pfleiderer[6] and J. Weiss,[7] who see, in the text as it stands, an expression of special ethical sonship, yet at the same time contending that it is not genuine.

There are other scholars who, adhering to the genuineness of the Lucan passage, derive therefrom the view of special ethical sonship. Such is Keim, who thinks that in Christ's first words "lay the inkling of an infinite claim on the near regard of the heavenly Father, of a Divine Sonship, outbidding far the earthly in enjoyment, in right, in duty."[8] Reinhard argues from the use of the words "My Father" that Jesus here "expresses a clear and

---

[1] Das Messiasbewusstsein Jesu und seine neueste Bestreitung.
[2] Die wichtigsten Fragen im Leben Jesu, see 95, 98.
[3] Jesus der Menschensohn oder das Berufsbewusstsein Jesu.
[4] Thus Farmer (Boyhood of J., HDG 1226), Anderson (The Man of Naz., 41–43), R. Mackintosh (Dawn of the Messianic Consc., ExpT XVI (1905) 212; cf. 215).
[5] Abbott (Life of C., 80), Neander (Life of C., 31), Boardmann (The Divine Man . . . , 225, 226), Hamyln (ExpT XXVII (1915) 43), Peabody (The Character of J. C., HJ I (1903), 645), Fairbain (Studies in the Life of C., 59), Kilpatrick (Character of C., HDC I. 284), Montefiori (Synoptic Gospels, II. 864), Carpenter (Christianity acc. to S. Luke, 172, 173).
[6] Primitive Christianity, II. 113.
[7] Die Schriften des n. T., I. 430–431.
[8] Jesus of Naz., II. 133. The view of Schleiermacher (Das Leben Jesu, 83–116) is a special relation to God, yet a natural human development.

full consciousness of His sustaining a higher relation to God than mankind in general."[1] Dickenson calls the words "the first human consciousness of the holy God as the Father of the individual soul."[2] Godet states that the word "My" in Jesus' reply gives to His consciousness "of His filial relationship with God a peculiar and, as it were, exceptional significance,"[3] and in another work he writes that "the words 'My Father' were the first revelation of a relation which surpassed all that Judaism had realized."[4] Giving Luke ii. 49 as an instance, Beyschlag states that "the name 'Father' on the lips of Jesus is the expression of a purely personal relation that has no equal."[5] Wendt infers from the text that from His childhood Jesus "was clearly sensible of the fatherly love of God and His filial relationship to God."[6] On the basis of this Temple episode, too, Denny considers Christ's consciousness of the Fatherhood of God "as something realized in Him as it was in no other."[7] Sheldon declares that the words of Jesus were "certainly quite foreign to the ordinary dialect of the Jewish child and indicated the dawning of a peculiar sense of intimacy with the Father in heaven."[8] The same ideas are emphatically upheld by Nösgen.[9] The exceptional character of the saying is pointed out by Réville,[10] and by Monnier.[11] Both Nebe[12] and Bovon,[13] while denying the word "Father," in the Boy Christ's reply, expresses the same signification that it had for Him afterward, yet affirm that it expresses a very special relation to God. Something unique, but only in a religious way, is likewise seen in

[1] Plan of the Founder of Christianity, 261 note.
[2] The Perfecting of J., AndR XVII (1892), 342. This writer holds that the Boy Jesus had not yet "the knowledge that His consciousness of God was peculiar to Himself . . . not yet the thought of His sinlessness" (Idem, 343). Both of which points are denied by the following scholars.
[3] Life of J. prior to His Ministry, Think VII (1895), 398.
[4] Comment. on Luke, 93. Godet's views on our passage are opposed by Brown, Life of J. prior to His Public Minist., ExpT VI (1904–5), 415 ff.
[5] N. Test. Th., I. 81.
[6] The Teaching of J., 97.
[7] Jesus and the Gospel, 184.
[8] New Test. Theol., 63.
[9] Geschichte J. C., 125.
[10] Affirmation ingénue d' une relation de fils à père qui l' unirait à Dieu très particulièrement. (Jésus de Naz., 410.)
[11] Il se sent fils de Dieu de la façon la plus immédiate (La Mission Historique de J., 30).
[12] Die Kindheitsgeschichte J. C., 417.
[13] Theol. du N. Test., I. 236.

THE MODERN VIEWS

the self-consciousness of the Boy Christ by H. Schmidt,[1] Schlatter,[2] Gelpke,[3] Furrer,[4] Hess,[5] P. W. Schmidt,[6] Paterson,[7] Reuss,[8] Evans,[9] Hitchcock,[10] Gilbert,[11] Garvie.[12]

3. "MERE MESSIANIC CONSCIOUSNESS"

Certain modern scholars claim that Jesus' earliest recorded words express Messiahship, yet nothing more than Messiahship. Some of those deny the genuineness of the words, others contend that only the dawn or first glimpse of Messianic consciousness is expressed, while others claim that full assurance of Messiahship is expressed.

Certain modern scholars, while denying the genuineness of Luke ii. 49, yet state that the text itself as it stands expresses Messiahship. This is the view of Paulus,[13] Strauss,[14] Bruno Bauer,[15] and Loisy.[16]

[1] Bildung und Gehalt des messianischen Bewusstseins Jesu, StKr LXII (1889), 429, 430.
[2] Theol. des n. Test., I. 483.
[3] Die Jugendgesch. des Herrn, 90.
[4] Das Leben J. C., 51-58.
[5] Jesus von Nazareth, 4-9.
[6] Geschichte Jesu, 52-56.
[7] Jesus Christ, HDB (sing. vol. 446).
[8] Histoire Évangelique, 159.
[9] Self-consciousness of J., AndthSB II (1891) 18.
[10] Psychology of J., 102. Cf. Self-consciousness of J., OT-NTSt XIII (1891) 272.
[11] Student's Life of J., 124-5.
[12] Studies in the inner Life of J., 110-114. Cf. Gospel according to St. Luke, 76. This writer confesses he is not able to tell when the consciousness of Sonship and Messiahship came to Jesus, but thinks they came gradually in correspondence with His development (op cit. 126, 309). Godet writes concerning the Boy Christ that, "even now in a distance, a mission dawns before His gaze" (Life of J. prior to His Ministry, Think VII (1895) 398). Monnier (loc. cit.) states that the Messianic consciousness came after the twelfth year, not stating when. The coming of this consciousness is placed after the baptism by P. W. Schmidt (Jesus in modern criticism, 38-39). With these exceptions the scholars given in this section date the birth of the Messianic consciousness at the baptism. Gore (Dissertation on Subjects Connected with the Incarnation, 78 and note) is to be classed here, but he expresses his view in a doubtful way.
[13] Das Leben J., I. 18, Exegetesches Handbuch ..., 280. He doubts the historicity, 282.
[14] Life of J., 195.
[15] Kritik der Evang., I. 293.
[16] Les Évang. Synopt., I. 183. J. Häcker says he finds in the Temple episode "nichts andres als eine Verherrlichung des Messiaskindes" (Die Jungfrauen Geburt und das n. Test. ZwTh XLIX (1906) 56), thus implying a denial of the genuineness.

44 THE BOYHOOD CONSCIOUSNESS OF CHRIST

Other scholars attribute to the twelve-year-old Jesus the beginning of Messianic consciousness. For instance, Edersheim characterizes the state of mind of the twelve-year-old Boy "the awakening of the Christ consciousness . . . partial, and perhaps even temporary." [1] After seeing in Luke ii. 49, "the breaking forth of the consciousness of Divine Sonship" Meyer adds in a note, "at all events already in Messianic presentiment, yet not with the conception fully unfolded." [2] The passage is called by Ramsay "a remarkable instance of the young Boy's awakening consciousness of His own mission." [3] While de Pressensé writes that during this visit of Jesus to the Temple He "perhaps for the first time became fully conscious of the greatness of His mission," yet in the next breath he calls it a "great moment in the development of Jesus, by revealing Him to Himself." [4] A. T. Robertson, referring to Christ's saying "as the keyword to His after life and teaching" and as expressing a most special relation with God, yet attributes to the Boy Jesus a "dawning Messianic consciousness." [5] E. F. Scott uses the words "awakened" and "henceforth" and this, after referring to the importance of Luke ii. 49, for the question of the development of Christ's Messianic consciousness.[6]

Certain scholars hold that Christ in His first words manifested full Messianic consciousness. For instance Briggs writes: "Jesus here at the age of twelve years, makes it known to His parents that He is assured of His Messianic calling." [7] From the Temple episode, Thomson infers that "Jesus was already aware of His mission and consciously preparing for it." [8] A "strongly developed Messianic consciousness" is the view of Baljon.[9] Wallis mentions "the dawning consciousness of the youthful Messiah" [10]

[1] Life and Times of J., I. 249.
[2] Comment. on New Test., I. 345.
[3] Was Christ born in Beth.? 80.
[4] Jesus Christ, 208.
[5] Keywords in the Teaching of J., 13, The Teaching of J. concerning God the Father, 47, Epochs in the Life of J., 6–8, Luke the historian, 158.
[6] Father's House, HDG I. 583.
[7] Messiah of the Gospels, 234.
[8] Art. Jesus Christ in SDB I. 164. This writer also holds that Christ's "consciousness of His Divine nature and power grew and ripened and strengthened until the time of His showing unto Israel."
[9] Commentaar ... Lukas, 72.
[10] About My Father's business, Exp. 2d ser. vol. VIII. 23.

and the deepening of "His assured sense of His Heavenly Father's mission."[1] A view peculiar to himself is Malan's: that the words of the Boy Jesus indicate the realization that His Father's Will is His.[2]

4. "REAL DIVINE SONSHIP"

There are modern scholars who interpret from Jesus' first words that there is expressed the dawning or beginning of consciousness of a real Divine Sonship. This Divine Sonship is variously viewed and is frequently diverse from orthodoxy.

The dawning consciousness of real Divine Sonship is the view of Olshausen, who says that the event in the Temple was the moment when Christ "became aware of His exalted Divine nature,"[3] that there His mental development ripened "into the clear knowledge that He was the Son of God, and that God was His Father."[4] Oosterzee calls Christ's saying the "expression of direct and infallible self-consciousness, now gradually developing into higher knowledge,"[5] and Lange, after saying it expressed the whole idea of His nature, predicates of it "the dawning feeling of that Sonship which was His alone."[6] Hartmann declares that Christ "in holy presentiment expressed His oneness with the heavenly Father."[7] In the first words of Jesus, MacDermott finds "the dawning consciousness of His unique relation to God,"[8] and Plumptre finds "a germ that there comes out so fully in such words as 'My Father worketh hitherto and I also work,' 'I and the Father are one.'"[9] That it was in the Temple that His Divine nature first dawned on Him is held by Davis,[10] Paynter,[11]

---

[1] Id., 24.
[2] "Un rapport direct du principe même de sa libre volonté avec la volonté de Dieu comme de son Père." L'Avénement, dans Jésus Enfant de la Conscience religieuse, RThQr V (1896) 282.
[3] Bible Comment. on Gosp., I. 149.
[4] Id., 150.
[5] Comment. on St. Luke, 51.
[6] Life of C., 324.
[7] Das Leben J., 68.
[8] Gospel accord. to St. Luke, 23.
[9] St. Luke, Ellicott's Comment., I. 258–9.
[10] The Story of the Naz., 60.
[11] The Holy Life, 123.

Geikie,[1] Keil.[2] Stier holds the view that from the very beginning Christ possessed a consciousness of the object of His life, but as to the knowledge of His nature, Mary's question was responsible for its origin. "This great truth rises before Him out of Joseph's name of father, that His own true Father is He whom no one in Israel had ever addressed by that name, and Himself never till now."[3] Somewhat similar is the view of Steinmeyer.[4] Reubelt holds that Jesus at twelve "had already some idea that God was in a peculiar manner His Father," only later He acquired "full knowledge of this."[5] Stanley Hall mentions that the Boy Christ "was already on the way to a sense of Divine Sonship."[6] While holding that Christ was destined for His mission "from the first conceivable moment of His earthly existence," Ewald states that Luke ii. 49 allows us to take a glance "into an opening life of an infinite and most exalted nature."[7] The opinion of Nolloth is that "the consciousness of the nature of His Person and of His mission was already awakened."[8] Such is the view also of Foxell.[9] Ebrard[10] and Brough[11] contend that in the Temple Jesus first recognized His own nature and His personal relation with God, but He was not yet conscious of His mission or Messiahship. A similar view is expressed by Sweet,[12] Frederich,[13] Mackintosh,[14] and Robinson.[15]

In the midst of a diversity and confusion of opinions, the view

---

[1] The Life and Words of C., 228. Adamson seems to hold a view on the same lines as these scholars (Studies in the Mind of J., 154–155; cf. also 144). Hanna (The Early Years of Our Lord's Life, 122) expresses this view in a doubtful way using the word "perhaps."
[2] Comment. über ... Mk. u. Lk., 244. Cf. also Kühl, Das Selbstbewusstsein J., BZSF (1907) III, Ser. N. II, p. 43.
[3] Words of the Lord J., 23, 25.
[4] Die Geschichte der Geburt des Herrn, 167.
[5] Scripture Doctrine of the Person of Christ, 385.
[6] Jesus the Christ in the Light of Psychology, I. 252, yet see p. 302.
[7] History of Israel, VI. 188. Cf. Die drei ersten Evang., I. 230–231.
[8] Rise of the Christian Religion, 183–184; he says Christ "is on the way to know Himself." Cf. Person of our Lord and Recent Thought, 115–119, where he puts Messianic consciousness at the baptism.
[9] Temptation of J., 34, 103.
[10] Gospel Hist., 191.
[11] The Early Life of Our Lord, 124–128.
[12] Birth and Infancy of C., 13, 258, 259.
[13] The Self-consc. of J., AndthSB II (1891) 2.
[14] The Doctrine of the Person of J., 26, 27, 17, cf. 481.
[15] The Self-limitation of the Word of God, 68–71.

THE MODERN VIEWS 47

that the Boy Christ expressed complete real Divine Sonship, is held by not a few non-Catholic as well as by Catholic scholars. As to the non-Catholic scholars, in a general way it may be said that the view of conservative Protestants concerning Christ's self-consciousness is as follows: Like everybody He was born an "unthinking infant." As soon as He reached the age of reason, that is, long before His twelfth year, He became conscious of His Divine Sonship, and in the Temple He gave expression to this consciousness. The following interpret real Divine Sonship from the text — yet sometimes not exactly in the traditional sense: Phelan,[1] Sadler,[2] Vallings,[3] Dorner,[4] Alfred,[5] Bengel,[6] Ellicott,[7] Barnes,[8] Clarke,[9] Jacobus,[10] Owen,[11] Foote,[12] Goulburn,[13] Ryle,[14] van Doren,[15] Besser,[16] Hahn,[17] Blunt,[18] Nevin,[19] Beet,[20] Döderlein,[21] Hall,[22] Schaff,[23] Riddle,[24] Homes,[25] Beecher,[26] Fleetwood,[27] Adeney,[28] Farrar,[29] Stalker,[30] Plummer,[31] Maclaren,[32]

[1] Discourse II. on Lk. ii. 49, Remains, I. 143. He holds that the Man Jesus was united with the Supreme Intelligence "from the beginning."
[2] Gosp. according to Luke, 68, 69.
[3] The Divine Man, 51.
[4] History of the Development of Doctrine of Person of C., Div. I. vol I. 54. For similar view see Christology, McClinton and Strong, Enc. of Bib. Theol. II. 278.
[5] Gr. Test., I. 419.
[6] Gnomon of New Test., 401.
[7] Hist. Lectures on ... J. C., 96–7.
[8] Notes ... on the Gosp., II. 33.
[9] New Test., I. 355.
[10] Comment. on Mk. and Lk., 159.
[11] Comment. on Lk., 44.
[12] Lectures on Luke, I. 125.
[13] Gospel of the Childhood, 166 ff.
[14] St. Luke, I. 81.
[15] Comment. on Lk., 73.
[16] Evang. St. Lucä, 96.
[17] Evang. des Lucas, I. 234.
[18] Lectures on the Hist. of Our Lord, 45.
[19] Popular Comment. on Lk., 79.
[20] The Father's Business, Homiletic Rev. XXXIV (1897) 242.
[21] Das Lern. d. Jesusknaben, NJdTh I (1892) 618, cf. Think III (1893), 173.
[22] The Kenotic Theory, 189; The Incarnation, 338.
[23] Comment. on Lk., 361, 362.
[24] Gosp. accord. St. Luke, 44.
[25] Jesus Christ, Kit. EB II. 549.
[26] Life of C., 74.
[27] Life of C., 00.
[28] St. Luke, 156.
[29] Life of C., 36. Cf. Gosp. St. Luke, 78.
[30] Christology of J., 101.
[31] Comment. on Luke, 77, 78.
[32] Gospel of Luke, 39.

48 THE BOYHOOD CONSCIOUSNESS OF CHRIST

D'Arcy,[1] Sanday,[2] Hastings,[3] Dalman,[4] Box,[5] Stewart,[6] Nicoll,[7] Du Bose.[8]

Catholic scholars of the modern period unanimously take the position that, in His first recorded words, Jesus expressed the full consciousness of His real Divine Sonship. Among them may be mentioned,[9] Bisping,[10] MacEvilly,[11] Veuillott,[12] Didon,[13] Le Camus,[14] Gigot,[15] Terrien,[16] Capicelatro,[17] Shanahan,[18] Bartmann,[19] Pohle-Preuss,[20] Brassac,[21] Schaefer,[22] Mangenot,[23] Lesêtre,[24] Picard,[25] Ward,[26] Thiriet,[27] Lagrange.[28] In answer to attacks on their view point, some scholars have dealt with the question at considerable length, as for example, Lepin,[29] Fillion,[30] Seitz,[31] Felder.[32]

[1] Consciousness, HDG I. 361.
[2] Life of C. in Light of Rec. Research, 133.
[3] Great Texts of the Bible, St. Luke, 127–129.
[4] Clearly implies this view, Words of J., 288; cf. 280–287.
[5] Virgin Birth, 106–107.
[6] The Temptation of J., 60, 68.
[7] Incarnate Saviour, 49.
[8] The Consciousness of J., 41, 42, 50, 51.
[9] It is implied by the thesis defended in many theological works, that Christ from the first moment of His conception enjoyed the infused knowledge, v.g. Billot, De Verbo Incarnato, 201 ff. Pesch, Praelectiones dogmaticae, IV. 150 ff. Coughlan, De Incarnatione, 153 ff., etc. It is implied by Knabenbauer (Comment. in Luc. ad loc.), 146, Curci (II. Nuovo Test., I. 321–322).
[10] Erklärung d. Evang. Mk u. Lk., 206.
[11] Comment. on St. Luke, 70.
[12] La Vie de N. S. J. C., 117, 118.
[13] Jésus Christ, 90.
[14] La vie de N. S. J. C., I. 190.
[15] Virgin Birth in St. Luke, IthQ VIII (1913) 434.
[16] La Mère de Dieu, I. 177.
[17] La Vita di Gesu Cristo, I. 101.
[18] Was the Son of man Brusque to His Mother? Cath. World CIV (1916) 346.
[19] Christus ein Gegner des Marienkultus? 48–51.
[20] Christology, 261.
[21] Handbook to the New Test., 257.
[22] Mother of J. in Script., 192, 227.
[23] Les Évang. Synopt., 123–124.
[24] Jésus Christ, VDB III 1444.
[25] La Transcendance de J. C., 165.
[26] Holy Gosp. of Luke, 35.
[27] L'Évangile médité avec les Pères, I. 389.
[28] Le Récit de l'Enfrance., Rb. IV (1895) 181; La Conception surnaturelle du C. Rb (1914) 201; Évangile selon S. Luc., 97.
[29] Christ and the Gospel, 122, 250 ff., 258, 332, 471.
[30] Le Développement intellectuel et moral de J. in RCIFr for April 1, 1914, 15–17; cf. Évang. selon S. Luc., 87.
[31] Das Evang. von Gottessohn, 194–209.
[32] Jesus Christus, I. 328–331; cf. 456–457.

THE MODERN VIEWS 49

That in Christ's first expression of real Divine Sonship, there is a reference to His Messiahship, is held by some Protestants, such as Jacobus, Clarke, Foote, van Doren, Nicoll, Holmes, Stalker, Hall, D. Smith;[1] while Catholic scholars of this period, in harmony with those of the preceding one, understand that the Boy Christ referred to the mission He received from His Father, such as MacEvilly, Didon, Brassac,[2] LeCamus, Bartman, Lepin, Felder.

A brief outline of the history of the exegesis of Luke ii. 49, which at the same time gives us the *status questionis,* is as follows:

The early Church saw in Jesus' first recorded words an expression of real Divine Sonship. This interpretation was supported throughout the centuries, and is upheld by certain conservative Protestant as well as Catholic scholars of the present day.

In modern times there have sprung up five other views; — the beginning of real Divine Sonship, a mere Messianic consciousness, the dawn of Messianic consciousness, a special ethical Sonship, an ordinary Israelitic consciousness. With the exception of the last mentioned, which would be implied by certain early heretical opinions, these modern views have no precedents or parallels in previous history.

[1] The Days of His Flesh, 23.
[2] Handbook of N. T. 257.

SECTION III
PRELIMINARY QUESTIONS

CHAPTER VI

THE CORRECT TEXT OF LUKE ii. 49

In endeavoring to find out which is the Greek text representing, as far as we know, the original, we shall examine all the variations in detail. Our authority, unless otherwise indicated, is Tischendorf, Novum Testamentum, editio octava major, II. 438–439.

1. (a) Syr. sch. and cu. omitt Καὶ.

(b) Instead of Καὶ εἶπεν the codices 13, 49, 346 read εἶπε δὲ. 13 and 346 belong to the Ferrar group; but here D, which is generally in harmony with them, has the common reading Καὶ εἶπεν which it is clear is to be preferred.

2. (a) For ὅτι 59 has ἔτι, which, being alone, must be regarded as a mistake of the copyist.

(b) For τί ὅτι, Δ (Greek) has τί ὅτε (it is followed by ζητεῖτε whose ε was confused (ὅτι ε) into the preceding word), but it is corrected in its Latin interlinear text δ which has: quid est quod. Childhood Gospel of Thomas[1] has simply τί. These are the only exceptions, and it is clear that the correct reading is τί ὅτι.

3. Concerning the next word matters are not so easy.

(a) We find the imperfect verb ἐζητεῖτε in ℵ° ABCDLXΓΔΠ unc. (five) it (nearly all)[2] vg. syr(utr) arm aeth go Origen,[3] Didymus,[4] Epiphanius,[5] Cyril of Alexandria,[6] etc.

(b) However the present ζητεῖτε is read in ℵ* 346 b[7] cop syr[cu.] also in the Childhood Gospel of Thomas[8] and St. Leo.[9]

[1] Cf. Évang. Apocryph. (edit. Michel), I. 188.
[2] Cf. Sabatier, Bib. Sac., III. 2, p. 272.
[3] Twice in Homil., XX. in Luc., M.PG XIII. 185.
[4] De Trinit., III. 20, M.PG XXXIX. 896.
[5] Two different times, Adv. Haer., I. ii. 30. Her. 50, M.PG XLI. 456; Id. II. ii, Her., 66, M.PG XLII. 93.
[6] Twice in his Comment., M.PG LXXII. 509, also in De Recta Fide, M.PG LXXVI. 1520.
[7] Cod. Veronensis, Oxford 1911, ad loc.
[8] Cf. Évang. Apocryph. (edit. Michel), I. 188.
[9] Ep. XVI. 2, M.PL LIV. 697.

Mentioning that Westcott-Hort has done the same, Power adopts the present ζητεῖτε, as well as the present tense, in the preceding verse, 48, ζητοῦμεν. We give his argument in detail. "In making the change Westcott and Hort, while fully alive to the strength of the opposition represented by the Cod. A C D, the Vulgate, Tischendorf and the English Versions of 1611 and 1881, have been content to abide by the reading of ℵ (prima manu) and B. The truth is that the imperfects cannot be defended except by those who have overlooked the force of the present and imperfect 'continuous' in Greek."[1]

Power then points out that λέγω can have three differently shaded time-concepts, "I speak," "I am speaking," "I have been speaking." He contends that this last has been lost sight of; and he goes on to say: "It becomes easy to understand how some early copyists rejected the present ζητοῦμεν in Luke ii. 48 and substituted the imperfect ἐζητοῦμεν. All they say in the ζητοῦμεν, now happily restored by Westcott and Hort, was 'we seek,' and how could Mary say, 'Son we seek thee' when she had met Him in the Temple? Thus the imperfect 'we were seeking thee' was dragged in, to the loss of the pathos of the phrase that represents the pained greeting of the Mother, 'Son sorrowing we have been seeking Thee (ζητοῦμεν). How the Child took up the phrase and turned it into a kind of verbal interjection, 'seeking,' has been emphasized before, when the English construction was said to be far more lifelike than the roundabout and inert substitution for inverted commas, ὅτι ζητοῦμεν."[2]

To this argument we answer as follows: (1) It is certainly too much to suppose the copyists of the Greek Codices did not know the value of the Greek present; it is also too much to suppose this ignorance on the part of all the Greek Fathers, who are unanimous in using the imperfect. (2) Power makes a mistake. Neither B nor W-H give the present ζητεῖτε in verse 49. They both have the present ζητοῦμεν in the previous verse, 48. In regard to this verse 48, for the imperfect ἐζητοῦμεν there are ℵ⁰ AC DL XΓΔΛΠ unc³ al fere omnia it^omn vg syr^omn etc., etc., and for the present ζητοῦμεν there are ℵ* B 6^pe vid. So that for verse 48, B has the

---

[1] "Who were they, etc.," IThQ VII (1912) 444–451.
[2] Id., pp. 450–451.

THE CORRECT TEXT OF LUKE ii. 49

present, and W-H on account of their cult of this Codex adopted this reading. But in spite of having the present in verse 48, both B and W-H retain the imperfect in verse 49, which fact is a strong point in favor of the imperfect in the latter verse.

(3) Comparing the two verses 48 and 49 in regard to the verb "seek": If originally there were different tenses, the present in one and the imperfect in the other, there is more authority for the present in verse 48, for B has the present here and the imperfect in 49, — which is the stand taken by W-H, Nestle, and B. Weiss; on the other hand, if the verbs in both verses had originally the same tense — the only authority for the present in both verses is ℵ (prima manu) which makes, it highly probable that the imperfect was in both verses. (4) It is also suggested from the meaning that the verb "seek" in 49 had originally the same tense as the verb "know" in the second half of the verse. Now it is fairly certain, and Power here agrees with us, that the imperfect ἤδειτε is to be preferred.

(5) All that Power's whole argument amounts to is that the present tense would not be incongruous; he does not, cannot claim that the imperfect continuous is incongruous. So that the matter is to be settled on the question of the authorities. For the present tense there are prima manu Sinaiticus (ℵ), only one of the Ferrar group (346), one syr. (cur.), and only one Old Latin (b). The rest of these groups are in unison in giving the imperfect, and this along with D and A B C L X Γ Δ Π and all the Fathers except a solitary Latin one, St. Leo. The evidence is clearly in favor of the imperfect, the one exception in each of the aforesaid groups being explicable by error of the copyist.

4. Instead of ἤδειτε (imperfect) we find the present οἴδατε in D 225,282 49[ev] a b c e f ff² l q syr[cu].

The remarkable and much discussed fact is found here again, viz., that here as in so many other points D, the Old Latin and syr[cu] agree against the common reading. But it is to be noted that syr[utr] and the Ferrar group arc, here with the consensus of authorities, for the imperfect, which fact lends great weight to the view that the imperfect is the correct reading.

The Fathers are arranged on both sides.

(a) The following give the present tense: Childhood Gospel of

Thomas,[1] Marcosians in Irenaeus,[2] Origen,[3] Cyril of Alexandria,[4] Theodoret,[5] Tertullian,[6] Juvencus,[7] Ambrose,[8] Gratiani.[9]

(b) The imperfect is found in Origen,[10] Cyril of Jerusalem,[11] Didymus,[12] Epiphanius,[13] Cyril of Alexandria,[14] Dialogus contra Maced,[15] Theodoret,[16] Photius,[17] Augustine,[18] Leo,[19] Victor,[20] Simeon Metaphrastes,[21] Greek catena (edit. Cramer).[22] It is a curious thing that Titus of Bostra insists that not the plural but the singular (οἶδας) was used. This disagreement of the Fathers may be explained by the fact that they frequently quoted from memory. Thus we find Origen and Cyril of Alexandria using both tenses. Hence this disagreement of the Fathers does not impair our reason given above for preferring the imperfect, ᾔδειτε.

5. In regard to the expression ἐν τοῖς, there are no variants in the Greek Manuscripts, but we find some in the versions and Fathers.

For ἐν τοῖς τοῦ Πατρός μου,

(a) The Curetonian Syriac has "in the Father's house"; [23]

---

[1] Évang. Apocryph. (edit. Michel), 188.
[2] Both Greek and Latin Adv. Haer., I. 20, 2, M.PG VII. 653.
[3] Homil. XVII. in Luc., M.PG XIII. 1849.
[4] De Rocta Fide, loc. cit., M.PG LXXVI. 1517.
[5] De Incarnat., M.PG LXXIV. 73.
[6] Adv. Prax., XXVI., M.PL II. 189.
[7] Gosp. Harm. ad. loc., Corp. Script. Lat., XXIV. 18 (edit. Huemer).
[8] Comment. ad. loc., Corp. Script. Lat., XXXII. p. 75 (edit. Schenkel).
[9] Accord. to Sabatier, III. 2, 272.
[10] Origen has the imperfect in Homil., XXI. M.PG XIII. 1851.
[11] Catech., VII. De Patre, VI. M.PG XXXIII. 612.
[12] De Trinit., III. 20, M.PG XXXIX. 896.
[13] Three times. Adv. Haer., II. i. Haer. 30 and 51, M.PG XLI. 456, and 925, and Adv. Haer., II. ii. Haer., 66, M.PG XLII. 93.
[14] Three times: once in De Recta Fide, M.PG LXXVI. 1517, and twice in his Comment. in Luc. ad loc., M.PG LXXII. 509.
[15] Nbr., 486, M.PG XXVIII. 324.
[16] Cited by Tischendorf as 5, 1063, but which I could not verify.
[17] Twice: Ad Amphil., CLVIII., M.PG CI. 832: and Contr. Manac, IV. 16, M.PG CII.B 213.
[18] Augustine uses the imperfect several times in Homil., LI. in Concord. Evang., M.PL XXXVIII. 342 ff. He also uses it in De Nuptiis et Concup., Corp. Script., Lat. XLII. 225 (edit. Vrba & Zycha).
[19] Epist., XVI., M.PL LIV. 697.
[20] Evangel. Harm. Interp., XII, M.PL LXVIII. 262.
[21] Vitae Sanctorum ..., M.PG CXV. 548.
[22] Catenae Graecae, 27.
[23] F. C. Burkitt, Evangelion da Mepharreshe, I., Cambridge 1904, 258–9, "Abba" here and often in this version is used for "My Father," cf. Burkitt's Work, II. 47.

THE CORRECT TEXT OF LUKE ii. 49

the Peshitto: "in the house of My Father";[1] the Sinaitic Syriac: "in the house of My Father";[2] the Armenian: "in the house of My Father";[3] the Persian: "in domo patris";[4] the Arabic Gosp. of the Infancy: "in My Father's house."[5]

(b) The Coptic (Boharic) has "in the things of My Father";[6] the Coptic (Sahidic): "in the (things) of My Father";[7] the Aethiopic: "in his quae (sunt) Patris Mei";[8] the Arabic: "in iis quae Patris mei";[9] the Old Latin: "in his quae Patris mei";[10] except Veronensis (b)[11] which has "in propria Patris mei," and both Vercellensis (a)[12] and Rehdegeranus (1)[13] which have "in Patris mei"; the Vulgate: "in his quae Patris mei."[14]

Concerning the Fathers, they are classified elsewhere[15] when we dealt at length with the question as to what is to be understood by this expression ἐν τοῖς τοῦ. It can be readily seen that the versions are not at all at one in their renderings of the expression. They already raised the question as to what is to be understood.

6. Instead of εἶναί με we find the transposition, με εἶναι in D i, 13, 69, 118, 6^pe it vg.

It is to be noted that D and the numbers of the Ferrar group, 13, 69, and the Old Latin are here again in agreement against the general consensus of texts which have εἶναί με.

Here, too, the Fathers are naturally on both sides.

---

[1] Tetraevangelium sanctum juxta, simpl. Syr. Vers. edit. P. E. Pusey, Oxonii 1891, 330.
[2] The Four Gosp. in Syriac transcribed from the Sinaitic Palimpsest, Cambridge, 1894.
[3] Waltoni Bibl. Polyglotta, V. 258.
[4] Id.
[5] Codex Apocryphus (edit. Thilo), 128.
[6] The Coptic Version of New Test. in the North. Dial., II. (edit. from MS. Huntington, 17, Oxford (1898), 32-33.
[7] The Coptic Vers. of New Test. in South Dial., II., Oxford (1911), 44-45.
[8] Transl. in Waltoni Bibl. Polyglotta, V. 259.
[9] Transl. in same, V. 259.
[10] In Sabatier, Bib. Sac. III., 2, p. 272.
[11] Edit. Oxford, 1911.
[12] Edit. Gasquet, Rome, 1914.
[13] Edit. Vogels, Rome, 1913.
[14] Novum Testamentum D. N. J. C. latine secundum edit. Hieron. (edit. J. Wordsworth, Oxonii, 1899-1908).
[15] In the IthQ for 1922, April and July.

58   THE BOYHOOD CONSCIOUSNESS OF CHRIST

(a) For με εἶναι, there are, Marcosians in Irenaeus,[1] Origen,[2] Didymus,[3] Cyril of Jerusalem,[4] Epiphanius,[5] Theodoret,[6] Dialogus contra Maced.[7]

(b) And for εἶναί με we have the Childhood Gospel of Thomas,[8] Epiphanius,[9] Cyril of Alexandria,[10] Theordoret,[11] Photius,[12] Simeon Metaphrastes,[13] Greek Catena.[14]

The Fathers quoted freely,[15] a practice which renders a mistake easy. The bulk of the texts put the με last, which makes it clear that this is the correct reading. This point may seem an unimportant matter, yet if με is last, it is emphasized, and this is, as we shall see, of some importance.

Summing up the matter of the text, the only serious difficulty is the question of the tense of the two verbs, "to seek" and "to know." In regard to these we have shown that it is most probable that the imperfect represents the original. At any rate there is nothing of great consequence involved. Whether the present or the imperfect was used will not seriously affect anything we have to say.

The resultant text as we take it (in agreement with Westcott-Hort, Tischendorf, Nestle, von Sodon, Vogels, etc.) is: Καὶ εἶπεν πρὸς αὐτούς· τί ὅτι ἐζητεῖτε με; οὐκ ᾔδειτε ὅτι ἐν τοῖς τοῦ Πατρός

---

[1] Both Greek and Latin Adv. Haer., I. 20, 2, M.PG VII. 653.
[2] Homil., XX. in Luc., M.PG XIII. 1852. Yet the other reading is found in another place, M.PG XVII. 324.
[3] De Trinit., III. 20, M.PG XXXIX. 896.
[4] Catech., VII, M.PG XXXIII. 612.
[5] Twice Adv. Haer., I. ii., Haer., 51, M.PG XLI. 925 and Adv. Haer., II. ii. Haer., 66, M.PG XLII. 93.
[6] 5, 1063, according to Tischendorf, Oct. Maj. ad loc.
[7] 486, M.PG XXVIII. 1324.
[8] Évang. Apocr. (edit. Michel), 188.
[9] He quotes twice the other way and once this way. Adv. Haer., I. ii., Haer., 30, M.PG XLI. 456.
[10] De Recta Fide, M.PG LXXVI. 1317. Also Comment. ad loc., M.PG LXXII. 509.
[11] De Incarnatione, M.PG LXXXIV. 73. Cf. M.PG LXXV. 1462.
[12] Twice, Contra Manac., IV. 16, M.PG CII.B. 213, also Ad. Amphil., CLVIII., M.PG CI. 832.
[13] Vitae Sanctorum, M.PG CXV. 548.
[14] Edit. Cramer, 27.
[15] Thus in one place in the Latin translation of Origen we find, "in his quae sunt Patris mei me esse oportet" (Homil. XXI. in Luc., M.PG XIII. 1852). Tertullian writes, "in Patris mei me esse oportet" (Adv. Prax. XXVI. M.PL II. 189). Besides quoting correctly Augustine gives, "in his oportet me esse quae Patris mei sunt" (Homil, LI. De Concord. Evang. X. M.PL XXXVIII. 343).

μου δεῖ εἶναί με; A literal translation would read thus: "And He said unto them: Why[1] did you seek me? Did you not know[2] that in the (things) of My Father I must be?"

[1] Τί ὅτι is for τί γέγονεν ὅτι as in John xiv. 22. It means "why." Cf. Robertson, Grammar of New Test. Greek, 739. Power, Who were they . . .? Ithq VII (1912) 278–279.

[2] Or "were ye not aware" (all the time). The present "wist ye not" of the Authorized and Revised must be sacrificed. Cf. Power, op. cit. IthQ VII (1912) 451.

CHAPTER VII

HISTORICAL TRUSTWORTHINESS OF LUKE ii. 49

1. LUKE'S EARLY CHAPTERS AS A WHOLE

THE first recorded saying of Jesus, spoken when a boy of twelve years, is found only in the Third Gospel. The bulk of scholars date this writing somewhere between 58 and 90 A.D.[1] and nearly all scholars are agreed that the author is Luke the Physician, the companion of St. Paul.[2] There is, however, not the same consensus of opinion touching the range of its historical accuracy. Even a scholar like Harnack charges St. Luke with "carelessness,"[3] but he is sharply taken to task by Ramsay and others;[4] and among a wide range of scholars the highest claims are made for St. Luke as a historian. Plummer even maintains, "that Luke is at variance with other historians has yet to be proven; and the merit of the greater accuracy may still be with him, even if such variance exists."[5] The physician and companion of St. Paul was a most appropriate person for a historian, as his education and profession, his literary ability, and his facilities for investigation, are happy combinations and strong guarantees for historical trustworthiness. In his classic introduction to the Gospel, he lays claim to painstaking research, and he assures the reader that he has written accurately and chronologically to the end that "thou

---

[1] For the different dates assigned by writers, see Jacquier: Hist. des livres du N. Test. II. 491. Conservative writers generally place the date between 60–70 A.D.

[2] Col. iv. 14; Philem. 24. The authenticity of the Third Gospel is denied or doubted by H. Holtzmann, Jülicher, Schmiedel, Pfleiderer and Loisy. These writers contend that an unknown gentile Christian (who made use of the memoirs of Luke) was the final editor or redactor of the Acts and the Third Gospel. However, this view is generally losing ground, especially since the vindication by Harnack of the Lucan authorship of both the Gospel and the Acts (Luke the Physician, especially 121–145).

[3] Luke the Physician, 112.

[4] Ramsay's work, Luke the Physician, is a criticism of Harnack. Likewise is MacRory's; Professor Harnack and St. Luke's historical authority, IthQ. II (1907) 223 ff. Cf. Robertson, Luke the historian, 29–41.

[5] Comment. on Luke, 6.

mayest know the verity of those words in which thou hast been instructed."[1]

It is in the Infancy section of the Third Gospel that the Temple episode is given. Since this section treats of the Virgin Birth and the miraculous attending circumstances, it does not meet the approval of those who reject miracles on a priori principles; and in fact this portion has been the storm center of attack on the New Testament; most radical scholars brand the first two chapters of both Matthew and Luke as "something superadded to the main body of Apostolic tradition,"[2] and attach little or no value to them historically.[3] But the fight has not been all one-sided. Since the beginning of the present century, the historicity of the Infancy narratives has had an ever increasing number of valiant champions,[4] and the result has been to bring into prominence the remarkable evidence for the stand of conservative scholars.

The first two chapters of Luke are found in all the texts of the Gospel that have come down to us. The Muratorian Canon implies that the Gospel began with them.[5] True, they were rejected by both the Ebionites and Marcion, but this was on account of special christological theories to which the contents of these chapters were opposed. Irenaeus (✠202) defends these

[1] Luke i. 1–4. Cf. Blass; Phil. of the Gospels, 7 ff. Plummer: Comment. on Luke, 1–5.
[2] Wellhausen (Das Evang. Luc.) drops these chapters without a word of explanation; Schmeidel is confident that the Gospel of Luke "once was without the first two chapters" (art. Mary in E. B., 2961); they "must come from quite other hands" thinks Usener (art. Nativity E. B.); Loisy maintains that at least the hymns and verses relating to the Virgin Birth must be attributed to the redactor (Les écrits des Luc, RHLr N. S. IV (1913) 367). Cf. also Lobstein (the Virgin Birth, 41), Lester (the Historic Jesus, 57–58), Soltau (Birth of J. C., 49–50).
[3] Cf. Conrady (Die Quelle der kanonischen Kindheitsgesch, J. 728); Bousset (Jesus, 1), Harnack (What is Christianity? 30), Loisy (the Gospel and the Church, 39), Campbell (The New Theology, 101), Martin (The Life of Jesus, 54–55); J. Weiss (Die Schriften des n. T., 412); O. Pfleiderer (Primitive Christianity, II. 109); Wernle (The Sources of Our Knowledge of the Life of Jesus, 100); Völter (Die Evang. Erzählungen von der Geburt und Kindheit Jesu, 131).
[4] Steinmeyer, Die Geschichte der Geburt des Herrn u. seiner ersten Schritte im Leben; Sweet, The Birth and Infancy of Jesus Christ; Durand, The Childhood of Jesus Christ; Steinmetzer, Die Geschichte der Geburt und Kindheit Christi; Orr, The Virgin Birth of Christ; Box, The Virgin Birth. The man who has done the greatest work in upholding and vindicating Luke's historical trustworthiness is Ramsay in his works: Was Christ born at Bethlehem? Luke the Physician, Luke's Narrative of the Birth of Jesus in Exp. ser. 8 vol. IV (1912) 481–507; The Bearing of Recent Discoveries on Trustworthiness of New Testament.
[5] The Muratorian Canon, I, says that Luke wrote in order and "began his narrative with the nativity of John," A–NF V. 603.

chapters against Marcion,[1] Justin Martyr (✠160) shows his opposition to Marcion [2] and quotes from the Infancy sections,[3] and an acquaintance with the early chapters of Matthew and Luke is implied by Ignatius Martyr (✠110–115), who frequently refers to the Virgin Birth.[4]

External evidence entitles one to trace these chapters back to the beginning of the first century, thus favoring the view that they belong to the original Gospel of Luke; but this is all but superfluous, since the internal evidence is so plain and convincing. That the early section "contains the same peculiarities of Luke as are apparent in the other portions of the Gospel and in the Acts of the Apostles," [5] cannot well be denied. In fact, as Hawkins points out, although Luke i–ii is one ninth part of the whole Gospel, it contains almost exactly one seventh of the characteristic words,[6] and even taking the Acts into consideration, the Lucan characteristic words are most frequently used in the Infancy narrative.[7]

Although the first two chapters form an integral part of the Third Gospel; although the wording is Lucan and reveals Luke's hand, yet strange to say the style is in great contrast to other parts of his work, especially to the prologue. Semitic idioms and expressions shine through the Greek clothing in almost every verse, suiting the ideas expressed which are not such as we would expect from a gentile like Luke, but are those of the Old Testament times and of Palestinian origin. The ideas, thoughts and occurrences are so Jewish and so Palestinian that there is little possibility that they were invented by Luke, grant him what genius one may. The poetic charm and the Israelitic spirit in the inserted psalms

[1] Adv. Haer. I. 27, 2 ff; III. 14, 4, etc. Cf. Tertullian, Adv. Marcion, IV. 5 ff.
[2] I. Apol. XXVI. LXVII.
[3] Clearly, he was acquainted with both Mt. i.–ii and Luke. i.–ii., Dial LXXVIII. C., etc.
[4] Ephes. XVIII. XIX; Trall. XIX., etc.
[5] Meyer, Comment. on Mark and Luke, I. 314. Harnack demonstrates that the Infancy section contains Lucan characteristics (Luke the Physician, 97–101 and 199–219), but on account of the presence of the two non-Lucan words, he rejects Luke i. 34–35. So, too, does Weinel (Ausleg. d. apost. Bekenntnisses u. ntl. Forschung ZntlW II (1901) 37 ff.) Zimmermann (Evangelium des Luk. 1 u. 2, StKr LXXVI (1903) 273 ff.), Loisy (RHLr N.S. IV (1913) 367), Hillman (JPrTh XVII (1891) 224), and others. The genuineness of these verses is vindicated by Gigot IthQ VIII (1913) 123 ff., Box, ZntlW VI (1905) 91–93, Bardenhewer, Mariä Verkündigung, 6 ff.
[6] Horae Synopticae, 24–25.
[7] Id., 175.

and narrative portion of Luke i. and ii, are comparable only to the finest parts of the book of Samuel. To quote Zahn, they "could not have been written by a Greek like Luke. They must have originated in Palestine, where men and women of prophetic temperament and prophetic gifts were closely associated with the beginnings and progress of Christianity." [1]

What were his sources for these first two chapters? First, as to the language of St. Luke's source: it was not Greek. It had been generally held to be Aramaic,[2] but Lagarde,[3] and after him Dalman [4] have pointed out that the coloring throughout Luke i.–ii. is distinctly Hebrew. Yet Dalman thinks that a Hebrew source is unproven and that Luke himself may be responsible for the Hebraisms, writing "with greater consistency than usual in Biblical style." [5] Others contend, and it would seem with good reason, that Dalman has gone too far in excluding a Hebrew source from the composition of the first two chapters of the Third Gospel.[6] Also scholars are not agreed as to whether the sources were written or oral; a fair number think they were written,[7] while others (principally Ramsay [8] and Harnack [9]) hold they were oral.

Who then is St. Luke's authority for the facts that appear in

[1] Introd. to New Test., III, 112. Cf. Bardenhewer, Mariä, Verkündigung, 28, 260; Machen, Origin of Luke i. ii., PrthR X (1912) 260; Sweet, Birth and Infancy of J. C., 136–138; Sanday, Life of Christ in Recent Research, 165–166.
[2] Thus Wright, Gospel of St. Luke, 2; Moffatt, Introd., 275, etc.
[3] Mitteilungen, III. 345.
[4] Words of Jesus, 39, and others.
[5] Id. It is also the view of Lagrange, Evang. Selon S. Luc. lxxxvii.
[6] Cf. Box (The Virgin Birth, 43), Briggs (New Light on the Life of Christ, 64). The latter holds there were original Hebrew poems, and Luke's Infancy section is no more than a setting for them. More likely is the view of Torrey that Luke translated into Greek a Hebrew document in which the poems were already set. (Translations from the original Aramaic Gospels, in Studies in Hist. of Rel., pres. to C. H. Toy, 290–295). Resch tried to reconstruct a Hebrew source at the basis of the Infancy section of Matthew, and Luke (Das Kindheits Evang., T.U.X. (1897) 203, 215), but failed. Cf. Mangenot (Luc. in VDB.IV 398); Machen (The New Testament Account of the Birth of Christ, PrthR III (1905) 649). Conrady's fantastic theory (Die Quelle der kanonischen Kindheitsgesch. J., 728), that the childhood narratives are based on the Protevangelium of James, is rejected by all. Cf. Durand (The Childhood of Jesus Christ, 185).
[7] E.g. B. Weiss (Introd. to New Test., 297), Zahn (Introd. to New Test. III, 113). Purves (The Story of the Birth, B.W. VIII (1896) 246), Plummer (Comment. on Luke, 7), Loisy (Les Évang. synopt., I. 384), Briggs (New Light on the Life of Christ, 164), Torrey (op. cit. 295).
[8] Luke the Physician, 13, Was Christ born at Bethlehem? 88.
[9] Luke the Physician, 102, n. 3.

64 THE BOYHOOD CONSCIOUSNESS OF CHRIST

the childhood account, facts such as the two annunciations, which could be known only to the families of John and Jesus, facts such as the very thoughts of Mary, which could be known to herself alone? It was not according to ancient custom for one to name his authority, but in such passages as i. 29; ii. 7, 19, 33, 50, 51, Luke plainly implies that Mary was at least his final authority, as is held by most scholars.[1] Plummer[2] says that Mary herself "may have been the writer of the documents used by Luke" while Ramsay[3] and Sanday[4] hold that there was a woman intermediary, the latter mentioning Joanna of Chusa. On this point there may be a difference, but in any case it is not necessary to suppose more than one document or intermediary "between Luke's finished narrative and Mary's artless story."[5]

About the year 57 A.D. St. Luke accompanied St. Paul to Jerusalem where they met St. James the brother of the Lord and the head of the church (Acts xxi. 17 ff.), and during the two following years while St. Paul was a prisoner in Jerusalem and Caesarea the Third Evangelist had an opportunity of learning the facts at first hand, either from documents or from witnesses, and of becoming acquainted with the incidents which could originally have been known only to Mary and the Holy Family. He had the qualifications necessary to avail himself of this opportunity, and that he did so is shown in his work.

How are we, then, to regard these Hebraistic chapters of Luke? The evidence strongly bears out the view of Plummer, "we have here the earliest documentary evidence which may justly be called contemporary";[6] and as a consequence we have the further

---

[1] To mention a few: Renan (Les Évang., 280), Olshausen (Gospels, I. 82), Godet (Introd. on New Test. II, 475), Harnack (Date of Acts and Syn. Gosp., 155), Zahn (Introd. to New Test. III. 113), Knowling (Our Lord's Virgin Birth, 22), George (The Gospels of the Infancy, OT–NT St X (1890) 282), Purves (The Story of the Birth BW VIII (1896) 426, Wright Luke, HDG II. 89), Briggs (New Light on the Life of Christ, 165), Nolloth (The Rise of the Christian Religion, 147), Milner (St. Luke, ii), Harden (art. Mary the Virgin) HDG II. 141, etc.
[2] Comment. on Luke, 7.
[3] Was Christ born at Bethlehem? 74–78, Luke the Physician, 13.
[4] The Virgin Birth, ExpT XIV (1902–3) 296 ff. Cf. art. Jesus Christ, HDB II. 644.
[5] Sweet, The Birth and Infancy of Jesus Christ, 321.
[6] Comment. on Luke, 7. Sanday concludes, too, that these early chapters of Luke "are essentially the most archaic thing in the whole New Testament, older really in substance — whatever be the date of their actual committal to writing — than 1 and 2 Thessalonians" (Life of Christ in Recent Research, 166).

conclusion that the tradition contained in these chapters, to use the words of Box, "has high claims to historical credibility."[1]

2. THE TEMPLE EPISODE

The account of the episode of the Boy Christ in the Temple comes at the end of the Infancy section.[2] At the outset it is significant to note that negative scholars, as a rule, attribute far more historical value to it than to what precedes. The previous portion reflects the Virgin Birth which these men are unwilling to accept. They claim that the section Luke ii. 40-52 does not contain, rather is opposed to, this doctrine,[3] and that representing the Child Jesus as submitting to the Law and developing in a human manner, it is older and may truly be considered a fragment of Judaeo-Christian literature which was inserted by the redactor without being harmonized with its surroundings.[4]

On the other hand, the genuineness or historicity of Luke ii. 40-52 is denied by B. Bauer,[5] Strauss,[6] Renan,[7] Loisy,[8] O. Pfleiderer,[9] H. Holtzmann,[10] Jeremias,[11] J. Weiss,[12] Völter,[13] Monte-

[1] The Gospel narrative of the Nativity, ZntlW VI (1905) 100. Ramsay does not hesitate to say that Luke "should be placed along with the very greatest of historians" and this on account of recent discoveries and vindications (The Bearing of Recent Disc. on Trustworthiness of New Test. 222). From these same facts Robertson also concludes, "Luke is shown to be the careful and accurate historian that he professed to be" (The Romance of the Census in Luke's Gospel, Bib. Rev. V (1920) 506).
[2] The similarities of expression in verses 40 and 52 can be accounted for by the fact that both summarize a number of years in Christ's life, and hence these verses need not indicate a separate source. Cf. Schleiermacher, Essay on Luke, 41.
[3] Cf. Lobstein (V. Birth, 49), Schmiedel (Art., Mary, EB), Loisy (Les Évang. Synopt., 382), H. Holtzmann (Hand Comment., 51), Réville (Jésus de Naz., 409, note), Barrows (Mythical and Legendary Elements in the New Test., NW VIII (1899), 292), Soltau (The Birth of Jesus Christ, 28, 29), Neumann (Jesus, 47). Conservative scholars on the contrary claim that this passage witnesses to and confirms Christ's supernatural conception. Cf. Gigot (The V. Birth in Luke ii. IthQ VIII (1913) 429-433), Durand (The Childhood of Jesus Christ, 121).
[4] Lobstein (op. cit., 49), Réville (op. cit., 409), Loisy (op. cit., 382), H. Holtzmann (op. cit.), Barrows (op. cit.). Cf. on matter, Budham (The Integrity of Luke i. and ii., ExpT VIII (1896-7), 177), Durand (op. cit., 120).
[5] Kritik der Evangelien, I. II. 313.
[6] Life of Jesus, 197-200.
[7] Life of Jesus, 60.
[8] Op. cit., 384.
[9] Christian Origins, 230.
[10] Op. cit., 51.
[11] Babylonisches im n. T., 109.
[12] Die Schriften des n. T., 430.
[13] Die evang. Erzählungen der Geburt., 75-81.

66   THE BOYHOOD CONSCIOUSNESS OF CHRIST

fiore,[1] and A. Martin.[2] Others express doubts and hesitate to say whether or not it is historical, such as Hase,[3] Réville,[4] Schmiedel,[5] Schenkel,[6] Guignebert,[7] Miller.[8] And others ignore the account altogether.

The reasons assigned for rejecting as unhistorical the episode of the Boy Jesus in the Temple are drawn mostly fron analogies and resemblances between the Gospel story and events related of other personages, namely Buddha,[9] Josephus,[10] Moses,[11] Samuel,[12] Solomon,[13] David,[14] and Alexander the Great.[15]

In the first place, in none of the cases brought forward is it a historical fact that the occurrence which is supposed to be analogous is connected with the twelfth year.[16] Secondly, the very fact

[1] The Synoptic Gospels, II. 863.
[2] Life of Jesus, 76–78.
[3] Life of Jesus, 51. He treats the question at length in Geschichte Jesu, 224.
[4] Jésus de Naz., 410 ff. Cf. Birth and Infancy of J., NW I (1892) 721.
[5] "Mary," E.B. c. 2966, also Die Haupt-probleme des Lebens Jesu-Forschung, 94.
[6] Das Charakterbild J., 35 (trans. 58, 59).
[7] Manuel d'Hist. anc. du Chrét., 175.
[8] Our knowledge of Christ . . . 51, cf. BW LXIII (1914) 76.
[9] Lalita Vistara, XI. The story is found in two forms. In the Pali form, Buddha, an infant of five months, was left by his nurses under a jambu-tree which continued to afford him shade despite the fact that the sun had gone round in the heavens. In the form of the Northern school, as a young man he retired from his father who after a search found him in a meditative trance in the arrested shade of the jambu-tree. (Cf. Aiken, the Dhamma of Gotama, 246–247). The analogy supposing dependence is held by Pfleiderer (Christian Origins, 230), Hase (New Test. Parallels, 31), Campbell (The New Theology, 101), Berg van Eysinga (Jüdische Einflüsse, 27), and others.
[10] In his own life (11) Josephus tells that "when fourteen he was consulted by the high priests and principal men of his city concerning points of the Law." Cf. Strauss, Life of Jesus, 197, note), Hausrath (Jesus u. die ntl. Schriftsteller, II. 93), Krenkel (Josephus und Lucas, 75 ff.).
[11] In his twelfth year Moses is said to have left his father's house and to be wise above his years: Philo (De vita Moses, app. edit. Mangey II. 2, p. 83), and Josephus (Ant. II. ix. 6). Cf. Strauss (op. cit.), Jeremias (op. cit., 109). Hase (Life of J., 51).
[12] Samuel is said to have prophesied in his twelfth year, Josephus (Ant. V. x. 4). Cf. Strauss (op. cit.), Hase (op. cit.); and as a boy Samuel is left in the Temple, I K. i. 22 ff. Völter, Die evang. Erzählungen der Geburt, 76–77.
[13] It is recorded in Ignatius' interpolated epistle Ad Magnes. III. that at the age of twelve David and Solomon gave expression to wise judgments. Cf. Strauss (op. cit.).
[14] Id.
[15] Young Alexander questioned the Persian Ambassadors to his father's court concerning their mode of fighting, etc. Plutarch's Vit. Alex. 5 (II. p. 842, B), Jeremias (op. cit.); O. Pfleiderer adds what Suetonius says of Augustus Octavius (XCIV.).
[16] Josias (according to 2 Paralip. xxxiv. 3) "in the twelfth year of his reign cleansed Juda and Jerusalem." This account is not an analogy, for Josias was then twenty years of age.

that other great geniuses gave or were supposed to give in boyhood a premonition of their greatness could not of itself account for St. Luke's story. Why did this fact have no influence on the other writers of the New Testament who pass over Jesus' boyhood? Then there is the difficulty of explaining how these legends, or occurrences, found their way into Palestine, were responsible for the story of the Boy Christ, and were the reason why it was incorporated in the Gospel account, while some of the Apostles were still alive and in the country where the Gospel events took place. Some of the analogies mentioned are far-fetched and we need not delay on them.[1] The one most frequently mentioned is that of Buddha; yet to quote Aiken, "it is plain that with the single exception of the search for the young prince . . . this legend is quite unlike the story of the lost Jesus."[2] The most striking analogy, at first sight, is Josephus' account of His being consulted on the Law as a boy of fourteen. But his work was written after the Third Gospel, or at any rate not long enough previously to have any influence on Luke; in any case, to use the words of O. Holtzmann, "there is nothing at all in common between the perfect simplicity of Luke's narrative and the vain self-glorification of Josephus."[3]

The best analogy mentioned, the one that in any way may have had an influence on the Gospel narrative is that of Samuel, — not because he is said to have begun to prophesy at the age of twelve which Josephus (Ant. V. x. 4) alone mentions. There are striking resemblances (especially between I K. iii. 19; ii. 26) of Samuel on one hand, and Lk. i. 66, 80 of John, and Lk. ii. 40, 52 of Jesus; also between Anna's Canticle I K. ii. 1–10, and Zachary's Lk. i. 68–79 and Mary's Lk. i. 46–55), yet there are striking differences. Extrinsic or literary dependence[4] would account for the facts. When St. Luke was writing the Infancy narrative of Christ in Whom Jewish history reached its greatest climax, he may have been influenced after a literary way by the childhood account of the great prophet Samuel who also witnessed a climax in the history of the Jewish people. The account of Anna and her "asked-of-God" child, one of the most beautiful and most impressive

---

[1] Cf. Meyer (Comment. on Mk. and Lk. i. 347), Keim (Jesus of Naz. 134–5), Steinmetzer (Geschichte der Geburt u. Kindheit C. 202) and others.
[2] The Dhamma of Gotamma, 247.
[3] Life of Jesus, 100. Cf. also a similar judgment by Zahn (Introd. to New Test. III. 134) and by Barth (Die Hauptprobleme des Lebens J., 269).
[4] Literary influence does not militate against the Catholic doctrine of inspiration.

narratives of the Old Testament, by its simplicity and realism especially appealing to an artistic temperament, could not but impress the author of "the most beautiful book ever written." The effect would manifest itself in the Evangelist or the author of the Hebrew original emphasizing certain points, recording certain facts, omitting others, thus (whether intentionally or not) bringing out resemblances interwoven in the accounts of John and Jesus.[1] Outside of this there is no influence and there certainly is no dependence of facts; the boy Samuel is left at the Temple (I. K. i. 22, 28) whereas the Boy Jesus only visits the Temple at feast time (Lk. ii. 42), living at Nazareth (ii. 39). In the Temple God speaks to Samuel (I. K. iii. 4–14), whereas Christ stupefies the doctors by His understanding and His answers (Lk. ii. 47). Samuel calls God "Lord" and speaks of Himself as "servant" (I. K. iii. 10) whereas Jesus refers to God as "My Father" (Lk. ii. 49). In spite of any literary influence that the childhood account of Samuel had on Luke's Infancy narrative, the facts recorded of the Boy Jesus are quite different from these recorded of Samuel; this is worth noticing, as it is an indirect argument for the historicity of the Lucan episode.

Other objections against the historicity of St. Luke's account, drawn from its alleged unlikeliness, namely, how the Boy Jesus could get lost,[2] how the parents could be a whole day without missing Him,[3] how they could be "three days" without finding Him,[4] the Boy's unnatural and unfilial attitude,[5] such objections are not serious ones and can be easily answered.

As to positive arguments for the genuineness and historicity of the section Luke ii. 40–52, we can quote the same textual and external evidence as we gave above to indicate that Luke i. and ii. is an integral part of the Third Gospel. Besides, this section is written in Luke's characteristic vocabulary; Harnack has gone

[1] The LXX. had a certain literary influence on St. Luke. Even in the view, which is very probable, that Luke merely translated a Hebrew original, a literary influence is all the more likely. The literary influence of any similar account in the Old Testament would probably tell on the writer of the classical Hebrew source.

[2] He was not lost, He deliberately "remained."

[3] Objection raised by Martin, Life of J., 76. But it shows what confidence they had in their Son.

[4] Martin, loc. cit. They had gone a day's journey, it took another to return, and they found Him on the third.

[5] Martin, op. cit., 77, 78, and others. But the attitude was not unnatural and unfilial for One who transcended earthly relations.

TRUSTWORTHINESS OF LUKE ii. 49

into each verse to demonstrate this.[1] Indeed there are words and expressions here which are not found in the New Testament outside of St. Luke, for instance, κατ' ἔτος (41), κατὰ τὸ ἔθος (42), ὑπέμεινεν (43), ἀνεζήτουν (44), ὀδυνώμενοι (48),[2] τί ὅτι (49). We may point out also other notable Lucan characteristics. The verb ὑποστρέφειν (43, 46) runs through the Third Gospel and Acts; it is found elsewhere in the New Testament, only in St. Paul (twice).[3] The Hebraic construction ἐν τῷ, with the infinitive as in 43, is found 25 times in Luke, once in Matthew and once in Mark.[4] Another Hebraism καὶ ἐγένετο (42, 46) is found 42 times in the Third Gospel, 21 times in Acts and only 5 times in Matthew, 4 times in Mark and not at all in John.[5] Another Lucan characteristic is καὶ αὐτός (50) where αὐτός has no real intensive force and where καὶ is merely copulative. Yet this Lucan Greek wording is only a covering for the Jewish background; Hebrew style, expressions, modes of thought betray themselves in every verse, the whole picture of the "parents" and the "Boy" in the Temple is intensely Hebraistic and Palestinian, the warm Jewish devotion and respect for the Law is breathed forth at every step, the entire background drawn in the text is most realistic for the early decades of our era.

After the early Hebrew atmosphere that pervades the account, the most striking feature of the narrative is its simplicity. The tone is sincere and in no way artificial. Moreover, there are points which the composer of a legend would not record, the Boy Jesus remaining behind without the permission of His parents, His abrupt words offering no apology,[6] yet His subjecting Himself, the parents themselves being surprised at the scene before the Doctors, their not understanding the saying Jesus uttered, — all these are marks of "psychological truth," [7] and strong indications

---

[1] Luke the Physician, 212–214; so have Zimmermann; Evangelium des Lukas. StKr LXXVI (1903) 263; and Machen, the Origin of the First Two Chapters of Lk. PrthR X (1912) 252–253.

[2] This word is also one of Luke's medical terms. Cf. Vogel, Zur Charakteristik des Lukas, 62.

[3] Cf. Plummer's Comment., 35.

[4] Cf. Dalman, Words of J., 33.

[5] Id., 32; Zimmermann, op. cit., 250.

[6] Schleiermacher sees in the "inexplicable indifference" on the part of Jesus a sure pledge that the whole story is not fiction (Essay on Luke, 42).

[7] Box, Virgin Birth, 108.

of genuineness. Seeing "its unadorned simplicity and its internal truth," Meyer[1] strongly defends its historicity; so does Keim, who declares that the episode "cannot have been devised by human hands which left to themselves were always betrayed into coarseness and exaggeration as shown by the apocryphal gospels."[2] The historicity is upheld not only by Keim and Meyer, but also by such men as Schleiermacher,[3] Tholuck,[4] Stapfer,[5] Furrer,[6] O. Holtzmann,[7] B. Weiss,[8] Nat. Schmidt,[9] Wendt,[10] Steinmeyer.[11]

The words of the Boy Jesus in Luke ii. 49 share the fate of the rest of the episode in regard to the question of historicity.[12] These scholars whom we have mentioned as denying or doubting the genuineness of the episode include therein the first recorded saying; and those who defend the historicity of the episode hold likewise the historicity of Christ's words. We quote one of the critics, Wendt, who regards it from his standpoint: "The calm assurance with which He spoke of God as His Father and of His sojourn in His Father's house as if it were a matter of course, and the childish naïveté and simplicity of judgment with which he perceived it a necessary duty to tarry in His Father's house in spite of His parents' departure and their anxious quest of Him, all these traits bear evidently the stamp of truth."[13] Farrar, from a more exalted point of view, says about it, "This answer, so divinely natural, so sublimely noble, bears upon itself the certain stamp of authenticity. The conflict of thoughts which it implies; the half-vexed astonishment which it expresses that they should

---

[1] Comment. on Mk. and Lk., I. 347.
[2] Jesus of Naz., 136.
[3] Über die Schriften des Lukas, 38–41 transl., 42.
[4] He defends the genuineness against Strauss (Die Glaubwürdigkeit der Evang. Geschichte, 211–221).
[5] J. C. before His Ministry, 39 ff.
[6] Leben Jesu Christi, 46.
[7] Life of Jesus, 99.
[8] Life of Jesus, I. 278.
[9] The Prophet of Naz., 251 note.
[10] The Teaching of Jesus, 95, 96.
[11] Die Geschichte der Geburt des Herrn, 158–208.
[12] This is speaking generally. There are exceptions, v.g. Neumann (Jesus, 47), who calls Lk. ii. 40–52 a "very valuable old record" yet says about verse 49: "we must simply concede that this answer of Jesus' was formulated by a later writer."
[13] The Teaching of Jesus, 99.

so little understand Him; the perfect dignity, and yet the perfect humility, which it combines, lie wholly beyond the possibility of invention. It is in accordance, too, with all His ministry . . ."[1]

There is a remarkable conformity and harmony between Jesus' earliest recorded saying and the sayings of His later life, especially Mark iii. 21, 31–35; yet this fact should not warrant one to cast suspicions on the historicity of the Boy Jesus' saying on the ground that it was invented on the basis of other sayings, — which is done by Loisy,[2] Pfleiderer,[3] Montefiore,[4] and Völter.[5] The uniqueness of the saying appears from the fact that the only parallels that can be discovered are ones among Christ's own words;[6] and can it not be argued that the harmony between the first saying and those of the public ministry is rather a mark of genuineness, since it is generally admitted that a great unity and uniformity runs through all of Christ's teaching? Besides the view of these writers requires deliberate deception and fraud on the part of the author of the Third Gospel. If he was an impostor, we say with Ramsay, "his work remains one of the most incomprehensible and unintelligible facts of literary history."[7]

Luke had the capabilities and the opportunities of getting approximately first-hand information; and it is incredible that one who was brought into intimate fellowship with a Jewish Christian group at Jerusalem "of whom a blood relative of Jesus was a prominent member, would have accepted any important item concerning His life without confirmation from the lips of James."[8] At any rate, it seems clear that no less a person than Mary is the final authority from whom directly or through an intermediary the Evangelist learned the answer of the Boy Jesus. The pithy abrupt saying was most strange and deep. Coming

---

[1] The Life of Christ, 36.
[2] Les Évang. Synopt., I. 381.
[3] Primitive Christianity, II. 113.
[4] Synoptic Gospels, II. 864.
[5] Op. cit., 78, 79.
[6] In spite of Pfleiderer's remarks (Early Christian Conception of Christ, 45), there is very little resemblance between Christ's saying and that reported of Buddha: "Cast aside thy ploughing, O my father, and seek higher." Völter is certainly straining a point when he bases Christ's words on expressions of Anna, I K. i. 22, 28, as well as on Mk. iii. 31–35 (op. cit., 79).
[7] Was Christ born in Beth.? 19.
[8] Sweet, Birth and Infancy of Jesus Christ, 321.

as the climax to a period of great worry and anxiety, it must have made a deep impression on the sorrowful mother; it could be easily preserved (ii. 51) to a time when it was understood in all its bearings (ii. 50). Such a saying, with such attending circumstances, could be without difficulty exactly remembered even though many years had elapsed since its utterance.

CHAPTER VIII

THE HISTORICAL BACKGROUND OF LUKE ii. 49

1. CIRCUMSTANCES LEADING TO THE UTTERANCE OF JESUS' FIRST RECORDED SAYING

AFTER describing Christ's birth (ii. 7 ff.), His Circumcision, when eight days old (ii. 21), and His Presentation in the Temple, when about forty days old[1] (ii. 22 ff.), St. Luke writes concerning the Holy Family: "and after they had performed all things according to the law of the Lord, they returned into Galilee, to their own city Nazareth" (ii. 39). This statement is to be understood in the sense that finally the "parents" and the Child returned to Nazareth, not immediately but after some interval; for in the meantime took place the flight into Egypt to escape the murderous hand of Herod the Great (Matthew ii. 13–18). As this king soon died the stay in Egypt was of short duration. When the Holy Family returned to Palestine they heard that the wicked "Archelaus reigned in Judea in the room of Herod his Father" (Matthew ii. 22), and in fear they "retired into the quarters of Galilee" (id.) "to a city called Nazareth" (Matthew ii. 23).

During the next nine years (B.C. 4–A.D. 6) under the sovereignty of Caesar Augustus of Rome, Archelaus reigned as Ethnarch of Judaea, Idumaea and Samaria.[2] He surpassed his father "in cruelty, oppression, luxury, the grossest egotism and the lowest sensuality, and that without possessing the talent or the energy of Herod."[3] Nor was there political peace and contentment in populous fertile Galilee, — where Jesus was growing up. The accession of Archelaus' brother, the incestuous Herod Antipas

---

[1] Other figures are suggested and there are various arrangements for the chronology of the Infancy section and for harmonizing the accounts of Matthew and Luke; cf. Maas, "Jesus Christ" in Cath. Enc. VIII. 378. Clemens, "Infancy" HDG I. 823, Durand, The Childhood of Jesus Christ, 250–258.
[2] Josephus, Ant. XVII. xi. 1–4; B. J. II. vi. 3.
[3] Edersheim, Life and Times of Jesus, I. 220.

74 THE BOYHOOD CONSCIOUSNESS OF CHRIST

(Luke iii. 19), the cunning "fox" (Luke iii. 32), as tetrarch (4 B.C.-A.D. 39) finds the country in revolt. The rebellion is quenched in the blood of the patriots, yet is followed by another of similar result¹ (cf. Luke xiii. 1, 2).

Having a large percentage of Gentile inhabitants and enjoying considerable commerce, Galilee was to a great extent free from the bigotry and fanaticism characteristic of the Southern Province, and, even more than Judaea, it came under the influence of the surrounding Graeco-Roman civilization.² It was Roman arms that conquered the Holy Land, but it was not Roman but Greek culture, language and ideas that held sway in the Empire.

The city (πόλις Matthew ii. 23; Luke i. 26; ii. 4, 39) of Nazareth must have been susceptible to this Graeco-Roman civilization, situated as it was on a great route of traffic and intercourse that led from the East to the sea.³ Here it was that Christ passed through the different stages of childhood and boyhood, stages for each of which the Jews have appropriate names.⁴

Was there an elementary school in Nazareth? According to a later Jewish tradition (Baba Bathra 21a, which was taken to be by no means incredible), Joshua ben Gamala (high priest from 63–65 A.D.) enacted that teachers of boys should be appointed in every province and in every town, and that children of the age of six or seven should be brought to them.⁵ Holding that this measure presupposes a somewhat longer existence of boys' schools, Schürer says "one may without hesitation transfer them to the age of Christ, even though not as a general and established institution." ⁶

---

¹ Josephus, Ant. XVIII. i. 1; cf. Edersheim, Life and Times of J., I. 241.
² Cf. Galilee, HDG I. 634; Mathews, Hist. of New Testament Times, 149; Mahaffy, Silver Age of the Greek World, 443–444. The ordinary inhabitants of the towns spoke Aramaic Greek and perhaps Latin; cf. Mathews, Hist. of New Testament Times, 160; Kennedy Education, HDB I. 451.
³ Cf. Edersheim, In the Days of Christ, 36, Galilee, in HDG I. 633; Bardenhewer: Mariä Verkündigung, 63–67, Kent, Biblical Geography and History, 239–241.
⁴ Cf. Edersheim, In the Days of Christ, 103–104. See also Brough, The Early Life of Our Lord. There is an excellent article on Boyhood (Jewish) and Boyhood of Jesus, by Farmer in HDG I. 221–230. Careful and scholarly work is shown at every step and apart from the "dogmatic conclusions" it is the best I have read on the matter. For works on Jewish education, cf. J. Simon: Education et l'Instruction des Enfants chez les anciens Juifs (Leipzig 1879), Feldman, The Jewish Child, 275 ff.
⁵ Cf. Edersheim, In the Days of Christ, 134. Schürer, Hist. of Jewish People, vol. II. Div. II. 49.
⁶ Op. cit. vol. II. Div. II. 49–50. Also Kennedy (Education, HDB I. 450). Other writers are not so positive, but hold the view to be probable; Edersheim

Whether or not there was one of these schools in Nazareth, indeed, irrespectively of any education received elsewhere, the obligation of instructing children remained with the parents.[1] The only text book was the Bible, wherein the Jews found solace and refuge from persecution and Hellenism and in which there was contained a literature that has had no equal. Every opportunity was used to make the child acquainted with the Sacred Scriptures. There were little rolls of parchment hung up in the doorway, and phylacteries were worn on the forehead and on the wrist containing choice portions of Holy Writ, which the child read and repeated as soon as he was old enough to do so. Hence Josephus could boast, that "from earliest consciousness" the Jews "learned the laws, so as to have them, as it were, engraved upon the soul." [2]

It is certain that there was a synagogue at Nazareth [3] (cf. Luke iv. 16), with services "not only on Sabbaths and feast days, but also on the second and the fifth days of the week." [4] These synagogue services, with their lections from the Law (Acts xv. 21) and the Prophets (Luke iv. 17-20; Acts xiii. 15), constituted an important factor in the training of Jewish boys. Indeed the Jewish religion was a ritualistic and ceremonial religion, "teaching through the eye in a way well adapted to the capacities of children." [5] And much of the ceremonial was for the home; thus in regard to the Pasch or Passover most of the service was conducted in the family circle.

According to the Law (Ex. xiii. 14, 17; xxxiv. 23, 24; Lev. xxiii. 4-22; Deut. xvi. 16) all male Israelites were obliged to appear in the Temple thrice a year, namely, at the feast of Pasch, the feast of Weeks and the feast of Tabernacles; though women and children did not come under the obligation, they often went, like

---

(Life and Times of J., I. 230-233), Hollmann (The Jewish Religion in the Time of Jesus, 10). Farmer says, "at least it is possible" (Boyhood, HDG I. 233). The view of these writers seems to be confirmed by the fact that Philo (Ad Caium XVI.) mentions "teachers and instructors" as well as "parents" who took part in training the Jews "from their very swaddling clothes."

[1] Numerous texts in Old Test. E.g. Ex. xiii. 8; Deut. vi. 20.
[2] Ag. Apion, II. 18. He says in same work, I. 12: "Our principal care of all is this, to educate our children well." Cf. Philo, Legatio ad Caium, XVI.
[3] Besides, Nazareth was one of the gathering places or centers of priests of one of the twenty-four courses whose duty it was to be on ministry in the Temple. (Cf. Edersheim, In the Days of Christ, 36; also Cath. Enc. art. Nazareth).
[4] Edersheim, In the Days of Christ, 277.
[5] Farmer, HDG I. 223.

Phenenna and Anna (I Kings i. 3, 4, 7, 21). Introducing the episode of the Temple visit with which we are concerned, St. Luke states, that Christ's "parents went every year (κατ' ἔτος), to Jerusalem at the feast of the Pasch (or Passover)" (Luke ii. 41). Does this imply that Mary and Joseph went only once a year? Farmer rightly thinks it probable that "the emphatic words of the sentence are οἱ γονεῖς. Joseph may have gone at other seasons and Mary usually (ἐπορεύοντο imperfect of 'habit') accompanied him." [1]

It is not recorded that the parents took the Child with them each year to the feast of the Passover, but it may be implied from the construction of the next verse, which begins the account of the episode, καὶ ὅτι ἐγένετο ἐτῶν δώδεκα, ἀναβαινόντων . . . (Luke ii. 42). It would seem that Jesus went with them; the fact that He was twelve years old — (the Evangelist says twelve years not about twelve) [2] being mentioned to mark the time when the episode occurred.

Lightfoot,[3] and after him Wetstein [4] and others represented that the twelfth year is mentioned because then Christ "became of age" in the Jewish sense; became a "son of the Law" or "son of the Commandment" (בר מצוה), this being His first fulfillment of the law which He was henceforth bound to observe. This view seems very doubtful for the following reasons culled from Edersheim,[5] Schürer [6] and Farmer.[7] (1) We have no evidence that in the time of Christ the term Bar-Mizvah was used for a boy reaching his twelfth year; the term, although already found in the Talmud (Aboth V. 21), was not generally used until the middle

[1] Art. Boyhood HDG I. 225.
[2] By stating the age definitely, Luke implied he is sure of it. He states a definite time, e.g., i. 26, 59; ii. 21, 36, 37; iii. 1. At other times he used the word "about," v.g. Christ was "about thirty," iii. 23; the daughter of Jairus was "about twelve," viii. 42. Does St. Luke's statement imply that Christ was exactly twelve years? In reference to the passage, St. Jerome says that Christ had completed twelve years (duodecim annos Salvator impleverat, Letter to Paulius, LIII., M.PL XXII. 543). Yes, the gospel text implies that Jesus was fully twelve, yet if He was twelve and a few months St. Luke's words would still be appropriate. If we could be sure that the Evangelist meant that Christ was exactly twelve, we could know the exact month of Christ's birth (Nisan).
[3] Horae Hebracae, ad loc.
[4] Nov. Test. Graec., ad loc.
[5] In the Days of Christ, 120; cf. Life and Times of J., I. 235-236.
[6] Geschichte des jüdischen Volkes, II. 496-497, Transl. vol. II. ser. II. 51-52.
[7] "Boyhood" HDG I. 224, also 225.

ages for a full grown Israelite. (2) Then this later authority assigns not twelve years but thirteen as the legal age.[1] (3) Not only are there no reasons for supposing that a child before he reached twelve might not be present at the feast of the Pasch, but we have indications to the contrary.[2] (4) Very likely it was not any definite age, but signs of approaching puberty that marked the boundary line for obligation and non-obligation. (5) The current view is based on a very doubtful assumption that, in this late Talmudic rule concerning the "Son of the Law," we find the explanation for the mention of Our Lord's age. Now Luke ii. 42, implies nothing as to whether Christ attended previous feasts or not, and there are other reasons for the mention of the age, e.g., to mark the time when the episode occurred. (6) Also the fact that Christ remained behind on this occasion, "the parents not knowing it," would seem to imply that it was not His first Passover; if it was His first, the parents would be likely to have made sure He was in the company before setting out. (7) Finally, the silence of the Evangelist, who does not say that the twelve-year-old Christ went to the feast to fulfil any law or custom. And certainly the incident is not mentioned on account of the age, but the age on account of the incident.

But even if this was Jesus' first attendance at the Passover in Jerusalem, there is another reason besides age why it would be so. Archelaus, whom the parents feared (Matthew ii. 22), no longer reigned in Judaea; he had been sent into exile 6 A.D., which was about the twelfth year of Christ's age,[3] and his banishment ushered in a security and safety obtaining more political and social improvement, — Roman law and justice ruling the land; for Judaea with Samaria and Idumaea were incorporated in the Roman province of Syria, under its governor or legate P. Sulpicius Quirinius, the immediate governing of Palestine being directed by the Procurator Coponius.[4]

---

[1] Thirteen and one day is the legal age. Farmer (HDG I. 224) points out that when this age was fixed the Rabbis found reasons for it, or rather for that of twelve. Obligations bound children before their thirteenth year; cf. Yoma, 82 A. Besides Jewish authorities did not agree that full responsibility began at thirteen and one day, some holding that responsibility for sin against God began later. Cf. Feldman, The Jewish Child, 364. For the Bar Mizvah Institution, cf. Löw, Die Lebensalter in der jüdischen Literatur, 210–217.

[2] Ex. xii. 3, 4.

[3] Cf. Dates, HDG I. 415, Chronology, Cath. Enc., Ramsay, Luke the Physician, 235.

[4] Cf. Josephus, Ant. XVIII. i. 1.

78 THE BOYHOOD CONSCIOUSNESS OF CHRIST

The Holy Land was ruled in this manner when Christ made the recorded visit to Jerusalem in His twelfth year; Augustus was still Emperor of Rome and the office of the High Priest was filled by Annas of New Testament memory. Nature and season were propitious,[1] as the Holy Family set out with the "company" from Nazareth on their pilgrimage to Jerusalem.

As the eighty-mile journey (which took three days) progressed, and they came nearer to the Holy City, festive bands choked in greater numbers the roads, and the more fervently arose the chanting of the Psalms of Ascent (Ps. cxix.–cxxiii.), especially the part "we will go into His tabernacle; we will adore in the place where His feet stood. Arise, O Lord, into thy resting place: Thou and the ark, which Thou has sanctified" (Ps. cxxxi. 7, 8). How intense a feeling must have been aroused in the breast of an Israelite, especially if he were a youth from a country town,[2] when on these occasions he mingled with his fellow countrymen, not only from other parts of Palestine, but even from distant countries, all assembled in their great historical city to worship the one true God! What aspirations of intense fervor were stirred up as he entered the great Temple where Jahweh's presence was to a great extent localized, as He took part in the beautiful impressive services of the Jewish feasts, especially this feast of Passover,[3] when the Paschal lamb was slain and offered, when the great songs of praise (the Hallel Ps. cxii. (cxiii.)–cxvii. and the Great Hallel cxxxv.) were chanted by the Levites to the response of the whole people, and when at the question of the youngest present, Why is this night different from other nights? the national history of the Jews was repeated and the symbols of the feast explained! A feast which commemorated the deliverance and emancipation of the nation, which acknowledged God's special care over His chosen people, and whose ritual made so many allusions to the Messiah, must have excited the most intense feelings of patriotism and devotion.

---

[1] The Passover was held from Nisan 15th to 21st (March–April).

[2] See Edersheim's description of the festive crowds, The Temple, 183, 187, In the Days of Christ, 108–109.

[3] As to what the Paschal services precisely consisted of in the time of Christ, one must heed the warning of Farmer (HDG I. 226) that they must have been somewhat different from the liturgy of later times, and also from that of the Egyptian Passover.

THE BACKGROUND OF LUKE ii. 49

As to what were the emotions of the twelve-year-old Boy from Nazareth, history is silent. Whether He and the "parents" remained the entire seven days of the feast, or left after the second day, is a disputed question. Luke simply writes "when they had fulfilled the days" (τελειωσάντων τὰς ἡμέρας Luke ii. 43).[1] But it is recorded that when the parents set out for home, "the Boy Jesus remained behind in Jerusalem (ὑπέμεινεν 'Ιησοῦς ὁ παῖς), the parents not knowing it." It may have been in the crowds at the Temple, to which all pilgrims used to go on the day of departure, that the "Son" and "the parents" became separated. However it happened, such was the case, and the "parents" thinking, He was in the company and that since He knew the time and place of departure, He was perhaps with the younger folk, they went a day's journey to their first resting place.[2] Here they looked around for Him among their relatives and acquaintances, and to their great grief they found that He was missing. They made a thorough search for Him along the road, all the way back to Jerusalem and through the Holy City (ἀναζητοῦντες, vs. 45). It was only "after three days"[3] that their sorrowful quest succeeded. The place where the Boy was found was "in the Temple," and He was "sitting in the midst of the Doctors both hearing them and asking them questions." The word for Temple is the generic term for the whole structure and leaves us in the dark as to the specific part in which the "parents" and the "Son" met. An outward part (porch or colonnade) of the Temple structure is rightly held

---

[1] Cornelius à Lapide, Lucas, Jansenius, Polus, Lightfoot, said the parents remained the seven days of the feast. On the other hand Simeon Metaphrastes and Cajetan said they left on the third day of the feast. Edersheim (Life and Times of J. I. 246–247) contends that it is "impossible" that on this occasion Mary and Joseph remained for the whole feast. He bases his argument on the fact that Christ is found among the Doctors three days after the parents' departure, and according to the Talmud members of the Sanhedrin came out on the terrace and taught during feast days; hence the feast was still going on. This Talmudical argument of Edersheim is not acceptable to Farmer (HDG I. 226), who says that while Luke's words are "perhaps compatible with Joseph and Mary having left on the third day," he prefers "to think that they 'stayed to the end' of the Feast."

[2] Different places are suggested. See Farmer, HDG I. 226, Edersheim, Life and Times of J., I. 248.

[3] This probably is to be considered from the time of departure from Jerusalem. They had gone a day's journey, they passed another day in returning and after the third day they found Him. For other ways of considering the matter, see Plummer, ad. loc. "After three days" may mean "on the third day" as it does in Mt. xxvii. 63; Mk. viii. 31; ix. 31.

to be the likely place.¹ It is stated ² that, on Sabbath days and especially on feast days, the Doctors or great Rabbis were accustomed to come out upon a terrace of the Temple and teach the people. How popular were these free instructions can easily be realized when one takes into account the Jewish reverence for the Rabbis and their love and aptitude for speculation and discussion. As to the personnel of the Doctors on this particular occasion one can only guess, the sacred record being silent.³ The part that Christ played will be examined in a later chapter where we study the effect on all those who heard Him and on the parents who discovered Him there.

Somewhat recovered from the surprise, and, it would seem,⁴ before leaving the place where He was found, and while still in the presence of the astonished Doctors, Mary gave expression to the feeling of her heart in a question to Jesus, "Son, why hast Thou done so to us? Behold Thy father and I have sought Thee sorrowing." The intense mental anguish experienced by both the Virgin Mother and the foster father is expressed by the strong word ὀδυνώμενοι (cf. Luke xvi. 24, 25), considered one of the Lucan medical terms.

¹ Lightfoot (Horae Hebr., 48) and Wolf (Curae Phil. et. Crit., 594) held there was a synagogue in the Temple and the scene took place there. This is refuted by Edersheim, Life and Times of J., 742–743. Cf. Wünsche (Neue Beitrage . . . aus Talmud und Midrasch, 419–420), Hausrath (Hist. of New Testament Times, I. 90), Schürer (Hist. of Jewish People, vol. II. part II. 326), Lesêtre (Le Temple de Jerusalem, 150).
² Cf. Edersheim, Life and Times of J., I. 247. Lagrange has a different view, Évangile selon S. Luc, ad loc.
³ Shammai was probably dead; the mild Hillel may have been still alive (died about 10 A.D.), his grandson Gamaliel, the teacher of St. Paul (Ac. xxii. 3), must have been then flourishing. Cf. Coulburn, Gospel of the Childhood, 105 ff. Maas, A Day in the Temple, 147.
⁴ Some authors have held that the words of Mary, and consequently the answer of Christ, were uttered after leaving the assemblage of the Doctors; v.g. Salmeron, Maldonatus, Cornelius à Lapide, Natalis Alexander. This view is not excluded by the text. Yet when one reads vs. 48, "and seeing Him, they were surprised and His mother said to Him," and after the words vs. 51, "and He went down with them," and when one hears Mary's formal expression "Thy father and I," one receives the impression that the first words were uttered in the presence of the Doctors and bystanders. The Apocryphal Gospels of the Childhood (Gospel of Thomas, First Greek Form (XIX.), Arabic Gospel (LIII.)) reflect this view, representing the Doctors as afterwards speaking to Mary. There is something in the remark of Ellicott (Historical Lectures 96, note 3) that the emphatic position of πρὸς αὐτὸν in verse 48, would suggest that the mother waited until they were alone before she spoke, yet the reading of this text as a whole would suggest the other view.

THE BACKGROUND OF LUKE ii. 49

2. CONTEMPORARY JEWISH CONCEPTION OF GOD'S RELATION TO MAN

It would seem that in Pentateuchal times the Jews considered that Jahweh their God was concerned with them, with their interests, their success. Whenever the term "Father" is applied to Him, or "Sons" (or "Son" or "Children") to them, the relation expressed is always in respect to the nation, never to the individual, and the reason for this relation is frequently the fact that God begot them by delivering them out of Egypt. Thus: "Israel is My Son, My first-born" (Ex. iv. 22); "Be ye children of the Lord your God. He chose thee to be His peculiar people of all nations that are upon the earth" (Deut. xiv. 1, 2); "Is not He thy Father that hath possessed thee, and made thee and created thee?" (Deut. xxxii. 5, 6, 18, 19; cf. Num. xxi. 29; and "as a Father" in Deut. i. 31; viii. 5).

In the last passage quoted, fatherly relation is expressed of God because He is the Creator. This is also done in passages of subsequent works, Is. xlv. 11; lxiv. 8; Malac. i. 6; ii. 10, 11; I Paral. xxix. 10. In these post-Pentateuchal works God is considered in a closer relation to the Hebrew people, namely as the husband, and since God is husband of the nation, individual Jews may be called children of God, — of course in the Jewish idea of husband, that is to say, with strong emphasis on the duty of the espoused Israelites not to prostitute themselves in idolatry. Thus: "And the bridegroom shall rejoice over the bride, and thy God shall rejoice over thee" (Is. lxii. 5; liv. 6); "But thou hast polluted thyself to many lovers; Return, Oh ye revolting children, saith the Lord: for I am your husband." (Jer. iii. 1, 14, 19, 20, 22; ii. 2; cf. Osee ii. 2; 19, 20; Ezech. xvi. 8, 20).

In the same books we have the fatherly relation predicated of God in the sense that He is the Protector of Israel. "I have brought up children and exalted them: but they have despised me . . . A wicked seed, ungracious children" (Is. i. 2, 4; xxx. 9); "Therefore at least from this time call to me: Thou art My Father, the guide of my virginity" (Jer. iii. 4; cf. Osee xi. 1, 3). And we also find the fatherly relation coupled with the idea of mercy and pity.[1] Thus: "and I will bring them back in mercy for I am a father to Israel, and Ephraim is my first-born" (Jer. xxxi. 9, 20; cf. Is. xliii. 6; lxiii. 8, 16; Wisdom (Father in the sense of Providence) xiv. 3, Tob. xiii. 4 acc. some MSS.).

In the prophecies of Jeremiah and Ezechiel it is clearly taught that Jahweh is concerned not only with the nation as a whole but also with its individual members. In the new covenant which Jeremiah promises, as God had written the law on the heart of the prophet, so He was to write it on the heart of the individual Israelite (Jer. xxxi. 32, 34). This individualism was developed by Ezechiel: "All souls are mine" (Ezech., xviii. 4).[2]

A higher step was reached when the fatherly relation of God was predicated of the individual. The book of Wisdom says that the just man "boasteth that he hath the knowledge of God, and calleth Himself the Son of God . . . and glorieth that he hath God for His Father" (ii. 13, 16; cf. ii. 18; v. 5). And the Son of Sirach addresses God thus: "Oh Lord, Father, and sovereign ruler of my life," "Oh Lord, Father and God of my life" (Ecclesiasticus xxiii. 1, 4). The original is not preserved but Dalman says that κύριε πάτερ καὶ δέσποτα (vs. 4, θεέ) ζωῆς μου is to be traced to יהוה אבי ואל חיי.[3] It is said of this passage in Ecclesiasticus that it "certainly witnesses to a real belief in the Fatherhood of God in regard to the individual."[4] These few passages are the only ones in the canonical books of the Old Testament where there is an expression of God's fatherly relation to the ordinary individual.

In the Apocryphal books of the Old Testament[5] (which help us to catch a glimpse of the religious conceptions of the Jews in the centuries immediately preceding the advent of Christianity), God is addressed as "Father" in 3 Mac. v. 7 (prayer is implied); vi. 4, 8; and the sense seems to be the merciful loving God of the

[1] And this tender idea is also expressed in some of the later Psalms: cii. (ciii.) 13; cvi. (cvii.) 41; lxvii. (lxviii.) 5.
[2] Cf. Charles, Religious Development between the Old and New Testament, 106–107.
[3] Words of J., 184–185. Dalman also says concerning li. 14, κύριον πατέρα κυρίου μου that "the original may have had יהוה אבי ואדני "Jehovah my Father and my Lord" (p. 185).
[4] Box and Oesterley, in Introd. to Sirach, in Apocrypha and Pseudepigrapha of Old Test., edit. Charles I. 304; cf. Toy, Judaism and Christianity, 84.
[5] Texts are collected but not well assorted by Wicks: The Doctrine of God in the Jewish Apocryphal and Apocalyptical Literature, London, 1915.

Jews "fighting on their side continually as a father for his children" (vii. 6). It is said in Jubilees i. 23-25, that God will be Father.[1] He is referred to as "Father" in Test. of Levi xviii. 6; Test. of Jud. xxiv. 2;[2] and the Jews are called "children," En. lxii. 11; Ps. of Sol. xvii. 29; Test. of Levi xviii. 8.

Thus a hasty survey of the canonical and Apocryphal books of the Old Testament would seem to suggest that among the Jews, there was a development in the revelation of God's relation to man: from acknowledging God's concern over the nation as a whole, they came to recognize His interest in the individual,[3] and from proclaiming God's fatherly relation to His chosen people they finally confessed His fatherly relation to the individual Israelite.[4]

We have been considering here only God's fatherly relation to ordinary individuals. Divine Sonship has been attributed to extraordinary individuals. Angels are called "Sons of God" in Gen. vi. L-4; Job. i. 6; ii. 1; xxxviii. 7; Ps. xxviii. (xxix.) i.; lxxxviii. (lxxxix.) 7; (cf. Septuag.); and many times in I En. Once (Ps. lxxxi. (lxxxii.) 1-6, cf. John x. 34) Judges are called Gods, synonymous with Sons of God and implying investment with God's power. Concerning the theocratic king typifying the Messiah, it is said in Ps. ii. 7, "Thou art My Son, this day have I begotten thee." And in Ps. lxxxviii. (lxxxix.) 21, 27, 28, "I have found David my servant, He shall cry out to Me: Thou art my Father, my God, and the support of my salvation, and I will make him my first born high above the kings of the earth." Again God said in reference to David, "I will be to him a Father, and he will be to Me a Son" (2 K. vii. 14). "Son" is applied to the Messiah in I En. cv. 2; 4 Esd. vii. 28, 29; xiii. 32, 37, 52; xiv. 9.

A word as to the Greeks, whose civilization had enveloped Palestine at the time of Christ and exerted an influence on the Jews. In general it may be said that the polytheism of the Greeks

---

[1] This passage is remarkable. It reads: "... I will create in them a holy spirit, ... and I will be their Father and they shall be My children, and they all shall be called children of the living God and every angel and every spirit shall know, yea, they shall know that these are My children and that I am their Father in uprightness and righteousness."

[2] Also in Sibylline Books (of uncertain date), V. lines 360, 498, 500.

[3] Yet, as Dalman says, "the individual Israelite was aware that it was only as a member of his people that he possessed the claim to and prospect of God's help and patronage." Words of J., 189.

[4] Cf. Candlish (HDB II. 217), who sees four successive stages in the Old Testament statements about sonship to God as applied to man.

led to doubt and unbelief rather than to a conception of a close or personal relationship with God. In the anthropomorphic theism of Homer, Zeus, although given preëminence as "the Father of Gods and of Men," is represented as having sons and daughters among the Gods, as having brothers and even as having a father, Kronos. In the religious system of the Greek poets of the sixth and fifth centuries B.C., "the concepts of the Gods are essentially the Homeric, except that Zeus plays a larger part in the divine economy than in Homer."[1] Neither in the absolute, the "Ideas" of Plato, nor in the "Mind" (the first cause) of Aristotle, nor in the polytheistic pantheism of Stoicism, is there to be found any conception of man's personal relationship with God.

One who more than anybody else tried to combine the Hebrew and Greek Theosophies, Philo, almost a contemporary of Christ, professed as his central doctrine (in which he was influenced by Plato) the view that God the First Cause of all is so transcendent, so widely separated from the world, that He is present in the world only in His acts and that He accomplished creation through powers or ideas, the chief being the Logos. In regard to God as Father, thanks to Carmon (Philo's doctrine of the Divine Father and the Virgin Mother (AJTh IX (1905) 491–518)) we have his texts on the matter collected and assorted. Philo uses the name of "Father" for God very freely. He uses it in the sense of creator,[2] as is seen from the fact that he often speaks of God as "the Father and Creator" as "the Father of the universe, of the world, of all things"; and based on this sense, he uses the word figuratively (v.g. Father of generic virtue). Indeed, far from holding there was a close relation between man and God, Philo put God at a distance from the world in his transcendental notion of Him.

Before the time of Christ, therefore, the name "Father" had been applied to God by both Jews and Greeks, by the Jews in mostly a national sense, by the Greeks in a vague and mostly

---

[1] Moore, Religious Thought of the Greeks, 75. For an account of the religious thought of the Romans see Döllinger, The Gentile and the Jew, etc., II. 9–6. Cf. also Dill. S. Roman Society from Nero to Marcus Aurelius, London, 1905. For social and religious conditions (and good bibliography) see Angus: The Environment of Early Christianity, 83 ff. See p. 99, for examples where God is called "Father."

[2] See especially, Ad. Caium, XVI. Bibl. S. Pat. Eccl. Graec. II. Phil, Jud. Opera VI. 98, where he says that the Jews were taught to believe "that there was but one God the (their) Father and the Creator of the world."

figurative sense; but the designation of God "My Father" is not found on the lips of any ordinary individual, unless perhaps in the case of Ecclesiasticus xxiv. 1, 4; and the only other reference to God's fatherly relation to the ordinary individual is Wisd. ii. 13, 16. It is indeed remarkable that any mention of God's fatherly relation to the individual is almost absent from the great religious literature of the ancient Jews, and that it is not found in the Psalms, those outbursts of the intense feeling and warm devotion of the Jewish heart. In them Jahweh is frequently addressed as "My God," xv. (xvi.), 2; "My King," v. 3; "My Shepherd," xxii. (xxiii.) 1; yet we never hear Him called "My Father." Outside the Messianic passages we do not find in the Psalms any reference to God's fatherly relation even to the nation as a whole, and we must admit the inference of Green: "If the religion of Israel had really attained to any clear conception of God as Father and of men as His children, it would most naturally find utterance in these compositions, in which we have at once the devoutest expression of the personal religious consciousness and the chosen vehicle of the worship of the congregation."[1]

Not only is the term "Father" comparatively rarely used of God by the Jews before the time of Christ but, as Dalman says, "The Targums show that great care was exercised against the single use of the word father, for God."[2] The examples which Dalman brings forward show that the word "Father" was avoided and even "My Father" (אבי) was changed into "My Lord" (רבוני).

Instances of "Our Father" in Jewish prayers are given by Dalman (the earliest is 118 A.D.),[3] but in Jewish parlance the usual designation of God was "Our Father in heaven," "the dicta of the Rabbis from the end of the first Christian century onwards are the earliest source of instances."[4] Dalman gives instances from this time on showing the conception of the fatherly relation of God to the individual Israelite. But as Beyschlag remarks,

[1] HDB Extra Vol. 125.
[2] Words of J., 191. When Jesus simply said, "My Father worketh until now; and I work" (Jn. v. 17), St. John in the next verse tells us that the Jews therefore "sought the more to kill Him, because He did not only break the Sabbath but also said God was His Father, making Himself equal to God." Could we infer from this that the expression "My Father" applied to God would be blasphemous in their eyes?
[3] Op. cit., 190–191.
[4] Op. cit., 186.

86 THE BOYHOOD CONSCIOUSNESS OF CHRIST

"it may be asked whether its origin in these is not due — as so many old Rabbinic sayings suggest — solely to the desire not to lag behind Christian ideas and modes of expression." [1]

The Targums (which throw light on theological views of contemporaries of Christ) not only show a dislike for the name Father applied to God, but give other evidence of a widespread tendency to exaggerate God's transcendence. Widening the chasm between God and the world, the Targums remove or paraphrase away the anthropomorphisms of the Old Testament; thus the creation of man in the likeness of God is changed into his creation in the likeness of the ministering angels.[2] Changes and paraphrases of a like nature are found even in the Septuagint (third century B.C.).[3] As Fairweather says in the post-exilic period "there was developed a tendency to conceive God as dwelling in the distant heaven as 'afar off' and remote from the life of men."[4] A strongly marked evidence of it is seen in names applied to God in quite general use. Many kinds of evasive and precautionary ways were taken not to refer to the name of God or to mention His Person. He was referred to as "most High," as "Heaven," as "Place," etc.[5]

Yet side by side with this abstract and transcendental view of God and inconsistently with it, there was another great characteristic of Jewish theology contemporary with Christ, namely the autocracy of the Law. The Law was exalted at the expense of everything else, even to the extent of drying up spiritual energies, of lowering spiritual ideas, of limiting religion to the traditional interpretation of the law, and of making God Himself subject to the Law.[6] At the time of Christ, then, there existed a tendency

[1] New Test. Th. I. 80, note 2. This view is also taken by Bousset. Die Religion des Judenthums in ntl. Zeitalter, 357.
[2] Many other examples are given by Sanday, who has a very good treatment of the "Tendencies of Contemporary Judaism" (HDB II. 203–208).
[3] For examples see Sanday, HDB II. 206–207; cf. Fairweather, Development of Doctrine, HDB Extra Vol. 279, also Background of the Gospel, 330, Gilbert, HDG I. 582.
[4] The Background of the Gospel, 208; cf. Maclean (HDG Sing. Vol. X, 301), Gilbert (HDG I. 582).
[5] Cf. Dalman, Words of J., 194–232. Sanday, op. cit., HDB II. 206, Fairweather, op. cit., 281.
[6] He was even represented as studying the Law, cf. Sanday, HDB II. 208, Oesterley, Judaism in the Days of the C., 87 ff. After mentioning the evils of this Jewish worship of the Law, this writer (p. 94) says that one should not "overstate their prevalence." And Herford contends that the exaltation of the Torah on the contrary deepened the spiritual life of the ordinary Jew (Pharisaism, 72).

to put God further and further away from earthly things, to consider Him as transcending them to make Him to a certain extent uninteresting, unlovable.[1]

Summing up, then, and reviewing all our evidence for the Jewish conception of God at the time of Christ, we should think that the prevailing view was the transcendental one of the Scribes and Pharisees. Yet, as we indicated above, there seemed to be a development and elevation of the notion of God's fatherly relationship through the centuries, until at a time, not many centuries distant from the Christian era, God's fatherly relation to the individual was predicated. This was done only a few times; yet there seems to be justice in the remark of Toy that "the conception of God's fatherly relation to individuals existed therefore a couple of hundred years before the beginning of our era, and we may suppose that it gathered force and fulness as the increasing purity and elevation of ethical ideas was transferred to the divine character. Still it does not seem to have been a favorite conception; the Jewish national feeling was strong enough to depress it. It was probably held by a select circle of thinkers, but it was kept out of general view by the circumstances of the time, the political excitements and the religious-ethical tendencies thence resulting." [2] It was, then, only within "a select circle of thinkers" that God's close, warm, fatherly relation to the individual could be preserved amid prevailing views of Judaism relegating God to the distance, making Him subservient to the Law.

[1] When the Pharisees answered Christ: "We are not born of fornication: we have one Father, even God," Jn. viii. 41, they employed the name Father for God in the sense in which it is frequently found in the Old Testament: God was Father of the Jews because they were children of a nation espoused to God. Cf. Mtt. xv. 26; Mk. vii. 27.

[2] Judaism and Christianity, 84; cf. Green, Children of God, HDB Sing. Vol. 125.

SECTION IV

CHRIST'S CONSCIOUSNESS AS EXPRESSED IN LUKE ii. 49

CHAPTER IX

REAL DIVINE SONSHIP EXPRESSED IN THE FIRST RECORDED WORDS

1. THE STUDY OF THE WORDS "MY FATHER"

IN Christ's first recorded saying: "Why did you seek Me? Did you not know that in the (things) of My Father I must be? (Τί ὅτι ἐζητεῖτέ με; οὐκ ᾔδειτε ὅτι ἐν τοῖς τοῦ Πατρός μου δεῖ εἶναί με; Luke ii. 49), the words that express His relationship to God are "My Father." In this expression we immediately strike the core of the problem we have in hand, we meet the whole issue and have to decide it before going further. What will remain to be done, will be only to reinforce the main argument outlined here.

(a) From the evidence brought forward in the previous chapter one can safely conclude that at the time of Christ, the title of "Father" was used of God. The usual way of referring to Him, would seem to have been "Our Father in heaven," which had gradually been adopted for the then obsolete tetragramaton. But, for an individual to call God His Father was not at all popular, as very few instances are to be found previous to the time of Our Lord, and the prevailing conception of God was against it. So that we straightway see that Christ's expression τοῦ Πατρός μου, "My Father" for God was not the ordinary one.

In making this departure, there were no great precedents for Christ to follow. Samuel, "the faithful prophet of the Lord" (1 Kings iii. 20), as a boy referred to God as "Lord," and called himself "servant," 1 Kings iii. 10. Although God told David through the Prophet Nathan that He would be a Father to him, and David would be to Him a son, yet David too cries "O Lord God" and refers to himself as "servant," 2 Kings vii. 18, 19, 25, etc. In prophecy the great Jewish mediator and saviour of the Gentiles is called by Isaias, "My servant," Isaias xlii. 1 ff.

According to St. Luke himself, priestly Zachary refers to God as "the Lord God of Israel," Luke i. 68; and pious Simeon views his relation to God as a "slave" to a "master" νῦν ἀπολύεις τὸν δοῦλον σου, δέσποτα, Luke ii. 29.

Certainly it was not on account of precedents, or by virtue of custom and usage that "My Father" fell from Christ's lips. If, in referring to God, He had used "Our Father in Heaven" which according to Dalman seems to have been used by the Jews of that time, He might be following usage and custom of the time, but when instead of "Our" He used "My," Christ did something out of the ordinary; not only have we but few examples of an individual expressing filial relation to God, but the Targums (as referred to in the previous chapter) show an aversion to the use of the words "My Father" in reference to God; and there is an evident indication of a prevailing view of God which is abstract and diametrically opposed to the close warm conception of Him as expressed by the words "My Father." When we see that this expression making this departure is used, not by a man of mature years, not after years of pious reflection and religious experience, but by a boy of twelve it would seem to be very exceptional. And when we see that the expression was uttered in all seriousness (as the whole context presupposes), it would seem hard to explain.

(b) The words, "My Father," on the lips of the twelve-year-old Jesus are not only the most important ones of His saying, but they are the most emphatic ones, because with these words He made a contrast with the words, "Thy Father," in the question of Mary His Mother. She said ". . . Thy father and I sought Thee sorrowing"; He said ". . . in the (things) of My Father I must be." The contrast between "My Father" and "Thy Father" is evident, and it is admitted by all scholars with the exception of two, H. Holtzmann[1] and Meyer,[2] both of whom base their opposition to it on the ground that it would be unnatural, which is an a priori reason.

To Mary's reference to Joseph as father, Jesus opposes a reference to God as His Father. The opposition or contrast is equivalent to a decisive correction of Mary's words, it is tanta-

---

[1] Hand Comment. I. 51.
[2] Gospel of Mk. and Lk. i. 336.

mount to a denial that Joseph was His father, and, what is of special importance, it is a reminder of the Virgin Birth. According to the Lucan account Jesus had been miraculously conceived by the Holy Ghost, which was, so to speak, a physical reason why the "Holy One born" of the Virgin Mary would be "the Son of God" (Luke i. 35). By the words "My Father" as a designation of God, in opposition to the imputation of fatherhood on the part of Joseph, the Boy Christ shows that He was conscious of His miraculous conception of the Holy Ghost and indicates that these words, "My Father" are to be understood in accordance with this supernatural conception. This contrast, therefore, points to the view of real Divine Sonship. "In place of the foster father," says Titus of Bostra,[1] "He brings forward the true Father," or as Theophylact[2] interprets the contrast, "since Mary had called Joseph 'father.' He replied 'he is not My true father otherwise I would be in his house, but God is My Father and for this reason I am in His house that is in His temple.'"

(c) The occasion of the twelfth year was not the sole time that Jesus used the expression "My Father" in reference to God. He did it frequently during His Public Life. Not being an isolated instance, we can determine that it was not by accident that He uttered it in His twelfth year. In Christ's later life no other name of God was more frequently on His lips than that of "Father." And nowhere does Our Lord's teaching appear in sharper contrast to current religious ideas than in relation to the Divine Fatherhood. To avoid repetition we have reserved the study of Christ's references to God's Fatherhood to a closing chapter (page 188). We now refer the reader to it, and we here avail ourselves of the results. We can determine this certainly from His later usage, that His departing from the usual way of referring to God was deliberate and intentional. Indeed, He told all others, even His disciples to say "Our Father," yet He deliberately made a departure when He Himself was concerned, using "My Father." As Dalman remarks, "Jesus never applied to Himself the title 'Son of God' and yet made it indubitably clear that He was not

[1] Titus von Bostra (ed. Sickenberger), 152.
[2] M.PG CXXIII. 733. Cf. Stanley Hall, Jesus the Christ in the Light of Psychology I. 430, etc.

94 THE BOYHOOD CONSCIOUSNESS OF CHRIST

merely 'a' but 'the' Son of God. The position assumed shows itself in the preference He manifested for the designation of God as 'His' Father in the use of which He never includes the disciples along with Himself... The unique position assumed by Jesus also follows in other passages from the invariable separation between 'My Father' and 'Your Father.'" [1]

A unique or special Divine Sonship is signified by the use of the term "My Father" certainly in the evangelical narrative of the Public Life, this nobody can deny. Now, when we hear this expression fall from the lips of Jesus for the first time, and this when only twelve years of age, what are we to think? The sacred historian who records this here without explanation or comment in the same work wherein he represents Christ as using "My Father" to distinguish His Sonship from even His disciples, would certainly seem to attribute to the youthful Saviour a consciousness of a special Divine Sonship. To contend that it is not allowed to argue this way, that the "childishness" of the twelve-year-old Christ forbids the taking any great or deep meaning from His words, to contend this is to argue a priori, is to argue independently of the records.[2]

---

[1] Words of Jesus, 280-281.

[2] A number of modern writers appeal to the "childishness" of the saying in favor of their view. Hase does this (Geschichte Jesu, 224). A "childish limitation" is mentioned by Keim (Jesus of Naz., II. 133). Lange refers to the saying as a "feeling still enveloped in the bud of childishness" (Life of Christ, 324). Réville sees in the Gospel episode "beaucoup de candeur et d'illusion juvénile" (Jésus de Naz., 410). Neander holds that Christ's words "contain no explanation beyond His tender years" (Life of Christ, 31). According to Dickenson (The Perfecting of Jesus, AndR XLII (1912) 278) the childishness of His answer "forbids us to interpret the words, 'My Father,' in any other but a purely human sense of Sonship to the Father . . ." To do so, says Barth, would be "roh und unkindlich" (Die Hauptprobleme des Lebens J., 270), etc. In answer we say in the first place that an oriental boy of 12 is not a child. In any case there are no indications in the Gospel that Lk. ii. 49 is to be considered a childish saying. For the parents, it was no childish saying; it contained something so great and deep that they could not understand it (vs. 50), it contained something of such value that the Mother carefully preserved it (vs. 51). As we shall later see, the Evangelist previously narrates that the Boy Jesus displayed most extraordinary understanding (vs. 47) and that as a child He was filled with wisdom (vs. 40). He had previously described Christ's miraculous conception of the Holy Ghost and the miracles that attended His birth. This context, and besides the same serious tone that attends all the narrative of this Third Gospel — these are sufficient indications that the words may be taken for all they stand for, that one may adopt the interpretation that best suits. Finally, is not the distance between child and man lost in the interval that separates both from the Deity? And if a child's consciousness could not contain a divine metaphysical element, neither could a man's (cf. Owen, Comment on Gospel of St. Lk. 44). The claiming that the childishness of Jesus' saying precludes any great or deep meaning is an a priori argumentation.

REAL DIVINE SONSHIP EXPRESSED

This special Divine Sonship in the first words of Jesus is admitted by Keim, Godet, Nösgen, Réville, Beyschlag, Wendt and other such scholars.[1] These men admit that in Jesus' first saying "the words 'My Father' were the first realization of a relation which surpassed all that Judaism had realized," to quote Godet,[2] or to quote Beyschlag,[3] "the name of 'Father' on the lips of Jesus is the expression of a purely personal relation that has no equal." Yes, these admissions are required by the historical evidence, but how explain them naturally? "From what," we have to ask with H. Schmidt,[4] "is Christ's consciousness of His peculiar quality?" Even if one agree with these men that the special Sonship expressed by the youthful Christ is only ethical, we would look in vain for a natural explanation. Special ethical Sonship, or the conviction of an ethical relation above all others, might be arrived at by a person who had spent many years of prayer and missionary experience, namely after knowing the spiritual experiences of others and comparing them with one's own. A special ethical relation must necessarily be the result or fruit of growth and development in the mental and moral faculty of man, and according to the laws of Psychology it would be difficult to explain how the consciousness of a relation to God more special than that of anybody else would be found in a boy of twelve. No amount of natural precociousness, no natural ingenuity, no depth or strength of religious feeling could explain it; he must necessarily lack experience or the knowledge of how others view their relation to God. The unnaturalness of the natural explanation is confirmed by this fact, that both J. Weiss and O. Pfleiderer, while admitting that the text as it stands signifies special Divine Sonship, on this account reject it as not genuine.[5]

The conviction of a most special relation to God is expressed by Jesus in the words "My Father," and this conviction at such a tender age would indicate that for Him development was precluded, the ordinary laws of humanity were not observed, a preternatural explanation was to be looked for.

[1] The modern scholars who hold to a special ethical Sonship are given above, pp. 41 ff.
[2] Comment. on Luke, 93.
[3] New Test. Th. I. 81.
[4] Bildung und Gehalt d. messianisch. Bewusstsein J. StKr LXII (1889) 428.
[5] See above, p. 41.

(d) Not being able naturally to account for the words "My Father" in the first recorded saying of Jesus, we are compelled to seek an adequate explanation somewhere even if it should be in the realms of the supernatural. An adequate explanation is readily and as it were naturally suggested to us by the usage of this selfsame expression, "My Father," by Christ during the Public Ministry.

According to the representation of the Evangelist, not only unique but even real Divine Sonship is signified by Christ when He uses the term "Father" or "My Father." For instance: All things are delivered to Me by My Father; and no one knoweth who the Son is, but the Father; and who the Father is, but the Son and to whom the Son will reveal Him (Luke x. 22). Certainly real Divine Sonship is expressed here, for Christ indirectly states that His nature is such that it could be known only by God the Father, which is equivalent to saying that He had Divine Nature.[1] We refer the reader to the last section of this work, where is adduced accumulative evidence to show how the Saviour of the Public Life understood His Divine Sonship, to show that His use of the expression "My Father" corresponds to the expressions "the only Son," "the only begotten Son," to show that this expression "My Father" on His lips is fraught with the significance of metaphysical relation to God, — this is according to the representation of the Third Evangelist and the whole New Testament (pages 188 sq.).

In the light of this meaning, how is τοῦ Πατρός μου in the saying of the twelve-year-old Christ to be interpreted? We ask with Fillion[2] why not attribute to the word "Father" here the significance it so often receives in the course of the Gospel narratives? This should be done, if the canon is observed that an obscure passage is to be explained by a clear one. Would it not be a mistake to extract it from the book in which it is written and consider it apart from the representation of the writer? According to ordinary methods, it is not allowed to do so unless we have a statement to the effect from the Evangelist. Where is there even

---

[1] This is admitted by a member of the negative school. See a work on this passage by Schumacher. Die Selbstoffenbarung Jesu bei' Mat. xi. 27 (Luc. x. 22).
[2] Le développement intell. et. moral de Jésus RClfr April (1914) 16. Cf. Felder, Jesus Christus, I. 328.

REAL DIVINE SONSHIP EXPRESSED

an intimation of this? By not informing us on the matter Luke would be deceiving us if the term has not the same meaning in the second as in any later chapter. Since there is no warrant whatsoever for saying that the title used of God, "My Father," changed in meaning for Jesus, and since He expressed real Divine Sonship in other passages where this title is used, would not one naturally expect that real Divine Sonship is likewise expressed in ii. 49?

The words "My Father" were Christ's most common name for God and hence did not drop accidentally from the lips of the youthful Saviour. Although a Jew of Christ's time, especially if he belonged to a select class, might speak of God as his Father — this is true, despite a few authorities to the contrary [1] — yet Jesus' employment of the title for God was something quite characteristic of Him alone. He even went beyond the usage in reference to the theocratic king. Not only did He make use of the name "My Father" more frequently and in a more confident manner than was ever previously done,[2] but the way He reserved it for Himself alone, and the content He gave it surpass anything of the sort that we know of any historical personage. Seeing that Jesus at the tender age of twelve does not say "Our Father," but deliberately uses "My Father," appropriating God as His own special Father, St. Cyril of Alexandria draws this inference: He makes God His own Father, for He alone was divinely born of God according to nature, and when He became man He retained His own true (by nature) Father, God.[3] This is our conclusion: The use of the term "My Father" for God was not at all ordinary; from the contrast with the words "Thy Father" recalling the Virgin Birth, and from His usage, of which this is only one instance, we are led to expect that the term was fraught with the meaning of real Divine Sonship.

[1] A few have said that Christ's words "My Father" were altogether foreign to the ordinary Jewish dialect of His time, v.g. Sheldon' New Test. Theol. 63, Stier (Words of the Lord J., 25), Brough (Childhood and Youth of Our Lord, 124). These writers are not precisely correct, as is indicated in the last chapter.

[2] Cf. Hollmann, "But apart from the fact that use of this name in Jewish literature is not very frequent, the glad confident child-like feeling which the name of Father on the lips of Jesus implied is nowhere to be found." The Jewish Religion in the time of J., 51. Furrer writes: Mit seinem Sohnsbewusstsein steht Jesus ganz einzig da in seiner Zeit, in seiner Welt (Das Leben J. C., 55).

[3] M.PG LXXVI. 1320.

2. THE OTHER WORDS OF THE TEXT

(A) In Jesus' first recorded saying: Τί ὅτι ἐζητεῖτέ με; οὐκ ᾔδειτε ὅτι ἐν τοῖς τοῦ Πατρός μου δεῖ εἶναί με; the last word is με. Christ does not say that man must be in the things of His Father, like the answer He returned to the tempter, "Man liveth not by bread alone," Luke iv. 4; no, He does not use an indefinite pronoun, but mentions Himself alone. The με by being placed last is emphasized as has been remarked by Döderlein.[1] This little word appears twice; what is asserted in the saying is centered in Him; there is no mistaking that.

(B) Ἐιναί ἐν τοῖς τοῦ. In another place I have discussed the question: what is to be understood by ἐν τοῖς, and although to some extent favoring there the view of "business" as against that of "house," I shall here leave the question open.

(a) If "business" be taken as the meaning, then Christ says that He must be in the business of His Father. "To be in," εἶναι ἐν, would signify "to be completely taken up with,"[2] as in the case of 1 Tim. iv. 15, ἐν τούτοις ἴσθι, which the Revised translates, "give thyself wholly to them."[3] Mary had asked: Why did you do this to us? Making a slight contrast, the Son replied, not that He must do the business but that He must be completely taken up with, immersed in the affairs of His Father. To explain this assertion as merely the outcome of intense religious feeling requires attributing a certain amount of unnaturalness to the twelve-year-old Christ as well as arguing independently of the text and context (as will be shown). On the other hand, according to the view that takes "My Father" in the literal sense, this expression is most fitting and natural for the Boy Jesus. The right and duty of a true son is to be taken up with his Father's business.

(b) What is the meaning, in the view that "house" is to be understood for ἐν τοῖς τοῦ? In the first place, be it noticed that in Jewish usage the Temple was not called "the Father's house"; there is not a single instance either in the canonical or apocryphal

---

[1] NJdTH I (1892) 617.
[2] As has been remarked by Pricaeus (in Biblia Critica, ad loc.) and also by Stier (Words of the Lord J., 23).
[3] Cf. a similar use in Rom. xii. 7 (where εἶναι is omitted) and in Philip iv. 11.

works of the Old Testament. By David, by Solomon, in the Psalms and even in the Psalms of Ascent, the Temple is designated as "the house of the Lord." Not only this departure, but the Boy Christ, using the plural article, not even using the word "house," refers to the Temple as His Father's house in a very familiar manner, ἐν τοῖς τοῦ Πατρός μου. The Temple of Jerusalem was the center of Jewish thoughts and aspirations, where Jahweh's presence was to some extent localized (3 Kings viii. 13), where His eyes and heart were to remain perpetually (3 Kings ix. 3; 2 Paralip. vii. 16); it is this Temple that Christ in a familiar manner spoke of as "His Father's house." He afterwards again called it His Father's house, τὸν οἶκον τοῦ Πατρός μου (John ii. 17) when forcibly ejecting the money changers who were defiling it. According to the account of the cleansing described by the Synoptics [1] (Matthew xix. 12, 13; Mark ix. 13-17; Luke xix. 45-46) Christ quotes the text "My house is the house of prayer." Christ always associated Himself with the Temple [2] and as He felt called upon to "cleanse" it in after life, so even at the age of twelve (if the view of house for ἐν τοῖς be correct) He felt He must be there. Why must He be there any more than anybody else, any more than Mary or Joseph for instance? A very close connection with Jahweh, a very exceptional self-consciousness of His relation to God is clearly expressed — and this, be it always remembered, in spite of a strong abstract transcendental view of God prevailing at His time.

As the real Son of God Christ would naturally, and as a matter of course, be intimately associated with the Temple and regard it as His Father's house where He must be, as is stated in Heb. iii. 6 (but where house is not taken as a material building) Χριστὸς δὲ ὡς υἱὸς ἐπὶ τὸν οἶκον αὐτοῦ. Or, as Juvencus paraphrases our passage, ". . . quod jure paternis sedibus et domibus natum inhabitare necesse est." [3] Yes, by right a son should be in

---

[1] The Synoptics seem to be describing a different cleansing from that described by John. Their account comes towards the end of the Public Ministry, while his is at the beginning. These are two different occasions, as is pointed out by Chrysostom (Hom. xxiii. on St. John NP-NF XIV. 80).

[2] Indeed as Schaefer points out "the, self revelations of Jesus as the Son of God are connected especially with the Temple in Jerusalem," Mother of Jesus in Script. 234.

[3] Corp. Script. Lat. XXIV. 18.

his father's house, and to a great extent he has a right to call the father's house his house. Hence it is that Origen says that Christ was in His own (ἐν ἰδίοις)[1] when He declared: "I must be in the house of My Father." If one would not be ready to admit that Christ claimed the Temple as His own house by calling it His Father's, at least one has to admit, that by referring to the Temple in a familiar way as His Father's house, He very closely associated Himself with Jahweh's great house and with Jahweh Himself, and this is best explained in the light of the real relationship of "Son" to the "Father."

(C) The Boy Jesus does not say it is proper, or it is becoming that I be in the (things) of My Father, but He says it is necessary, δεῖ. Let the usage of the Evangelist be our criterion for arriving at the exact significance of this word.

Christ uses this word δεῖ when telling Zacchaeus that He must abide in his house, δεῖ με μεῖναι (Luke ix. 5.) He uses it when telling the people of Capharnaum who wished to detain Him there, that in other cities as well must He preach (εὐαγγελίσασθαι) the kingdom of God, and the reason of the necessity was because for this was He sent (Luke iv. 43).

Referring again to His work, and vaguely alluding to His passion, Christ again uses this word when in answer to the Pharisees who warned Him to depart and go into Judaea for Herod had a mind to kill Him, He said ironically it cannot be (οὐκ ἐνδέχεται) that a prophet be put to death outside of Jerusalem, howbeit it is ordained by Divine decree that I go on my way hence (πλὴν δεῖ με) as Herod desires, not however, because you suggest it, but because My work at this time requires it. (Luke xiii. 33.)[2] To express the necessity there was on Him to suffer many things, to die and rise again, the Son of Man used this word δεῖ in Luke ix. 22, and again in Luke xvii. 25.

Christ felt and expressed that He must go to His sufferings and death as it was part of a Divine decree, as it was determined for Him (κατὰ τὸ ὡρισμένον, Luke xxii. 22) and He uses the word we are considering to designate the necessity of His fulfilling the text of Scripture: He was reckoned as a malefactor (δεῖ τελεσθῆναι ἐν ἐμοί, Luke xxii. 37). And the Risen Saviour makes use of it in dispelling the misunderstandings of the Apostles and disciples

[1] Given in M.PG XIII. 1852, note.
[2] We are giving here Plummer's paraphrase of the verse (Comment. ad loc., 354).

REAL DIVINE SONSHIP EXPRESSED 101

explaining how according to Moses, the prophets and the Psalms, it was necessary for Him to have acted and spoken as He did, to have died, risen and entered into His glory, Luke xxiv. 26, 44, and again in vs. 46, — where the same idea is expressed but where the best texts leave out the δεῖ.

We may add that besides this use of the word by Christ in reference to Himself, we find it on the lips of St. Peter when preaching that the heaven must receive Christ, ὅν δεῖ οὐρανὸν μὲν δέξασθαι, Acts iii. 21, and on the lips of St. Paul "declaring and alleging that Christ must needs have (τὸν Χριστὸν ἔδει) suffered and risen from the dead," Acts xvii. 3. St. Paul writes this word when referring to the necessity of Christ in reigning (δεῖ γὰρ αὐτὸν βασιλεύειν) "till He had put all his enemies under His feet," 1 Cor. xv. 25.

From the usage of δεῖ in the New Testament, we see the justice of the remark of Gigot that according to the Third Evangelist this word in the language of Christ "invariably refers to the Divine decree according to which Jesus had to carry out His mission on earth,"[1] and likewise we see the justice of the inference of Plummer from this word concerning Christ, "His work and His sufferings are ordered by Divine decree. The word is thus used of Christ throughout the New Testament."[2] Christ with this word expresses the necessity of His doing something because "for that He was sent," because "it was so determined," because "the Scriptures must be fulfilled." Now when we hear this "sacred must"[3] among the first words of Jesus, we can see that those commentators, who held that here Christ referred to His mission or even those who explain the "business" that Christ alludes to, as the Redemption, were only arguing from the usage of this word, as represented by our Evangelist. However this may be, one thing is certain, this word put by St. Luke in the mouth of Christ is a very strong word, it expresses His "absolute constraint"[4] to be taken up with His Father's business or in His Father's house. By this expression of absolute constraint

---
[1] The Virgin Birth in Lk. ii. IthQ VIII (1913) 433.
[2] Comment. 140.
[3] So called by Stier, Words of the Lord J., I. 23. H. Schmidt calls it "das göttlichen δεῖ (Bildung und Gehalt des messianisch. Bewusstsein J., St. Kr. LXII (1889) 429); so does Baljon (Commentaar, 72).
[4] Vincent, Word Studies, I. 279.

Jesus indirectly claims a very close association and relation with God, claims, as Briggs [1] points out, that His mind is ethically one with the will of God. And this as a boy of twelve, how explain it? Why should He feel this way more than any other boy who ever lived? Who can explain how He should arrive at this frame of mind, lacking experience as a boy necessarily does? We are not going beyond what the usage of the word allows us, when we say that the expression indicates a self-consciousness unique in history, indicates (as similarly we found in the case of the words "My Father") that at twelve Christ's mind had already reached the maturity of His public years, that development in His self-consciousness is excluded. When we learn from the text that the saying was received by the parents not with ridicule but with respect (as shall be later referred to), we are led to an explanation in harmony with the conclusion we arrived at from the study of the words "My Father," namely that the obligation, the necessity which Jesus felt, arose out of His very nature, because He was the real Son of God. The obligation was natural, the word "must" being in keeping with the words "My Father." At any rate, this much can be concluded with absolute safety, that Jesus expressed a Sonship with God closer and more binding than anybody else in history.

(D) The strong word δεῖ intensifies the εἶναι ἐν τοῖς, and they both, together with the με and the τοῦ Πατρός μου, are intensified and strengthened by the governing phrase, οὐκ ᾔδειτε; did you not know, or were you not aware? These words reflect the spontaneity and assertiveness of Jesus' reply. Besides they imply that the reason for remaining which He assigns was known or should have been known to Mary and Joseph.[2] For instance, when St. Paul wrote, "know you not (οὐκ οἴδατε) that you are the temple of the Holy Ghost" (1 Cor. iii. 16), or "know you not (οὐκ οἴδατε) that they that run in the race, all indeed run but one receiveth the prize" (1 Cor. ix. 24), he was only drawing attention to a fact, for he was conscious that the people he addressed knew that they were the temples of the Holy Ghost, and that

---

[1] The Ethical Teaching of Jesus, 34. Cf. Keil. Comm. Evang. Mk. u. Luc. 243-244.

[2] The οὐκ of course requires the answer "yes."

only one wins the prize. So the words of Jesus express that the parents should know that He must be in the things of His Father God. How could they know this? Judging from the Gospel narrative the only way they could know this was from His supernatural conception of the Holy Ghost and the miracles that attended His coming into the world. These He is evidently recalling to their minds by His words "did you not know?"[1] Here again we come to a suggestion, an intimation which is most important for the understanding of the relationship with God expressed by "My Father" in Jesus' words. There is here a reference to the Virgin Birth previously described by St. Luke. Mary and Joseph ought to know that Christ was in the things of God, His Father, for they knew that He was supernaturally born of God, that without a human father, He was born through the power and operation of the Holy Ghost, in which birth, there is, as we have said, a certain physical reason and basis for the real Divine Sonship of Jesus. And it is strict exegesis to interpret the Boy's words "My Father" in the light of this supernatural Divine Birth, which He indirectly recalls.

(E) Finally, we reach the even more assertive and matter-of-course question, τί ὅτι ἐζητεῖτε με; According to Adamson,[2] Mason,[3] Plummer,[4] and Robinson,[5] this question, "Why did you seek me?" implies that Christ did not know that his parents were seeking for him and hence implies ignorance as well as perplexity on His part. But these words need not have been uttered in a tone of surprise, and even if they were, it could be done to make the answer more emphatic. Any ordinary boy, who was absent from his parents for three days, could scarcely but advert to the fact that they were looking for him, much less a boy of the "understanding" (Luke ii. 47) of Jesus. There is no ignorance implied in Christ's words. The words are explicable in the light of what follows: "Did you not know," where there is given the reason why the parents should not have searched for the missing

---

[1] This was early seen by Titus of Bostra, who paraphrased Jesus' words, "didst thou not conceive as a virgin" (Titus von Bostra, 152).
[2] Studies of the Mind in C., 11, 12.
[3] The Conditions of Our Lord's Life, 148.
[4] The Advance of Christ, Exp. ser. 4, IV., p. 5.
[5] The Self-limitation of the Word of God, 72.

Boy. In her question, Mary had pointed out that Joseph and she had "sought Him sorrowing." To make His answer more emphatic He took up her "long-drawn-out word 'seeking' " [1] and as the first part of His answer, He points out the uselessness of what they had done, and this He did in the form of a question, Why did you seek me? It is to be remarked that Christ not only objects to their seeking Him with sorrow but to their seeking Him at all. From the ordinary and natural point of view these "parents" had a right to seek for Him on missing Him, yet by His rhetorical question He indirectly points out that they should not have sought for Him; that it was needless, and that they would not have done so, if they had attended to what they should know, viz., His Divine origin and nature, on account of which there was an obligation (by Divine ordinance) to be in the (things) of his Divine Father. In presence of this relation with God, which they should know, His relation with them and their claims on Him were of minor importance, — this is what is insinuated by Him, as shall be brought out in the following pages.

3. THE CONTRAST WITH THE PRECEDING VERSE

Jesus' first recorded saying was not a moral dictum or a generalization; it was intended as a reply to His mother, the Evangelist introducing it thus: And He said unto them.

VS. 48, (b)	VS. 49
Καὶ εἶπεν πρὸς αὐτὸν ἡ μήτηρ αὐτοῦ· τέκνον, τί ἐποίησας ἡμῖν οὕτως; ἰδοὺ ὁ πατήρ σου κἀγὼ ὀδυνώμενοι ζητοῦμέν σε.	Καὶ εἶπεν πρὸς αὐτούς· τί ὅτι ἐζητεῖτέ με; οὐκ ᾔδειτε ὅτι ἐν τοῖς τοῦ Πατρός μου δεῖ εἶναί με;

As has been referred to, the words τοῦ Πατρός μου in the Son's reply mark a contrast to ὁ πατήρ σου in the Mother's question, and this contrast is equivalent to a denial that Joseph is father and a reminder of the Virgin Birth.

In Jesus' reply there is more than a disavowal of Joseph. Mary in her question had appealed not only to the claims of

---

[1] As Power says, "All He did was to take up her long-drawn-out word 'seeking' and show it was not entirely appropriate." Who were they . . . ? IthQ VII (1912) 279.

Joseph, but also to those of herself. Reminding Him of His relation to her, she calls Him Son (τέκνον), She was His true and real mother; Joseph though only foster father had all the rights of fathers according to Jewish law. According to the Jewish law and custom the "Son" was bound to obey, respect and please them in all things. Why is it then, what could be the reason, that He surreptitiously remained behind after the "parents'" departure and caused both of them the great anxiety and weariness of the three days of sorrowful searching? Mary's question is a plea for her violated parental rights; and she could scarcely have put the matter more emphatically than she did with her question of "why," "why did you do so to us (ἡμῖν)?"

What does Jesus say to this charge? Does He admit a culpability, a forgetfulness, a lack of dutifulness? He does not. He does not even "express sympathetic regret at His parents' sorrow on His behalf."[1] In a short succinct reply He justifies His action. The reason that He assigns is His relation to God. In opposition to Mary's parental claims (τέκνον . . . ὁ πατήρ σου κἀγὼ) He points to God who has a relation to Him not less than Fatherhood (τοῦ Πατρός μου), with a claim on Him that by necessity (indeed by Divine ordinance), He be in His house or about His business; rather than be with them returning home, He must be in God's house, or rather than be employed in their affairs, He must be employed in God's affairs. This higher relation and claim, and what they entailed for Him, the parents should have known and adverted to; if they had done so, they would not have searched for Him. To the mother's question He replies with a double question. To the mother's emphatic "why" (τί), He rejoins with an emphatic why (τί ὅτι), "Why did you seek me?" Her reason was grounded on "Thy father and I." His was, "My Father and I." She was insistent and emphatic on the human parental rights, He was more insistent and emphatic on His duty arising from the parental right of God. This justifying Himself by setting the claim of His Father, God, over against the claims of His earthly parents with the implication that the for-

---

[1] Wilkinson: Concerning J. C., the Son of Man, 42. Also Maclaren (Gospel of Luke, 40) says "the answer might well startle her. It has not a word of regret nor of apology."

mer stringently bound Him even to the sacrifice of the latter, this certainly lays most remarkable emphasis on His Divine relation. From the human point of view the obligations of a child to his parents are the most binding on earth; could Jesus therefore lay greater emphasis on His relation to God than by saying that in comparison with it His relation to His earthly parents was of little concern? The Boy "knew God as His Father, and this in a manner so intimate and so peculiar that ordinary human relationships are as nothing in comparison with the relation to God."[1] Since He is making a contrast or comparison between two relations, it is clear that the one on the side which He justifies Himself would have to be the closer and stronger. To be closer and stronger than the one that binds a child to his parents, it would seem we would have to postulate a supernatural relation to God. As Felder says, the "tertium comparationis" is not ethical but physical fatherhood,[2] and so real Divine Fatherhood is to be understood on the side of God.

The significance of the contrast or comparison between Jesus' words and the words of Mary, is brought out by Cyril of Alexandria, who says that, in His reply, Christ showed "He was above human measure" and taught that His human mother "had been made the handmaid of the dispensation; . . . but that He was by nature and truth God and the Son of the Heavenly Father."[3] It is done by Ambrose who, commenting on our passage, writes: "There are two generations in Christ, the one paternal, the other maternal, the paternal the more Divine" and that "here the mother is censured because she demands what is human."[4] It is more clearly done by Augustine, who writes that Christ in His words to Mary and Joseph did not mean "you are not My parents, but you are My parents temporarily, He My Father eternally; you, the parents of the Son of man, He the Father of the Word and Wisdom."[5] It is done by Theodoret, who, referring to Mary's question, says that Jesus was "blamed by His mother," and referring to the Son's reply says, "He defends Himself ($\dot{\alpha}\pi o \lambda o \gamma \epsilon \tilde{\iota} \tau \alpha \iota$) and quietly reveals His Divinity."[6] But especially is it done by

[1] D'Arcy, art. Consciousness, HDG I. 361.
[2] Jesus Christus, I. 330.
[3] M.PG LXXII. 509.
[4] Corp. Script. Lat. XXXII. 75.
[5] Corp. Script. Lat. XLII. 225.
[6] M.PG LXXXIV. 73.

REAL DIVINE SONSHIP EXPRESSED   107

Simeon Metaphrastes, who says explicitly that Christ "corrected the saying of His mother, recalled the truth to their minds and pointed out that rather the parents were to be blamed for not saying or thinking the truth of things."[1] The significance of Christ's words as considered as a reply to His mother, is held by all those who paraphrased Christ's words; "I dismiss you on account of the eternal Father," or who say that He opposed the business of God His Father, to the business of His parents; the significance is recognized by those who cast doubt on the historicity of the passage, on the plea of its strangeness and unnaturalness; Bruno Bauer is a good example.[2]

As we have seen, Meyer and H. Holtzmann deny that there is a contrast on the ground that it would be unnatural. Having only this a priori reason to offer, they imply that the contrast is there, and at the same time bear witness to its force. It is unnatural; it is not what we would expect from a natural point of view, namely if Christ was not conscious of being the true Son of God. It is supernatural, and from the point of view of His strict Divine Sonship this taking up and applying to God the term "Father" and this setting His relation to God over against His relation to the "parents" were perfectly natural.

How gratuitous is the assumption of Lange[3] and Loisy[4] that the contrast, which is in the text, was not intended! What is their foundation for this? Where is there anything to this effect stated in the text? There is not the slightest hint in the narrative that words are set down which are not intended. On the contrary, the context warrants us in taking Christ's words for all they are worth, as will be evidenced in subsequent chapters.

In the words of Jesus there is a contrast with the words of Mary. Is there more than this? Is there a reprehension or reproof or rebuff? The affirmative seems to be held by Ambrose,[5] Nilus,[6] and Theodoret.[7] Impelled by theological bias Erasmus

---

[1] M.PG CXV. 548.
[2] Kritik der Evang. I. 293–294.
[3] Life of Christ, 324.
[4] Les Évang. Synop. 1. 38.
[5] "Hic mater arguitur," Corp. Script. Lat. XXXII. 75.
[6] In two different places Nilus writes that Christ reprehended (ἐπιτιμῶντος) Mary for seeking Him among His relatives, M.PG LXXIX. 229 and 776.
[7] In the passage "at one time He gives honor to His mother as to her that gave Him birth, at another time He rebukes (ἐπιτιμᾷ) her as her Lord" (M.PG LXXXIII. 144).

and many of the early Reformers loudly advocated this view, but nowadays there is scarcely any scholar [1] who holds it.

Whether Christ was brusque or not to His parents on this occasion,[2] would depend on the tone in which He uttered the words. This has not been preserved for us, but we would judge it to be mild from the way the words were received; they were received with reverence by Mary (51). Was there need of a reprehension? Mary was insisting on her natural rights, was appealing to custom and the way of action followed by everybody. Jesus reminded her of another claim that was on Him, a supernatural one which nullified all natural claims; hence He recalled to her something to which she was not adverting; He corrected her thoughts concerning Him; this could be done in a quiet but decisive manner and not brusquely, which would seem out of harmony with the context.

It was not a rebuff but a certain correction in this antithesis which on the lips of a Semite need not sound brusque. In what did this correction precisely consist? Considering that it was Mary herself who heard the explicit announcements of the angel Gabriel (Luke i. 26–38), considering that she was personally acquainted with all the facts concerning her Son's conception and birth, no one knew better than she His miraculous origin, His supernatural relation to God, indeed His claim and right to be called "the Son of God" (Luke i. 35). Mary had not to be reminded of this Divine origin and His relation of "Son" to God, but she had to be reminded of what this relation to God entailed. It entailed the obligation and responsibility of being concerned in His Father's work at all costs; it entailed that in His life's work, the end for which He came into this world, He was independent of everything earthly, even of maternal relationship. Mary should have known this, and if she reflected on the matter she would realize it; that is why He says: "Did you not know that I must be in the (things) of My Father?" But she was accustomed to

---

[1] He writes that Christ in His words "imo plene objurgat objurgantes," Annotationes, ad loc. in Biblia Critica, VI. 275.

[2] Wallis mentions "rebuke" but says it was "in the gentlest form" (About My Father's business. . . . Exp. 2d ser. VIII. 26); Farmer mentions "a slight touch of rebuke" (HDG I. 238); Wilkinson sees "a certain sweet and gracious reflection of reproach" (Concerning J. C. the Son of Man, 44).

REAL DIVINE SONSHIP EXPRESSED 109

seeing her Boy generally acting as an ordinary boy, and she was adopting the ordinary attitude herself; her complaint in her question is according to the rights of parents, namely her "Son" should have remembered the ties of relationship that bound Him to Joseph and herself, and should have advised them concerning His tarrying in the Temple. In an emphatic way, yet by simply pointing to His obligation of being in the (things) of His Father, Jesus intimates that this closest tie on earth for Him, not only did not count, but must be sacrificed; that the responsibilities arising from His great relation to His Father He must fulfil, "even though at the cost of some severance from the tender ties of home, yea, even at the cost of some pain to the mother whom He loves so dearly."[1] This then was the correction of the motherly point of view of Mary; she is to learn that she is not to be consulted, that the spiritual end will be followed by Christ, "whatever the cost to human emotion, whatever the price affection would have to pay, even a mother's and a son's."[2]

Christ's self-consciousness would receive all the more force and emphasis in the view that He administered a rebuke to Mary and Joseph; but, as D'Arcy says, the contrast in Christ's words was more "the inevitable reaction of His consciousness than as a deliberate correction of His mother. If so it is all the more impressive. It shows how fundamental was the position in His mind of the filial relation to which He stood to God."[3] Christ did not reprehend His mother, but by not excusing Himself or offering an apology for the neglect of parental rights, more than this, by His emphatically announcing to His parents that He was independent of and superior to any relation to them, in this He revealed a superhuman, a supernatural self-consciousness. The neglect, the sacrifice of the closest ties on earth, that of mother to son, is insinuated by Christ's words and this when they simply raise the parents' mental vision to what He owes Him of whom

---

[1] Hastings, The Great Texts . . . St. Luke, 108. As Bartmann (op. cit., 48) says, "So selbstverständlich als es der Mutter erscheint, dass ihr Sohn mit ihnen die Heimreise antreten musste, so selbstverständlich ist es dem Sohne, dass erzurückblieb."

[2] Shanahan "Was the Son of Man brusque to His Mother?" Catholic World, CIV (1916) 354.

[3] Art. Consciousness, HDG I. 361.

He is the eternal Son.¹ How could this Sonship be more emphasized, or conceived to be of a more special quality? We have here indirectly, and hence all the more strongly, a confirmation of the conclusion we arrived at from the individual words of the first saying, that they contain an expression of real Divine Sonship.

This first lesson Christ teaches His parents is in perfect agreement with the sentiment of all the later sayings in reference to His earthly relations. When at the marriage feast of Cana, the mother, by pointing out there was no wine, indirectly asked her Son to supply miraculously the deficiency, He replied, "Lady! What is that to Me and to thee? My hour is not yet come" (John ii. 4). He thus intimates that in regard to His work Mary's maternal rights are not to count (this is what His words express, though as a matter of fact, at her request, He did advance "His hour").² Again, when according to the synoptics (Matthew xii. 46–50; Mark iii. 31–35; Luke viii. 19–21), His mother and His brethren came to Him "while He was yet speaking," He said in answer to a voice in the crowd which advised Him of the approach of His relatives (here again making a contrast with words already used), "Who is My mother and who are My brethren? whosoever will do the will of My Father Who is in heaven, he is My brother and sister and mother," — intimating that besides the natural there was another bond which was to be preferred, the spiritual one or that relation having reference to God, His Father.³ Similarly, on the occasion that a woman in the audience raised her voice in praise of His mother, "Blessed is the womb that bore thee . . . ," not denying or contradicting what was said, the Saviour makes a transition to emphasize a spiritual point,⁴ "yea, rather blessed are they that hear the word of God

---

[1] As Bede writes: "Non quod eum quasi filium quaerunt, vituperat, sed quid ei potius cui aeternus est filius debeat, cogit oculos mentis attollere." M.PL XCII. 350.

[2] As Gregory the Great paraphrases the passage: "In the miracle which I have not of thy nature, I do not acknowledge thee" (Ep. xxxix. NP–NF XIII. 49).

[3] Comparing Lk. ii. 49 with this passage, Streatfeild says, "truly the Child was father of the man" (The Self-Interpretation of J. C., 128).

[4] Cf. what Chrysostom says concerning this passage, "for the answer was not that of one rejecting His mother, but of one who should show that her having borne Him would have nothing availed her had she not been very good and faithful" (Hom. XXI. on St. John, NP–NF XIV. 75).

REAL DIVINE SONSHIP EXPRESSED

and keep it" (Luke xi. 27, 28). Lastly Christ intimates this usual stand, when from the cross addressing Mary, He does not call her mother, "Lady, behold thy Son" (John xix. 26).

So that the position that Christ assumed to His relatives in Luke ii. 49, is the one He took in their regard during His later years. In His first words He "strikes the keynote of all His after life."[1] He outlines a policy He was always to follow. He is clear and emphatic on the matter, more explicit and more emphatic than in His later utterances. This certainly affords a strong confirmation of our view that Christ expressed real Sonship; that Jesus at the tender age of twelve should outline a policy He was to follow all His life, this policy one which is contrary to the ordinary mode of action of mankind, particularly contrary to the habits and instincts of youth, and this done in an unhesitating matter-of-course fashion, there would be clearly evidenced that He was in possession of a supernatural self-consciousness, for such a strange attitude, already determined on so early, could not be the result of meditation or experience and would exclude the workings of the laws of human development and psychology.

To summarize briefly the matter inversely from the order we have followed: In answer to His mother, who complained of parental rights violated, not in an apologizing attitude but with emphasis, Christ mentions a parental right binding Him even to the neglect and sacrifice of earthly connections. Making a correction of Mary's words, He insinuates that Joseph is not "father," mentioning another, God. That His relation with God goes back to His origin, to His "Virgin Birth," is recalled to the parents' minds by the words: "Why did you seek me? Did you not know?" It was a relation that bound Christ by absolute necessity, indeed by Divine ordination that He be in God's house (mentioned in a familiar manner), or that He be entirely engrossed in God's business. His relation and all that it implies is expressed in the crowning words of the saying, "My Father." This expression — a great departure from the usual Jewish way of referring to God, and of considering God, an expression which specifies God as His own individual Father, is uttered by the

[1] Smith, The Days of His Flesh, 23. Cf. Robertson, Keywords in the Teaching of J., 13.

twelve-year-old Saviour in the same self-confident off-hand matter-of-course manner as was Christ's wont during His whole life; judging from this we are directed and led to the view of real Divine Sonship.

These words that fell from the lips of the Boy Jesus show that there was no growth in His self-consciousness and no growth in His outlook on big questions of His life. At the tender age of twelve His mind is decidedly made up on His special characteristic title for God, "My Father," for expressing His special relation to Him, — indeed this was the most characteristic of all Christ's teachings. He is emphatic with His "must," for expressing His responsibility and obligation arising from His Divine origin and relation; He is clear and explicit in enunciating His attitude towards His earthly relations who are to be always sacrificed when God and God's work are concerned. Fundamental attitudes and policies that are characteristic of His later life, and that mark Him off from every other historical person, Christ emphatically announces as a boy. The laws of human development and psychology were certainly outwitted and frustrated by Him.

We wish to draw attention to the fact that our conclusion in this chapter is based on the study of the words of the text, is arrived at from the evident reading of what is before us, is deduced from the representation of the Evangelist. We are not concerned with the question how Christ's words appealed to the Doctors and bystanders who probably heard them; most likely they did not understand them to express real Divine Sonship, although the special and close relation to God that the Boy Jesus announces must have astonished the Doctors and bystanders just as much as His understanding and answers had previously done. Nor are we so much concerned with the question how Mary and Joseph understood Christ's words, although with the knowledge that they possessed, they could hardly have taken the relation to God He expressed in any other sense than the metaphysical. But what we are concerned with, and what we wish to insist on, is that the text as it stands, the words in the setting given by the Evangelist, would clearly point to the view that Jesus expressed real Divine Sonship. A strong confirmation of this is found in the fact that even members of the negative school hold this view. Usener, who rejects the historicity of the episode of the twelve-year-old Jesus, says it is introduced "for the purpose of allowing the consciousness of Divine Sonship to receive its first manifestation (vs. 49)."[1]

[1] Art. Nativity, EB III. 3344.

CHAPTER X

MESSIANIC CONSCIOUSNESS INCLUDED IN CHRIST'S
FIRST SELF-INTERPRETATION

In Jewish tradition it was held that when the Messiah would come, He would stand in a very close relationship to Jahweh, and frequently this relationship was declared to be that of "Son" to "Father." For instance, in Ps. ii. 7 (and there is no doubt that the Jews held this passage to be Messianic), we read, "The Lord hath said to me: Thou art My Son, this day have I begotten Thee." Here is certainly designated a most special personal relation to God. Frequently in the Old Testament Apocrypha (which reflect Jewish ideas in the centuries immediately preceding the Christian era), do we find this designation of "Son" of Jahweh applied to the Messiah. In 1 En. cv. 2, we find "For I and My Son will be united with them forever," in 4 Esd. vii. 28, "For My Son the Messiah shall be revealed," etc. This fact seems clear, then, that the Jews had expected that their "Anointed One" would enjoy a very close relationship with God, and many of them considered this relationship as that of Son.

Now, when as a Boy of twelve years, Jesus expressed a relationship with God that was far closer than that expressed by any of the Prophets or great leaders of Old Testament times,[1] when he claimed a unique relationship, declaring special Divine Sonship, then in the light of the Jewish hope and expectation, it is clear that He claimed Messiahship; in the light of Jewish writings this title of "Son" designating a very special relation with God would be nothing else than another name for "Messiah." Indeed most of the modern liberal scholars take Christ's title "Son of God" as meaning only Messiahship; and almost all of them understand the references to Divine Sonship in the ac-

[1] As we referred to above, even Samuel and David took the attitude towards God as that of "servant" towards "Lord."

counts of Christ's baptism (Thou art My beloved Son, Luke iii. 22) and temptation (If Thou be the Son of God, Luke iv. 3, 9), as signifying Messiahship. Why should one not similarly understand Jesus' own statement of His Divine Sonship, when in His first words He said "My Father"? There is no reason except an a priori one, why one should not. In declaring Himself to be the special Son of God, Christ assumed the characteristic name given to the Messiah in promise and prophecy; furthermore He gave a fuller and truer designation of whom He was, besides Messiah, the real Son of God.

According to the hope of the Jews, the Messiah was to be privileged with a special relationship to God, but he was primarily one sent to do a certain work for God, to fulfil a certain mission. If there is reference to His mission in Jesus' first words, then there would be conclusive proof that He reflected there Messianic self-consciousness. We think there is this reference in the first recorded saying. Broadly speaking, Christ's mission was to preach the Kingdom of God, to suffer and finally to die. Now whenever He refers to the mission for which "He was sent," which was "ordained" for Him, which was according to the "Scriptures," He generally uses the word δεῖ to express His obligation to fulfil His Mission, hence it would seem that He does likewise in the first words. This inference would seem to be all the more safe for two reasons: first, in Luke ii. 49, the δεῖ is connected with or rather flows from Christ's very special relation to God (My Father), secondly, considering the passage in relation to Mary's question, the δεῖ here has an extraordinary force, signifying Jesus' obligation to be in the (things) of God at the sacrifice of His earthly parents. Now as to the first reason, Jesus' obligation arising from His great relation to God, here He would express His Messiahship just as much as if He said He must do something because He was sent therefor, or because He must fulfil a Scriptural text. His Mission could flow from His origin and nature just as much as from mandate or ordinance. As to the second consideration, the obligation from Christ's relation to God causing anxiety and sorrow to the parents, this anxiety and sorrow would not be caused if there was no question of special work to be done for God. When the people of Capharnaum wished the Saviour to remain with them, He said, "to other cities must I also preach the Kingdom of God, for this am I sent" (Luke iii. 32), using "must" in a parallel sense to being "sent" and hence referring to His Mission. He would seem to have also referred to His mission, to special work for God, when in answer to the "parents" who had considered that He should have accompanied them on their way home and should not have remained behind, Jesus replied, "I must be in the (things) of My Father," here designating the necessity ("must") as springing from His relation to God ("My Father"). If "business" is to be understood for ἐν τοῖς, then the meaning of Luke ii. 49 is that Christ feels that as "Son" of God He must be engaged in His Father's affairs, and here then would be a clear reference to His mission or Messiahship. If rather it is "house" that is meant, then this center of Jewish devotion, this great national shrine of Jahweh is styled by Jesus, "My Father's house," and this in a familiar way which one would a priori expect from the Messiah.

When all is considered, especially the most special relation to God as "Son," and the use of δεῖ expressing His obligation flowing from this relation, and this considered in the light of the Old Testament, in the light of Christ's later life, in the light of the following verse (50) which states that the parents "did not understand," intimating that the full scope of Christ's words was only understood afterwards (as we shall later see), when all is considered it seems clear that in Luke ii. 49, Christ expressed with His Divine Sonship, Messianic self-consciousness. A strong confirmation is afforded by the fact that a number of the negative scholars hold that the text as it stands (although they object to its historicity) signifies Messiahship. Giving it a kind of paraphrase, Paulus interpolates in the text: The Messiah, "the Son of God."[1] Strauss very explicitly states that Christ's words "must have a special meaning which can here be no other than the mystery of the Messiahship of Jesus, who as Messiah was υἱὸς Θεοῦ in a special sense."[2] In his comments on our passage Bruno Bauer calls Christ, "the Messianic Child."[3] Loisy is most

---

[1] Das Leben Jesu, I. 18. Cf. Exegetisches Handbuch, 280.
[2] Life of Jesus, 195.
[3] Kritik der Evangelien, I. 293.

emphatic on the matter; "the reply of Jesus is full of significance, because He was already conscious of being the Messiah; to see there the simple expression of precocious piety is to compromise the economy of the account."[1] But these men just quoted will not accept the genuineness of the passage on the plea that one could not naturally account for this Messianic consciousness in a twelve-year-old boy. Strauss particularly has pointed out this: That there are certain vocations or callings in life of which exceptional men might early give evidence of being aware, but there are other vocations such as that of statesman for which only experience and knowledge of facts can excite even an inclination. Strauss rightly says that the calling of Messiah belongs to the latter class and he concludes concerning the twelve-year-old Christ that the Messianic consciousness "could not be so early evident to the most highly endowed individual because for this a knowledge of contemporary circumstances would be requisite, which only long observation and mature experience can confer."[2]

This is clear, then, that one cannot naturally explain how Jesus at twelve could possess consciousness of being the Messiah. It is clear, too, and also acknowledged by these scholars that the first recorded words do contain Messianic consciousness. Instead of resorting to the extreme of rejecting the historicity (in favor of which we have abundant evidence as shown above, pp. 60–72) we look for an explanation more than the merely natural. In seeking for this we are led back to the source from which Christ's mission flowed, on account of which He felt the great obligation to be engaged in God's special work, namely to His great relationship with God, τοῦ Πατρός μου, His real Divine Sonship. This Sonship is not only the basis, but also the perfection of Messiahship; it certainly affords an explanation why Jesus at twelve could be conscious of being the Messiah; so that we do not agree with Edersheim,[3] Briggs[4] and the other scholars who assert that in the first words nothing more than Messiahship is expressed. Besides a mission, Jesus also expressed a relation to

[1] Les Évang. Synopt., I. 183.
[2] Life of Jesus, 195.
[3] The Life and Times of J., I. 249.
[4] Messiah of the Gosp., 234.

God; indeed, as Harnack points out, it is "impossible to imagine how Christ would have arrived at the conviction that He was the future Messiah without first knowing Himself as standing in an unique relationship to God."[1] At any rate in Christ's first recorded words there is expressed the consciousness of both real Divine Sonship and Messiahship, the first giving rise to and explaining the supernatural occurrence of Messianic consciousness of a boy of twelve.

The Fathers did not mention that Messiahship is expressed in Jesus' first words, because it would seem that they had no reason to do so. From the thirteenth century onward, many writers have interpreted Messianic consciousness in the first recorded saying, holding that Christ expressed consciousness both of Divine Sonship and Messiahship.[2] Many of those scholars who hold that Christ expressed the consciousness of His Messianic mission, refer to this mission as the salvation of the world or Redemption; they have a twofold reason; first, Christ referred to a mission, and as a matter of fact His mission was to suffer and die for mankind; secondly Christ used the "must" which He so frequently employed in regard to His sufferings and death.[3] This remarkable fact that at such an early age Jesus gave evidence of His full conviction of His mission, — we say "full" for Christ's explicit and emphatic words give no room for the view of a "doubting" or "budding" self-consciousness, is another confirmatory reason for the conclusion in the previous chapter. This full conviction of His Messiahship at the age of twelve, inexplicable on natural premises, as is pointed out by negative scholars, is conclusive evidence that here, too, Jesus had no development in His self-consciousness, and was not subject to the laws of psychology.

[1] Sayings of J., 301.
[2] See especially Calvin, Comment. in Harm. Evang. Opera Omnia, XLV. 106; Lucas, Comment. ad loc. given in Migne, Cursus S.S XXII. 465; Cornelius à Lapide, Comment. in S. Script. VIII. 535; Fillion, Art. in RClfr April I (1914) 15; and Felder, Jesus Christus, I. 278–281.
[3] As Steinmeyer expresses the matter: Wer jedoch dieses, πατήρ μου in dem einzig möglichen Sinne fasst, der erkennt auch an dem δεῖ den Heiland und den Erlöser der Welt (Die Geschichte der Geburt des Herrn, 168).

SECTION V
JESUS' FIRST RECORDED WORDS AND THE IMMEDIATE CONTEXT

CHAPTER XI

THE SCENE AMONG THE DOCTORS

ALTHOUGH the sacred record does not inform us in what part of the Temple Mary and Joseph found the missing Boy Jesus, it lets us know something about His position and what He was doing when found; "sitting in the midst of the (teachers or) doctors," hence in a sitting posture, and "hearing and questioning them." The present participle of both verbs is used (ἀκούοντα, ἐπερωτῶντα), denoting continuous action; listening to them and asking them questions, not merely asking a question. This verse (46) must be understood in the light of the effect produced by the twelve-year-old Boy which we immediately proceed to examine.

1. WORD SCRUTINY OF LUKE ii. 47, 48 (a).

47 Ἐξίσταντο δὲ πάντες οἱ ἀκούοντες αὐτοῦ ἐπὶ
   τῇ συνέσει καὶ ταῖς ἀποκρίσεσιν αὐτοῦ.
48 (a)—Καὶ ἰδόντες αὐτὸν ἐξεπλάγησαν.

What is the meaning of ἐπὶ τῇ συνέσει καὶ ταῖς ἀποκρίσεσιν? The last word, ἀποκρίσεσιν, signifies "answers." The question of the meaning of σύνεσις is not so easy. The Curetonian Syriac and Armenian render it by "wisdom," the Vulgate by "prudentia," the Douay by "wisdom," and the Revised by "understanding."[1] Since there is no general agreement in the versions concerning the precise meaning of this word, and since its verb συνίημι in Luke ii. 50 is diversely interpreted, a summary of the usage of the noun and the verb in the New Testament will doubtless be useful.

Now, first, as to the use of the verb συνίημι in the New Testament; it is used in Mtt. xii. 19, 23, 51; xv. 10; to signify "bring

[1] The Old Latin Codex Palatinus (e) has "prudentia et os et responsa." Tyndal's — the first English translation from the Greek — has "witt."

home to oneself," or "realize" (a parable). In Mtt. xvii. 13, it signifies, "understand the connection or reference" and with much the same meaning it is found in Mtt. xvi. 12; Mk. viii. 17; in both of which it is identified with νοέω. In the same sense, Mark uses it another time, vi. 52; and in vii. 14, he employs it to express "realize, bring home to oneself."

The meaning of Lk. ii. 50 will be treated in the next chapter. In Lk. xviii. 34, συνίημι is identified with γιγνώσκω and seems to bear the signification "to realize the contents, or see the whole bearings of a saying." Again in Lk. viii. 10, γιγνώσκω is used synonymously with συνίημι; here as well as in Acts xxviii. 27, 29; Mtt. xiii. 14, 15; and Mk. iv. 12; this latter verb is employed to translate the Hebrew verb בין of Is. vi. 9, 10 (rendered in Jn. xii. 40, by νοέω), and in these passages συνίημι has the force of "to be convinced of a thing." We find our verb closely connected with νοῦς, the intellect, in Lk. xxiv. 45, and here means to have a proper insight into, to rightly interpret. Twice in Ac. vii. 25, this verb we are considering is used in the sense of to have sufficient insight or foresight so as to know.

St. Paul uses συνίημι in Rom. iii. 11, to translate שכל of Ps. liii. 3, with the meaning to be possessed of or convinced by spiritual knowledge. In Rom. xv. 21, he uses it to translate בין of Is. lii. 15, with the meaning to be convinced or believe in. We have the sentence μὴ γίνεσθε ἄφρονες, ἀλλὰ συνίετε τί τὸ θέλημα τοῦ Κυρίου, in Eph. v. 17; the last part is opposed to, ἄφρονες, imprudent, and means, to realize and try to live up to, what is the will of God; so that here συνίημι contains a reference to action. Also in 2 Cor. 12 συνίημι has a reference to action and means to be prudent. Συνετός is used in Mtt. xi. 25, Ac. x. 21, 1 Cor. i. 19, in sense of worldly wise, yet in Ac. xiii. 7, in sense of spiritually wise.

'Ασύνετος is used in Mtt. xv. 16, and Mk. vii. 18 with meaning, without understanding; in Rom. i. 14, and 22, it has meaning of spiritually foolish. In Rom. i. 31, this word is used for one who has a sinful lack of spiritual knowledge and in Rom. x. 19, without proper spiritual knowledge.

As to the noun σύνεσις outside of Lk. ii. 47, it is found six times in the New Testament. Only once, Ephes. iii. 4, it means knowledge; all other times, understanding. Twice, understanding in general, Col. i. 9; Mk. xii. 33 (by metonymy, mind) twice, spiritual understanding or insight, Col. ii. 2; 2 Tim. ii. 7, and once worldly understanding, intelligence, 1 Cor. i. 19.

THE SCENE AMONG THE DOCTORS 123

The New Testament usage would create the presumption that in Luke ii. 47, σύνεσις has the meaning of understanding. The fact that it is mentioned that the Child was found hearing and asking questions and the fact that σύνεσις is connected with "answers," is proof enough that this word is not to be taken as prudence (namely, containing a reference to action), and would indicate that the meaning is either wisdom or knowledge or understanding. In a few verses previous, verse 40, and a few verses subsequent, verse 52, St. Luke uses σοφία to signify "wisdom." The combination ἐπὶ τῇ συνέσει καὶ ταῖς ἀποκρίσεσιν would indicate that σύνεσις here means understanding, that is, insight, discernment, intelligence (in primary sense, to read between), which amazed the doctors as well as the product of this insight or discernment, the answers.[1]

Now the question is, of what kind was this discernment or combinative insight which the Boy Jesus displayed? Was it ordinary, was it remarkable, or was it more than remarkable? In the Gospel narrative, understanding is not qualified by an adjective, but it is stated that the Boy's understanding (or insight) and His answers produced an effect which of course reflects the cause.

First of all there is a little difficulty in regard to the general meaning of the passage under consideration. The phrase πάντες οἱ ἀκούοντες is very general, referring to all who heard Him; of them the verb ἐξίσταντο is predicated. As to καὶ ἰδόντες αὐτὸν ... Campbell tried to make this phrase refer to the bystanders. He constructed the sentence this way, "and all who heard Him were astonished, but they who saw Him were amazed at His understanding and His answers."[2] He admits that the text is susceptible of the common interpretation, and indeed his view has had very few followers. It would require a gratuitous transposition of the text, and the construction of the sentences beginning with the verb ἐξίσταντο gives the impression that the phrase which it covers is, as it were, parenthetical, after which Luke

[1] It is also the view of most scholars. Cremer (Biblisch. Theol. Wörterbuch de ntl. Gräcität., 501). Preuschen (Vollständiges Handwörterbuch zu den Schriften des n. T., 1059). Vincent (Word Studies, I. 278). Edersheim (The Life and Times of J. (new edit.) 1,247, and note). Carr (Gospel St. Luke, 44).

[2] The Four Gospels, ad loc., p. 116.

124   THE BOYHOOD CONSCIOUSNESS OF CHRIST

continued his narrative, καὶ ἰδόντες, referring back to the subject of εὗρον (vs. 46) which was mentioned in vs. 43, οἱ γονεῖς.

Now, there are two different verbs used: ἐξίσταντο to express the emotions of all who heard the Boy Jesus, at His understanding and His answers, and ἐξεπλάγησαν, to describe the feelings of the parents coming on the scene. We shall have to investigate the usages of these words in the New Testament before we can decide what are their exact meanings or whether they are synonymous. By having a correct idea concerning the signification of these words, we shall be able to form a correct idea of the understanding and the answers of the Boy Jesus.

First as to ἐξίσταντο which is used of all those hearing Him. In one case, Mk. iii. 21, this verb is used in a very strong sense and seems to mean, to be out of one's senses, to be beside oneself — the literal meaning, as in the parallel passage John (x. 20), has μαίνεται. In a very strong sense, too, it seems to be used in 2 Cor. v. 13, but here the meaning is not agreed upon. In all other New Testament instances, ἐξίστημι represents the state of mind of persons in the presence of miraculous inexplicable events. In the active transitive it is thrice used by St. Luke to describe the effect of a wonderful occurrence, namely, twice (Ac. viii. 9 and 11), the effect of the sorceries of Simon Magus on the people (miracles for them), and once (Lk. xxiv. 22), the effect on the downcast disciples of the women's account that they saw at the tomb of the Crucified a vision of angels who said He was alive. The active second aorist intransitive form of the verb is employed by Mark, namely in v. 42, to express the effect, on those who witnessed it, of the wonderful miracle of the raising to life of Jairus' daughter, and thrice by Luke, namely, once in his Gospel (viii. 55) to describe the effect just mentioned (he does not add ἐκστάσει μεγάλῃ as is found in Mark and we can easily give the former more credit for knowing the value of Greek words), and twice in his Acts, in x. 45, to depict the emotions of the Jews who were present when the Holy Ghost came upon Gentiles — indeed wonderful and inexplicable to them, and in xii. 16, to depict the emotions caused by Peter's sudden appearance after his miraculous delivery from prison.

The imperfect middle of ἐξίστημι (as in Lk. ii. 47) is found once in Mtt. xii. 23 to represent the state of mind of the crowd who witnessed the curing of one possessed of a blind and dumb devil, and twice in Mark, namely, in ii. 12, to express the effect of the

THE SCENE AMONG THE DOCTORS 125

cure of the man sick with the palsy, in vi. 51, to describe the feelings of the Apostles at the double miracle of Christ walking upon the water and His calming the tempest.

Likewise, in this same form, this verb is used by Luke four times outside of ii. 47, namely, Ac. ii. 7, and 12, to signify the state of mind of those Jews from every country under the sun who heard the Apostles speak different languages at once; Ac. viii. 13, to describe the feelings of Simon, magician, as he was, at seeing "the miracles and great works" of Philip, and in Ac. ix. 21, to express the emotions of the Jews of Damascus, also confronted by a miracle of the moral order, namely, when they heard Paul, previously the fanatic persecutor, preach that Christ is the Son of God.

So that, the verb ἐξίστημι expresses the feelings of those who are brought face to face with a miraculous, inexplicable occurrence in every New Testament passage in which it is used outside of Mark iii. 21; 2 Cor. v. 13, where it has a much stronger signification. Is there any reason why we should not adopt the same meaning for the verb in Luke ii. 47? We do not see any. Luke unhesitatingly uses the verb here of those who heard the Boy Jesus, as he uses it (unqualified) concerning those who were present at the raising to life of Jairus' daughter. At least, we cannot see any reason why this verb in ii. 47 does not express the same degree of astonishment and bewilderment as in the cases where this Third Evangelist uses the very same form: when the Jews witnessed the miracle of tongues, or when Simon Magus saw the great miracles of Philip, or when the Jews of Damascus were confronted with the miraculous change in Paul. According to the New Testament usage, therefore, and according to the use of the writer of the Third Gospel, this verb ἐξίσταντο predicated of those standing around the twelve-year-old Jesus, should represent, on their part, such emotions and feelings as are emitted by those who are in front of a miraculous inexplicable occurrence.[1]

What caused these feelings? The Boy's understanding and

---

[1] This agrees with the meanings given by Knabenbauer (Comment. ad loc., p. 144): "quasi extasi capti et sui prae obstuperfactione jam non compotes"; Preuschen, Op. cit., 404, "kamen ausser sich"; Plummer (Comment. ad loc., p. 76), this is "a strong word expressing great amazement."

answers. Keeping the proportion of effect to cause, we must say that to cause the degree of astonishment expressed by ἐξίσταντο Christ's insight and answers were miraculous and inexplicable as far as "all those hearing Him" were concerned. So that in answering our inquiry, as to what kind were the understanding and the answers of the youthful Nazarene, from a study of the word used to express the effect on the audience who were no less than the learned Jurists of Jerusalem, we are brought to the conclusion that the talents displayed were most extraordinary and inexplicable, indeed (New Testament usage leads us to say), miraculous.

We have another opportunity of endeavoring to ascertain what was the nature of His actions and His displayed ability from a word expressing wonder applied to the parents coming on the scene, who, it would seem, are not included under the expression, ἐξίσταντο. A different word, ἐξεπλάγησαν (48) is used to express the wonder of the parents, and their wonder was not because of "hearing Him," but because of "seeing Him," hence because of His position among the Doctors, of what He was doing, and, it would seem, of the effect He was causing, that is, taking the passage literally. As to this word ἐξεπλάγησαν, its literal meaning, as Warfield points out,[1] is "to be struck out (of the senses) by a blow." An examination of its usage reveals the following:

Of the twelve times this word is used in the New Testament, six times it has for object the doctrine (διδαχὴ) of Christ: Matthew vii. 28; Mark i. 22; Luke iv. 32; Matthew xxii. 33; Mark ix. 18; Acts xiii. 12; twice the emotions depicted were on account of a strange inexplicable saying of Christ; Matthew xix. 25; Mark x. 26, and two other times the effect which it expresses was caused by the wisdom and miracles of Jesus; Matthew xiii. 54; Mark vi. 2 (where it means "perplexed"); three times, Matthew xix. 25; Mark x. 26; Mark vii. 37 it is qualified with a strong adverb to express very strong emotions, from which fact it is legitimate to infer that the verb itself would not express these feelings. So that we can conclude that according to the New Testament usage of the word, it signifies amazement or per-

[1] Astonishment, HDG I. 131.

THE SCENE AMONG THE DOCTORS

plexity, very great, but, it would seem, not always exceedingly great.

Coming back to the verb as used in Luke ii. 47, what meaning has it here? It is used of the "parents" coming on the scene where Christ is sitting in the midst of the Doctors, who in their looks and bearing were wearing an air of stupefaction and great amazement at His intelligence and answers. This meaning, great wonder, that ἐκπλήσσομαι has in every other passage of the New Testament, seems to suit also this passage. This verb, however, would seem not to express the same degree of wonder and bewilderment as ἐξίστημι used of the Doctors, which fact may account for the reason why St. Luke used different words, for as we have seen ἐξίστημι is always used to describe the emotions resulting from the performance of a miracle and sometimes from a very great miracle, whereas, whenever ἐκπλήσσομαι is used to express very strong feelings a qualifying adverb is added, seemingly to give it strength.[1] The Doctors were stupefied beyond measure, the parents were greatly astonished, rather were greatly surprised, because, for the only time in the New Testament there is used the first aorist of the verb, which brings out the suddenness and noncontinuity of the wonder, especially, and all the more so, since the verb of itself has the idea of suddenness of access and lack of continuity.[2]

What was it at which the parents were greatly surprised or awe-struck? The text does not say that hearing Him they wondered or that they wondered at His intelligence and His answers, but "seeing Him they wondered." What was He doing when they saw Him? Sitting in the midst of the Doctors hearing and interrogating them and stupefying them by His combinative insight and answers. If there was nothing extraordinary about

---

[1] What Warfield intimates (HDG I. 47, 48), what Nebe (Kindheits Geschichte ... 408) states, and what Power (in art. in IthQ VII (1912) 455) says, that ἐξεπλάγησαν is a good deal stronger than ἐξίσταντο is so according to the uses of the classics but does not seem so according to New Testament usage. Cf. what Erasmus writes (Biblia Critica, VI. 275). Farmer (HDG I. 227, note) supports our view that the latter verb "may be the weaker of the two" for the reason that we have assigned, that in Mtt. xix. 25; Mk. x. 26; vii. 37, it needs an adverb to strengthen it.

[2] In giving the meaning of this word in the New Test. Warfield mentions that it contains the element of "alarm," that it signifies a sudden access of fear, to be "awestruck," HDG I. 48.

Him, if He was among the Doctors in the mien and posture of any ordinary Jewish boy who was there to listen to and be instructed by the learned Rabbis, or, if "seeing Him," is taken as referring to the effect He was causing, if this was not great, arising from His "intelligence and answers," why should Mary and Joseph greatly wonder? In this assumption we could not explain this statement of St. Luke. Their surprise and wonder makes the extraordinary character of Jesus' action stand out in bold relief; they were His parents who knew His everyday actions and who knew the exact amount of education He had received, if any; indeed, if He had learned to read they had helped Him to do so. This being the case, then, from the fact that they were struck with surprise and wonderment at the scene that met their eyes, we must infer that their Son's action was most extraordinary; a display of natural talents no matter how brilliant, no matter how exceptional, would seem not to explain the situation, for the Son's qualification could not have escaped the notice of the parents.

2. EXPLANATION OF LUKE ii. 46

The parents were greatly surprised when they saw their Son; verse 46, to which we now return to examine, states that they found Him "sitting in the midst of the Doctors, hearing and questioning them." This verse, as we said above, is to be explained in the light of the verse which follows, wherein is described the effect produced. "Sitting in the midst of the Doctors," whether He was among the learned Rabbis as a disciple, or whether He occupied the place of one of them, is not made clear in the text, nor is it agreed upon among scholars.[1]

[1] First as to the question, were the Doctors also sitting, John Lightfoot had pointed out that from Moses to Gamaliel, the Rabbis instructed while standing, but from the latter's death they sat (Horae Heb. 48). This view, says Schürer, is only "according to later Talmudic tradition," and he holds that the custom was for the pupil to sit upon the ground and the teacher in an elevated place (Hist. of Jew. People, Div. II., v. II., p. 326 and note). The matter had been previously stated by Wetstein. This view is held by many: Hausrath (History of N. T. T. I. 90), Felten (Ntl. Zeitgesch. I. 345). In the second place, what is the meaning of "sitting in the midst of the Doctors" or rather what is the force of "in the midst of" $\dot{\epsilon}\nu$ $\mu\dot{\epsilon}\sigma\psi$? In Lk. xxii. 27, it means "among" and in Ac. iv. 7 it signifies presence in a central conspicuous position. The fact that Luke writes that Jesus was in the midst of the Doctors and not of the listeners, added to the fact of the "surprise" to the parents

THE SCENE AMONG THE DOCTORS 129

"Hearing and asking questions." Is not hearing emphasized by being placed first? And is not this phrase written for the purpose of drawing attention to the fact that Christ was among the Doctors of Jerusalem to obtain information impelled by a sense of His own ignorance and a thirst for knowledge? This is not only a possible interpretation, but is the view of a number of scholars.[1]

Let us first take up the last part of the phrase, "asking questions." The present participle of the verb ἐπερωτάω has the force of not merely asking a question, but asking questions. This verb is sometimes used in the New Testament to signify the asking of a captious question, e.g., Matthew xii. 10; xxii. 35; Luke xx. 40. More than this, in John xvi. 30, to ask (ἐρωτᾷ) has the meaning of "to teach." In what sense is the verb used in Luke ii. 46,

coming on the scene, led many to understand that Christ was in the place of the Doctors. On the other hand the fact that the Boy was "hearing" and "asking questions" has led others to hold He was among the Doctors in the rôle of a disciple. That He was given a place amongst the admiring Doctors is held by Bossuet (Élévations sur les Myst. S. XX. 4, p. 337), Trollope (Analecta Theologica, 485), Schleiermacher (Das Leben J. ... 81), Tholuck (Die Glaubwürdigkeit der Evang. 216), Ewald (History of Isr. V. 188), Ellicott (Historical lectures, 95), Whitefoord (Exp. ser. v. II. 69–70). Matt. Henry (Gospel of Luke, ad loc., 350), Picard (La Transcendance de J. C., 105), Power (Who were they, etc., IthQ VII (1912) 455), Strauss (although denying historicity of the account, Life of J., 193). On the contrary, the following hold that Jesus was among the Doctors in the rôle of a disciple: Maldonatus (Comment. in Quat. Evang. II. 122), Cornelius à Lapide (Comm. ad loc., transl., 132), Menochius (Totius S. Script. Comment. ad loc.), Lucas (Annotationes, etc., ad loc.), Natalis Alexander (Expositio litteralis et moralis S. Evang. II., p. 137), Patritius (De Evang. III., p. 411); in fact, most present-day writers take this view. Yet Lagrange (Évangile selon S. Luc., 95) points out, what seems to have been overlooked, that Christ was not among a group of disciples, for then He would have had only one master.

[1] Here are the express statements of some of them. O. Holtzmann refers to the Boy as "consumed by a thirst for knowledge" (Life of Jesus, 100, note). Olshausen points to Christ's "receptivity" and states (what is frequently quoted) "an instructing demonstrating child would be a contradiction which the God of order could not possibly have placed in the world" (Comment. on Gosp. I. 151). Likewise, H. Holtzmann says that the Boy "is to be imagined as searching and asking, not as teaching and preaching" (Hand-Comment., 51). Kent contends that Jesus improved this opportunity to gain satisfactory answers to the many questions that were already stirring in His mind (The Life and Teachings of J., 53). Keim, "There is no question of a superior wisdom that could brook no further instruction" (Jesus of Naz. II. 135). Réville thinks that Christ's ingenuity showed itself in the "idée naïve qu'il se fait de la science profonde de ses docteurs" (Jésus de Naz., 411). Döderlein holds, "He wished to learn what He did not yet know" (The learning of the Boy, Think. III (1893) 173). Plummer says that Christ went through the form of asking questions because of "ignorance" (The Advance of Christ, etc., Exp. IV. ser. vol. 4 (1901) 4; Comment., 76); cf. Adeny, St. Luke, 155, etc.

asking for information's sake or asking captious questions? One thing is certain, if there is question here of mere asking questions to obtain information, we cannot explain verse 47, namely, we cannot explain the very strong word ἐξίσταντο — a verb used by Luke and the other writers of the New Testament always in connection with a miraculous and marvelous occurrence, nor can we explain His intelligence, which must be in proportion to the effect caused.

We cannot say that previously He had been giving answers and displaying intelligence, but when the parents came on the scene, He was merely hearing and questioning. They found Him "hearing and questioning," and "all those hearing Him were in amazement at His intelligence and His answers. He could not be listening and asking questions at the one time; nor at the same time was He asking questions and giving answers. The text does not say precisely that the Doctors were stupefied at His questions but at His intelligence and His answers. This might mean either the intelligence displayed by His questions and His answers, or the intelligence of His questions, besides this, His answers, or His intelligence as seen from His answers alone, i.e., His intelligent answers, which seems preferable. But must not His intelligence have also appeared in His questions? As Origen remarks, "Ex uno quippe doctrinae fonte manet et interrogare et respondere sapienter: et ejusdem scientiae est scire quid interroges quidve respondeas. Oportuit primum Salvatorem eruditae interrogationis magistrum fieri, ut postea interrogationibus responderet.[1] In another place, he explains Christ's procedure: "Interrogabat magistros et quia respondere non poterant, ipse his, de quibus interrogaverat, respondebat. . . . Interdum interrogat Jesus, interdum respondet, sicut supra diximus. Quamquam mirabilis ejus interrogatio sit, tamen multo mirabilior est responsio."[2] This explains the text very well. In the text it is not only said that the Doctors were amazed at His understanding and His answers; but it is also said that the Boy asked questions. Now, is it not likely that He who showed such miraculous combinative insight, asked questions that were intended to draw out

[1] Hom. XIX. in Luc., M.PG XIII. 1850.
[2] Id., 1848.

THE SCENE AMONG THE DOCTORS 131

the Doctors and elicit from them queries which He could wonderfully answer? The questions themselves, although wisely selected, are not mentioned as being wondered at, which is true to life, for this reason that, although great combinative insight is required for such questions,[1] yet not in the deep unsuspected question, but in the clear witty reply, is it seen in its dazzling brightness.

This mode of procedure would correspond to Christ's usual way of teaching, as when the Pharisees were watching Him to see if He would heal on the Sabbath day, seeing their thoughts, He said to them, "I ask you a question: 'is it lawful on the Sabbath day to do good or to do evil?'" Luke vi. 9. This weapon, the pointed question, so serviceable in His after life, Jesus wielded even in His twelfth year.[2]

The intelligence displayed certainly was most extraordinary to bewilder these Doctors; and to express this bewilderment, Luke not only uses a very strong word, ἐξίσταντο, he also emphasizes this word. About this there is no doubt, for he makes it the first word of the sentence, "and they were all amazed, hearing Him." . . . The amazement of the Doctors is certainly the salient and striking point in the text; in its light must everything else be explained. The phrase "hearing and asking questions" seems to be emphasized too, and the "hearing" being given first seems to have special emphasis; so that in this we agree with the objection advanced. But, if there is question here of an ordinary boy and an ordinary action, why is hearing emphasized? Is it not to

[1] Photius connects "insight" with the questions, Cont. Manich. IV. 16, M.PG CII. 212, also Melanchthon says, "est autem magnae artis, questiones proponere" (in Sermon for 1st Sunday after Epiphany, Opera Omnia, XXIV., p. 367).

[2] This view has many supporters. Beecher: "His questions were always like spears that pierced the joints of the harness. It seems that even so early He began to wield this weapon" (Life of Christ, 73). Blunt: "Doubtless some of His questions would be of that searching character which He used afterwards to instruct those who would learn from Him and silence those who opposed Him" (Comment. Lk. ad loc.). Cajetan: "Monstrabat enim magnam intelligentiam . . . formando interrogationes" (Comment. ad loc. III. 188). Hofmeister: Non dubium est quin Jesus pregnantes questiones Legisperitis proposuerit et tales, quae Judaeos ad cognitionem messiae perducere potuerint, quas quidem cum illi non intelligerent ipse explicuit et interpretatus est prudenter (in Evang. Lucae, 212). St. Jerome, "in Templo senes de quaestionibus legis interrogans magis docet dum prudenter interrogat" (in a letter to Paulius, M.PL XXII. 543). Origen: "Interrogabat, inquam magistros non ut aliquid disceret sed ut interrogans eruderet," and again, "eos quos interrogare videbatur docuit, in medio eorum loquens, et quodammodo concitabat eos ad quarenda, quae usque ad id locorum, utrum scirent, an ignorarent, nosse, non poterant," Hom. XIX. xx. in Luc., M.PG XIII. 1851.

be supposed? Why is it even mentioned in this context where the greatest emphasis is laid on the amazement of the bystanders? Is not the impression given something like the following? The twelve-year-old Boy was evidencing such intelligence as astounded those who spent their lives in weighty discussions, yet He was not monopolizing the conversation; when the Doctors had a mind to speak, He gave them an opportunity to do so, and listened attentively. Hence the text depicts the Boy not as one who is excited over the stupefaction of those around Him which by chance He has caused, but as a submissive, docile, modest Boy, one who has Himself under control, one who is self-composed, self-conscious, deliberate. To quote Erasmus, "Paraphrase," "also the partyes that stode roundeabout . . . were veraye muche astouned, not onely for respect of the chylde's wisedome (being suche as had not afore bene hearde of) . . . but also for the rare and syngulare sobrenesse of hys countenaunce, of hys gesture, and of hys tongue, whiche thynges gave a more ferther grace of acceptacyon unto hys understandyng." [1] If this soberness and modesty is emphasized, then there is emphasized a very remarkable trait, seldom found among precocious boys, — a trait which was a characteristic of Jesus in the Public Ministry.

In the eyes of the Doctors the "hearing and questioning" does not detract from the extraordinary character of the affair, rather, for them and for us, this rare combination of modesty and intelligence makes the extraordinary character shine out all the more strongly and brilliantly.[2]

[1] Paraphrase upon the Gosp. and Acts. ad loc. fol. XXXVII. Cf. also J. G. Michaelis, Exercitatio theol. Phil. op. cit., 268; also van Doren: Comment. on Luke, 72.

[2] The scene has been interpreted supernaturally all down the ages. Knabenbauer, "aliquid naturae suae altioris manifestasse" (Comment. ad loc., p. 145); Campbell, "Those whose eyesight convinced them of His tender age, were confounded as persons who were witnesses of something preternatural" (Notes on St. Luke, 117); Schottgenius, "Professi ergo sunt illo tempore Judaeorum doctores, adesse aliquem, qui ipsos docere posset, et extraordinario isthoc honoris genere Jesu exhibito, se divini quid apud ipsum deprehendere" (Horae Heb. et Talmud. II. 886); Calvin says these proud Doctors would not listen to Him, "nisi vis aliqua divina ipsos coegisset" (Opera Omnia, XLV. 105); Photius, . . . ὡς ἐκστασὶν τε καὶ θάμβος αὐτοῖς φιλόθεον ἐμβαλεῖν . . . εὑρίσκουσι δὲ πράττοντα, ἅπερ τε ἦν πράττειν, εἰκὸς, τὴν σωτηρίαν τοῦ κόσμου καὶ δόξαν τοῦ Ἰσραὴλ, καὶ ὁ λόγος προαπῆγγειλεν, Cont. Manich., IV. 16, M.PG CII. 212–213; Bede, "Divinam lingua sapientiam proderat . . . quasi Deus quae seniores et docti mirantur respondet" (Comment. in Luc., M.Pl XCII. 350); Leo the Great, "Sedens cum senioribus et

THE SCENE AMONG THE DOCTORS 133

In all sober history, there is no parallel to the account of the Boy Jesus in the midst of the Doctors, and those who compare it with examples of precociousness in youthful artists and genuises do not attend to what is written in the text.

On account of Jesus' preaching during His Public Ministry, it is recorded that His listeners "were amazed (ἐξεπλήσσοντο) at His teaching, for His word was with power" (Luke iv. 32; cf. Matthew vii. 28, 29; Mark i. 22). Yet St. Luke uses a stronger word to express the astonishment of, not an ordinary audience, but the learned Doctors of the Temple, in face of the "understanding and answers" of the twelve-year-old Christ; and he uses the same word to express the surprise to the parents at the scene. The question that came to men's minds during His later years (Matthew xiii. 54; Mark vi. 2) is of more consequence in regard to His twelfth year: how came Jesus by this wisdom? That He should display a wonderful, indeed supernatural, understanding before the Doctors is a confirmation of the conclusion that when shortly afterwards He uttered His reply to Mary, He evidenced a wonderful and supernatural self-consciousness.

Before turning away from the text,[1] now that we have en-

inter admirantes disputans invenitur" (Letter to Bishops of Sicily, M.PL LIV. 697); Theodoret, προσεδρεύει τῷ ἱερῷ τὴν Ἰουδαϊκὴν ἐλέγχει παχύτητα (M.PG LXXXIV. 73); Cyril of Alex., Εἶταθ αυμαζόμενον ἐπὶ ταῖς ἐρωτήσεσιν ὑπὸ πάντων καὶ ταῖς ἀπολογίαις (Comment. in Luc. M.PG LXXII. 508); Chrysostom, τῶν διδασκάλων ἀκροώμενος, καὶ διὰ τῆς ἐρωτήσεως ἐδόκει θαυμαστὸς εἶναι (M.PG LIX. 130); Augustine applies to Jesus among the Doctors the words of Ps. cxviii. 99. "I have more understanding than my teachers" (M.PL XXXVII. 1565); Augustine also writes "disputabat cum senioribus, et admirabantur super doctrina ejus" (Serm. LI., M.PL XXXVIII. 342); a few lines farther, he also uses "disputantem." We have already quoted Jerome; Epiphanius, in reference to Christ's action, uses the word disputing διαλεχθῆναι, M.PG XLI. 500; προσδιαλεγόμενος (M.PG XLI. 925); he also says, ἐρωτῶν αὐτοὺς καὶ ζητῶν μετ' αὐτῶν καὶ ἐξεπλάττοντο ἐπὶ τῷ λόγῳ τῆς χάριτος, τῷ ἐκπορευομένῳ ἐκ τοῦ στόματος αὐτοῦ and this he uses as an argument that Christ received the Logos before the baptism (M.PG XLI. 456); Athanasius, ἐνέκρινε περὶ τοῦ νομοῦ (M.PG XXVI. 433); Juvencus, "Invenit insertum legumque obscura senili tractantem coetu" (Corp. Script. Lat. XXIV. 18); quotations from Origen, we have already given. Opposed to this consensus of the Fathers is Gregory the Great, who says Christ was found not teaching but asking; he even adds, "puer doceri interrogando voluit" (Regula, Past., III. 25, M.PL LXVII. 98; cf. in Ezech. i and ii. 3, M.PL LXXVI. 796; Simeon Metaphrastes also says Christ did not teach the Doctors, Comment. ad loc., M.PG CXV. 548). But Gregory only wishes to point out that Christ did this as an example for us.

[1] It has not been recorded what was the theme of the questions and answers. Commentators as a rule suggest either the Law, or the Messiah, or paschal topics. Farmer (HDG I. 227) thinks that specimens are given in Mtt. ii. 4–6; Mk. ix. 11; Jn. vii. 42; Lk. xx. 22, 28–33. Would Lk. ii. 49 itself be an example?

deavored to ascertain its exact meaning, we wish to point out how baseless and purely conjectural are such opinions, as, for instance, that of Ebrard, that Jesus while among the Doctors "recognized with joy His Father's holy nature and His own," [1] or that of Stier, "in the course of this questioning, which is but the asking after Himself. . . . He makes the discovery of Himself, in the first consciousness, not yet mature, but now truly commencing — I am He!"; [2] or Godet's, that He learned to know more "intimately than before the God of His Father and His mother as His God and His Father"; [3] or Edersheim's reference to His being "absorbed by the awakening thought of His Being and mission." [4] Where in the Gospel account of the scene before the Doctors is there an intimation to warrant these views? "There is no evidence," truly says Plummer.[5]

Neither is there in the Gospel narrative of all that Jesus did in the Temple during the visit of the twelfth year, the slightest reference to any influence the Temple service or anything that happened in the Temple might have on His knowledge and self-consciousness. What is written in many works concerning the effect of the festal devotions, what is asserted concerning the effect of contact with the learned Doctors, what is contended that during this visit Mary for the first time informed her Son of His Virgin Birth and its attending circumstances, all this is imaginative, has no foundation in the text, and hence, as far as history is concerned, does not account for Christ's self-consciousness. The view that Jesus' self-consciousness arose during His visit to the Temple has no evidence in the historical record; it would seem to be excluded. Christ's first recorded action and His first recorded words, far from betraying any doubting or dawning attitude towards Himself, manifest supernatural understanding and self-consciousness. The origin of Jesus' knowledge and self-consciousness must be sought elsewhere than the Temple episode.

[1] Gospel Hist., 191.
[2] The Words of the Lord J., I. 20.
[3] The Life of Jesus prior to His Minist., Think. (1895) 397.
[4] The Life and Times of J., I. 248; cf. Hitchcock (The Self-consciousness of J., OT–NTSt XIII (1891) 272), and others.
[5] Comment., 76.

CHAPTER XII

THE "PARENTS" AND THE "SON"

1. THEIR MUTUAL ATTITUDE

TWICE in the narrative of the episode (41 and 43), Mary and Joseph are called the "parents" (γονεῖς), of Jesus, and once (48) Mary refers to Joseph as "Thy father" (ὁ πατήρ σου). Outside of those who knew the secret of the Virgin Birth and in the eyes of the Law, from the very fact that Jesus was born of Mary the betrothed (ii. 5) of Joseph and that they continued to live together, the latter would be regarded as father, even if he was not really so. Luke here employs the terms that are actually used' "parents," "father," and there is no contradiction to the account of the Virgin Birth in the previous chapter.[1] In the presence of those who were not acquainted with this mystery, it would be very awkward to use a term in reference to Joseph which would indicate that he was not the real father. As St. Jerome writes: Non quod vere pater Joseph, fuerit Salvatoris, sed quod ad famam Mariae conservandam pater sit ab omnibus aestimatur.[2]

These "parents" are described as faithful Jews, each year traveling to Jerusalem at the feast of the Pasch. On the occasion of the twelfth year, after they had celebrated for either two days, as was customary for pilgrims, or for seven days, as was prescribed by the Law, Mary and Joseph set out for home; and it was only after they had gone a day's journey, and after instituting a search among the relatives and acquaintances of their company, that they discovered their Son had not accompanied them. How was He left behind? Was it by neglect or by accident or by design on His part? St. Luke seems to excuse the mother and

---

[1] Cf. Gigot, The Virgin Birth in Lk. ii, IthQ VIII (1913) 412–434.
[2] In a treatise on the Perpetual Virginity of B. V. M.PL XXIII. 188. See other remarks of Fathers, p. 16 ff.

foster-father from culpable neglect,[1] stating that "the parents did not know" (οὐκ ἔγνωσαν, vs. 43), and they thought He was in the company (νομίσαντες δὲ αὐτὸν . . . vs. 44). From this fact that they did not make sure that Jesus was with them, we can catch a glimpse of their attitude towards Him, for "this shows," says Plummer, "what confidence they had in Him, and how little they were accustomed to watch Him. . . . They were accustomed to His obedience and prudence and He had never caused them anxiety."[2] The sacred writer, likewise, excludes the view that it was by accident that the Boy was left behind, for he makes it clear that the remaining behind was deliberate and intentional.[3] This is shown from the active verb "stayed" or "remained" (ὑπέμεινεν, vs. 43), is reflected in Mary's question, "why hast Thou done to us so?" and is far from being denied in Christ's words. This deliberately separating Himself from His natural mother and foster-father (taken in connection with other points in the episode), indicates the very exceptional consciousness of the twelve-year-old Boy and is an argument in favor of our conclusion above.

The sorrowing "parents" retraced their steps to Jerusalem in search of their missing Son and to their great surprise and alarm they stumbled upon a scene of which he was the central figure. Considering what these parents previously knew, their astonishment certainly casts illuminating rays on the most extraordinary character of Christ's position or action. It might imply that He usually did not act in a preternatural manner, but not necessarily that He never did a preternatural act before.

Jesus being perfectly human and ordinarily acting in a human

[1] That Mary showed negligence was held by Melanchthon (Mary sinned "per ignorantiam," in Serm. I. Dom. Epiph. Opera Omnia, XXIV. 367), Luther (in Serm. I. Dom. Epiph. Werke, I. 153), Calvin (Comm. in Harm. Evang., Opera Omnia, XLV. 106), Erasmus (Biblia Critica, VI. 276), Strauss (Life of Jesus, 192). This is said to be unwarranted by Meyer (Comment. I. 343). Early Suarez had pointed out that the Evangelist excuses the parents of neglect (De Myst. Disp. IV. quest XXVII. art. VI., n. 4, Opera omnia, XIX. 60). Also Canisius (Comment. de Verbi Dei corruptelis, II. 673–681).

[2] Comment. ad loc. 275; cf. also Olshausen, Comment. on the Gospel, I. 152, yet previously (p. 150) he says that Mary "sinned" through "neglect."

[3] Origen (M.PG XIII. 1850), and S. Metaphrastes (M.PG CXV. 547), hold that Christ hid from His parents miraculously. There is no word in the text for "lost" or "left behind" often used in this connection. The compound verb occurs only here and in Ac. xvii. 14.

manner, the parents were not always looking for supernatural feats from Him and supernatural interventions on His behalf; so that not only can we easily understand why they were surprised on this occasion,[1] but also we can readily understand how, when He was missing, they sought for Him and sought for Him with sorrow. "Behold Thy father and I sorrowing have been seeking Thee."[2] When they could not find their treasure, it was perfectly human that apprehension and grief should take possession of them, should blind them to the real facts of the case, should lead them on in their sorrowful and anxious search.

However, the interpretation of Origen,[3] and after him Theophylact,[4] Maldonatus,[5] Estius,[6] Cornelius à Lapide,[7] and Bernadini,[8] that the "parents" sorrowed after their Child, not thinking that something might have happened to Him, but fearful lest He had left them to go to others, etc., is not excluded by the text, and might have a foundation in Mary's question, "Son, why hast Thou done to us so?" Of course, the tone in which this was uttered would count a great deal in its understanding, but coming from one who was just recovering from astonishment at a preternatural action of her Son (47), from one who took care to preserve in her heart all that happened on this occasion (51), coming from one in such a frame of mind, we can judge that the tone was not one of harshness and reprehension.[9] She draws attention to the fact that Joseph and she had been sorrowfully seeking Him, and in a motherly way, asks why He had done this to them.

Mark, she does not say what one would expect a mother to

[1] Cf. Lagrange: Le récit de l'enfrance de Jésus, Rb IV (1895) 181, Durand, The Childhood of J. C., 141.
[2] "Relatives" is mentioned in Codex Ephraemi, Syr. harcl. and Palatinus (e). To "sorrowing" is added "sad" ($\lambda \nu \pi o \acute{\nu} \mu \epsilon \nu o \iota$, tristes) in D g r and the Old Latin a d e ff² g l q v got Syr. Cur. Ambr. L. (M.PL XVII. 364), Pseud-August. (Corp. Script. Lat. L. 125); cf. Vogels, BZ XI (1913) 42.
[3] Comment. M.PG XIII. 1850; cf. Scholia Vetera, M.PG CVI. 1189.
[4] Comm. M.PG CXXIII. 733.
[5] Comment. ad loc.
[6] Comment. ad loc.
[7] Comment. ad loc.
[8] Comment. ad loc.
[9] That Mary administered a rebuke is held by Haymo (Serm. for First Sunday after Epiphany, M.PL CXVIII. 124), Bonaventure (Comment. in Luc., ad loc.) and Erasmus (cf. Biblica Critica, VI. 275). But this is generally denied, v. g. Maldonatus, Comment. ad loc. Bartmann, Christus ein Gegner des Marienkultus? 47.

say, who has found her son after three days of anxiety and solicitude, namely, "How were you lost? What happened to you? How did you fare in the meantime? Her words, "Why hast Thou done to us so?" would indicate that at least when she was uttering them she knew that He had not been lost by chance or accident, for she credits Him with deliberately remaining behind and deliberately doing all this.[1] Her words have about them a certain amount of reserve; they imply that the Son must have a great reason for what He did; they breathe a certain amount of respect and deference for Him. As Farmer writes, "No doubt they were proud of Him in their hearts but Mary thought it necessary mildly to chide Him for having caused them so much anxiety. We say 'chide' as the nearest expression of our thought, but few parents in the East or anywhere else would speak of what they deemed to be a child's error so courteously and with such an absence of 'temper.'"[2]

As we referred to above, no objection against the Virgin Birth can be drawn from the fact that she mentions Joseph as "father."[3] An argument in favor of this doctrine is found in the fact that it is Mary who speaks and not Joseph, in whom, if he were the father, would repose all authority according to Jewish custom and law. To quote the last mentioned writer: "If Joseph had been the natural father of Christ, he would have spoken to a son of that age at least in addition to the mother."[4] The argument would be especially strong if the question was asked in front of the wondering Doctors, as the formal words "Thy father and I" would suggest.

Mary's plea was a plea for parental rights disregarded, and thus she began by addressing Jesus as, τέχνον, "child" or "son." He does not deny she is His mother, although not calling her so in His reply, but He takes up the word "father" which she had

[1] Cf. Saurez, De Myst. Disp., IV., quest., XXVII., art. VI., n. 4, Opera Omnia, XIX. 60.

[2] HDG I. 227-228.

[3] Or from the fact that she places Joseph before herself "Thy father and I"; as Augustine says, "Non attendit sui uteri dignitatem; sed attendit ordinem conjugalem." (Serm. LI, M.PL XXXVIII. 343.) The order is reversed in a few versions and Fathers (p. 17, 18). The first person is put first in Mtt. ix. 14; Jn. x. 30; 1 Cor. ix. 6.

[4] HDG I. 228.

used of Joseph and referred it to God, thus correcting her and recalling His Virgin Birth. Over against the claims of the earthly parents He places the claim of His Heavenly Parent; the obligation arising from His relation to God binds Him to the sacrifice of all things else, and this the parents should have known if they had reflected on the information they already possessed concerning Him.

When Jesus answered first the latter part of Mary's question ("Behold Thy Father and I sorrowing have been seeking Thee"), by pointing out that there was no reason for seeking Him at all, and then the first part ("Why hast Thou done to us so?") by recalling what they knew, that He must be in the (things) of His Father, it is recorded that "they did not understand the word that He spoke to them" (50). The text gives the impression, and it is the opinion of most scholars, that the non-understanding refers to the parents.[1]

What is it that the parents did not understand? Is it that Christ referred to God as His Father?[2] The text does not state this, and if it was intended it would have been made clear, as, for instance, at a later period when the Jews did not understand that Christ referred to God as His Father, St. John (viii. 27) makes it clear that "they understood not that He called God His Father."[3] The non-understanding of the parents does not refer

[1] It is not the opinion of all scholars. The Catenae Graecae (edit. Cramer, p. 27), Geodfridus (in sermon for Sunday after Epiph., M.PL CLXXIV. 107), Aelredus (De Jesu Puero Duodennis, M.PL CLXXXIV. 855), and Faber (Comment. ad loc.), think that αὐτοί refers to the bystanders. Cajetan (Comment. ad loc., tom. III. 189), holds it refers to either Joseph or the bystanders but not to Mary. Bourdaloue says it was Joseph who did not understand (Sermons pour le premier dimanche après Epiph. 6.); Power ("Who were they who understood not," IthQ VII (1912)) defends the contention that it is the bystanders who are meant. The view is not favorably received, cf. Gigot, The Virgin Birth in Lk. ii. IthQ VIII (1913) 432.

[2] That the parents did not understand the relation to God expressed by Christ's words is the opinion of most of the negative school. Cf. B. Weiss, Life of Christ, I. 283; Zahn, Das. Evang. des Luk. ad loc. The non-understanding of the parents is opposed to the Virgin Birth, thinks Usener (Art., Nativity EB III. 33–44). On account of the parent's non-understanding, Strauss calls the whole matter "a marvelous legend" (Life of J., 197). Meyer says "It is altogether incomprehensible how the words of Jesus would be unintelligible to the parents" (Comment. I. 346). Concerning this negative position, Alford rightly says, "It is a remarkable instance of the blindness of the Rationalistic commentators to the richness and debt of Scripture" (Gr. Test., 420).

[3] Cf. Gigot, The Virgin Birth in Lk. ii., IthQ VIII (1913) 432; Jn. xvi. 16 is even a better illustration.

to any single word in Lk. ii. 49; "the word" τὸ ῥῆμα signifies Christ's saying taken as a whole.

A possible explanation which suits the text and context is that the parents did not understand the appropriateness of the saying. We have given already a summary of the New Testament usage of the word συνίημι. We have shown that it sometimes means, to see the connection. The parents did not understand the connection between Christ's words and His remaining to astound the Doctors by His understanding.[1] The weak point in this explanation is that in verse 50 there is no reference to the scene before the Doctors.

A better explanation and one which is in keeping with the use of συνίημι, as well as in harmony with the context and the whole Gospel narrative, is as follows. Every word in Christ's saying was intelligible to the parents. In His words taken as a whole He referred to a mission. They understood the reference to His mission but they did not realize the bearing and scope of this mission, why it should entail sorrow, what should be the consequences in the future. To state it briefly, the words they heard did not sufficiently instruct and convince their Jewish minds concerning the nature of Jesus' Messianic career.

How do we get this far-reaching signification from the simple words οὐ συνῆκαν? We are going no further than New Testament usage would guarantee. As was pointed out according to the New Testament, this verb has often the meaning of "realize" (v. g. a parable), as Matthew xiii. 19; Mark vii. 14. It sometimes means to see the bearing or connection or consequences. A good example is Mark vi. 52, namely when Jesus performed the double miracle of walking on the water and calming the tempest, the Apostles were amazed beyond measure, and this reason is added, οὐ γὰρ συνῆκαν ἐπὶ τοῖς ἄρτοις; the meaning is they did not realize the bearing and consequences of the miracles of the loaves or they would bear in mind that Christ could perform very great miracles. A very strong confirmation of our view is the use of συνίημι in Acts vii. 25, in the sense of "to be sufficiently instructed so as to

---

[1] This view has not a few supporters: Jansenius (Comment. ad loc.); Farrar (Life of Christ, 78); Rice (Comment. on S. Luke, 59); Ryan (Gospels of the Sundays, 130); Fillion (Évang. selon. S. Luc., 87); F. Field (Notes on Trans. of New Test., 50).

THE "PARENTS" AND THE "SON" 141

foresee," but especially in illustration of our view do we point to Luke xviii. 34, when the same Evangelist who wrote ii. 50 states that the Apostles did not understand Our Lord saying that He must go up to Jerusalem and be scourged and crucified. The non-understanding of the parents is no more a matter of surprise than the non-understanding of the Apostles. The latter understood every word in the saying of Jesus that He must go up to Jerusalem and be scourged, etc., but the reasons, bearing and consequences, they did not realize. They had hoped that the Master would establish His kingdom without suffering or death (Luke xxiv. 21); and His expression to the contrary was not allowed (naturally or supernaturally)[1] to prepare them for what was to come, so that when the fatal day which He clearly foretold did come they were scandalized in Him. This is the force of the statement that the Apostles did not understand Christ saying He must be scourged and crucified.

Likewise, although every word in their Son's saying was intelligible to the parents, it did not bring home to them the nature and the consequences of the mission to which He referred. It did not enlighten them as to why the mission of His Father should entail suffering for them, and, no more than Simeon's prophecy, did it prepare them for what was to come. This is the force of the parents not understanding that Christ must be in the (things) of His Father at the expense of bringing sorrow and grief to them.[2]

This non-understanding, as we have explained it, was indeed very natural. The fact that it is mentioned shows the historicity of the whole account, suggests that Mary at least was the final author, and also indicates that the words became "intelligible" afterwards. Yes, as in the case of the Apostles so in the case of the parents, the unfolding of events cleared up matters. Only when the shadow of the cross had passed over her life did the mother realize what her Son's mission involved; and when giving the account to St. Luke or an intermediary she recalled that at the time they were uttered, the words of the Boy were in-

[1] Cf. Wright (Gosp. St. Luke, 19).
[2] This view is substantially in harmony with the views of Maldonatus (Comment. ad loc.); Nat. Alexander (Comment. ad loc.); Cornelius à Lapide (Comment. ad loc.); Polus (Comment. ad loc.); Canisius (op. cit., pp. 681–694); Lagrange (Le Récit de l'Enfance, Rb IV (1895) 182); Steinmeyer (Die Geschichte der Geburt, 180–181); Terrien (La Mère de Dieu., II. 63); Gigot (The Virgin Birth in Lk. ii., IthQ VIII. (1913) 432–433); Plummer (Comment., 78); Farmer (HDG I. 229); Box (Virgin Birth, 107), Bartmann (Christus ein Gegner des Marienkultus? 52–54).

deed not understood, they did not bring home to her, nor prepare her for the realities which resulted from His necessity of His being in the (things) of His Father.

This non-understanding by those who should know all about Him, brings out in bold relief the mysterious depth of Christ's prophetic words,[1] and hence we have again in this reference to the attitude of Mary and Joseph, another reflection of His most extraordinary character. This non-understanding is also evidence of the strongest kind that it was not the parents who implanted in Jesus' heart the knowledge of His mission and relation with God.

Although the mother and foster-father did not realize all that their Son's words implied, His reference to His mission and His mentioning His true Father seems to be enough to satisfy them, for far from there being any evidence of their insisting on and demanding another explanation, far from there being any hint that they subjected Him to chastisement, far from there being any indication that they considered His answer trivial and frivolous, in the text there is given positive proof of the high value that Mary attached to the first recorded words as well as to the other incidents of the episode, namely, Καὶ ἡ μήτηρ αὐτοῦ διετήρει πάντα τὰ ῥήματα ἐν τῇ καρδίᾳ αὐτῆς (51). The word διετήρει "expresses careful and continual keeping."[2] The mother's carefully preserving "all the things spoken of" heightens our appreciation of all that happened; it throws more light on the preternatural character of Christ's action, and it gives additional strength and force to the other arguments that His first words expressed real Divine Sonship.[3]

A final reference to Christ and His parents and one which contains an epitome of the nature of their relation is given in the sentence, "and He went down with them and came to Nazareth

[1] On account of the non-understanding of the parents, both Strauss (Life of Jesus, 195), and Loisy (Les Évang. Synopt., 383) see in Christ's words a declaration of Messiahship. It certainly shows that Lk. ii. 49 is not to be interpreted as a mere childish saying and is a strong indication that "business" is to be understood by ἐν τοῖς τοῦ.

[2] Plummer, Comment. ad loc. 78.

[3] As Origen says, "Plus aliquid quam homine suspicatur, unde et custodiebat omnia verba ejus in corde sua, non quasi pueri qui duodecim esset annorum sed ejus qui de Spiritu Sancto conceptus fuerat" (ad. loc. M.PG XIII. 1852); cf. S. Metaphrasetes, M.PG CIX. 549.

THE "PARENTS" AND THE "SON" 143

and was subject to them." The last phrase reads literally "and He was subjecting Himself to them" (καὶ ἦν ὑποτασσόμενος αὐτοῖς). As Edersheim has pointed out, the present participle middle brings out the "voluntariness of His submission,"[1] and as Plummer remarks, "the analytic tense gives prominence to the continuance of the subjection."[2] The form of this verb excludes the idea that Luke wishes to bring out a contrast between Christ's obedience at Nazareth and His disobedience at Jerusalem during the memorable visit. Besides it would be against the reverential tone of the whole narrative. Why does Luke mention Christ's subjecting Himself, which would seem superfluous, if Jesus was an ordinary boy? The Evangelist is aware that He acted in the Temple not like an ordinary boy, he is aware that His words are not the words of an ordinary boy, that they are a declaration of strict Divine Sonship. Realizing, then, what a great act of condescension it was, he records that though conscious of His Divine dignity and nature, Jesus subjected Himself to the earthly parents. Thus the relation that existed between them is fitly described. Being born through the operation of the Holy Ghost, being truly the Son of God and conscious of this fact, this God-man did not owe obedience to any human person. When He subjected Himself to Mary and Joseph, it was a great act of condescension on His part and a fact worthy of recording. He was breaking no moral precept if He did not obey them,[3] especially, as in the episode, when He must be in the (things) of His true and real Father.

2. MORALITY OF THE EPISODE

As to the relation of parents and children among the Jews we need only to quote Edersheim, "What Jewish fathers and moth-

---

[1] The Life and Times of J., 250, note.
[2] Comment., 78.
[3] As Didymus Alex. says concerning Christ's subjection to His parents: ἑκὼν δὲ δῆλον ὅτι, καὶ οὐκ ἀνάγκῃ, De Trin. III. 20, M.PG XXXIX. 893. Jerome writes: Venerabatur matrem cujus erat ipse pater, colebat nutricium quem nutrierat. (Epist. cxvii., Corp. Script. Lat., LV. 425, edit. Hilberg.) We find in the Constitutiones Apostolicae, "He who had commanded to honour our parents, was Himself subject to them" (VI. 23, M.PG I. 971). Ambrose points out that Christ's subjection is not a subjection of infirmity but of piety; and deference and piety are not weakness (Exp. Evang. Luc. ad loc. Corp. Script. Lat. XXXII.⁴, p. 75); cf. Cyril of Alex. (De Trin., V., M.PG LXXV. 993–6).

ers were; what they felt towards their children; and with what reverence, affection and care the latter returned what they had received, is known to every reader of the Old Testament. The relationship of father has its greatest sanction and embodiment in that of God towards Israel; the tenderness and care of a mother is that of the watchfulness and pity of the Lord over His people. The semi-Divine relationship between children and parents appears in the location, the far more than outward duties which it implies in the wording of the Fifth Commandment. No punishment more prompt than that of its breach (Deut. xxi. 18–21); no description more terribly realistic than that of the vengeance which overtakes such a sin (Prov. xxx. 17)." [1]

Jesus in His first words was giving an answer to Mary's inquiry: Why He had remained in Jerusalem and caused His parents three days of intense sorrow. Does the saying suit the purpose? Does He give a sufficient reason to account for His action? Or must His action be considered immoral? Wallis remarks, "A vague feeling of dissatisfaction, however consciously subdued, is apt to rise in the minds of many readers, at what may be called the moral character of the episode. In plain terms, the ordinary acceptation of the story makes it difficult to recognize the dutifulness or the consideration of our Lord's conduct, when we remember His youthfulness and His acknowledged relation to Joseph and Mary.[2] On account of the "revolt against paternal authority"[3] which he sees in the episode, Renan condemns the narrative as mythical. Martin also rejects the account, asking, "Is there not a touch of the unfilial in the tone of this reply . . . ?"[4] Certainly for an ordinary boy of twelve, it would be at least implicit disobedience for him to remain behind after his parents had set out for home, and thus cause them anxiety and sorrow, and ordinarily on finding him the parents would justly chastise their son.

To give the reason why this is not so in His case, to account for, to justify His actions, Jesus merely mentions that, as they

[1] The Life and Times of J., I. 227.
[2] The Father's business, etc., ExpT ser. 2, vol. VII. (1884) 20.
[3] Life of Jesus, 60; cf. Art., Nativity in E.B.
[4] The Life of Jesus, 75.

should know, He must be in the (things) of His Father, God. His reason for not fulfilling the highest of obligations, obedience to parents, was sufficient only in the explanation that He held a most extraordinary and superhuman relation to God, in other words, the view of real Divine Sonship or something very near it. In any other explanation His saying would be "mockery,"[1] as Riddle points out, and, as Felder states, His action would be "immoral";[2] His deliberately separating Himself from His parents without even informing them, thus causing them seemingly unnecessary grief of heart, certainly would not be in accordance with the laws of ethics,[3] and this act of immorality could hardly be explained. But for the Boy Jesus, it was not an act of immorality. Far from this being the case, He rather was fulfilling His filial obligation, He rather was obeying His real and true Father.[4] The claims of this true Father are most immediate and pressing, and, in comparison with them, the claims of Mary and Joseph are negligible. Carrying out His Father's will, He condescends to obey those whom He has given the privilege of being His earthly parents, — the verb employed, ἦν ὑποτασσόμενος, bringing out the voluntariness of the action — but when the Father's will and mission which he must carry out require, these parents are to be sacrificed now, as Mary was afterwards sacrificed at the foot of the cross.

If anything short of a superhuman and preternatural relation to God is expressed by Christ, His words would not explain His action, neither would they satisfy His earthly parents. Far from the text giving us indications that the parents justly chastised their Son, it depicts them as receiving the saying, although not understanding it, in a respectful, reverential attitude, Mary even thinking it worth while to preserve in her mind the whole account — sufficient indication that for the parents, Christ's reply carried

---

[1] Comment. on St. Luke, 361. (Gospel . . . Luke, 43.)
[2] Jesus Christus, I. 330.
[3] And this no matter how strongly one should feel a religious vocation. In the case of Christ it is clear that there is not question of merely a religious calling, as he immediately goes back to Nazareth to obey His parents.
[4] As Bartmann (op. cit., 50) says, "Aus diesem Umgange mit der Gottheit entstanden für ihn oft Situationen und Verpflichtungen, die in keinem Sittenkodex für Kinderpflichten, gebucht waren." Cf. Sylveira: Comment. in Text. Evang., I. 353.

more than sufficient explanation for this seeming disobedience and injustice towards them.[1]

The morality of the episode on the part of Christ is explained in the view we have been led to adopt in regard to the self-consciousness He expressed. Any abruptness, any lack of filial consideration seen in His action, any air of superiority interpreted from His words, all would be explicable and not unbecoming in one who had the conviction of being the real Son of God. This knowledge of being in such a wonderful relation to God explains the "Son's" attitude towards the "parents" during His whole life, namely when He uttered such sayings as "What is that to Me and to thee?" "Who is My mother, and who are My brethren?" He voluntarily subjected Himself to them, but He always made it clear that He was superior to their claims, that in His Divine obligation the ties of flesh and blood did not count. He was above the claims of the natural; He had a supernatural self-consciousness.

How explain the attitude of the "parents"? How is it that they were struck with astonishment at seeing Jesus among the Doctors? How explain that they sought for Him with sorrow and anxiety? How is it that they did not understand His words? For the better understanding we will examine their attitude in its perspective. Mary heard the angel announce that she would conceive a son who "shall be called Son of the Most High, and who shall reign in the house of Jacob forever" (Luke i. 31, 32; cf. Matthew i. 18, 20, 21, 23, 25), and although the angel explained how this Virgin Birth would take place, he did not inform her how the Son's kingdom would be established, nor what the nature of this kingdom would be, nor what it entailed for Him and for her. In these matters, consequently, she shared the contemporary Jewish views.[2] Knowing the fact of the Virgin Birth, knowing her Child to be the long-looked-for Messiah (Luke i. 35, 48), when the shepherds came to the newly born Babe, relat-

---

[1] Also from the fact that Christ was sinless we are obliged "to seek an explanation of His deportment on the present occasion," Wilkinson: Concerning J. C., the Son of Man, 42.

[2] Concerning Mary's knowledge, see Terrien: La Mère de Dieu, II. 4–66, Bartmann (op. cit., 21, 42, note). She was supernaturally endowed with intellectual gifts befitting her great position and association.

ing what they had seen and heard, Mary did not share the wonder of those who heard these things "but kept all these things pondering them in her heart" (Luke ii. 18, 19).

The secret of the Virgin Birth and the other parts of the Annunciation lay in her heart, being known only to Joseph, and hence when the "parents" heard the inspired Simeon proclaim the Child to be the Messiah, they wondered, they marveled at what he said (Luke ii. 25-33). Neither did holy Simeon's announcement of the career of "light" and "glory" of their "Son" impress them in such a way as to influence their every action, no more than his prophecy that Jesus would be set up "for a sign which shall be contradicted" and for the transpiercing of the mother's soul (Luke ii. 34, 35).

Accustomed to Christ's acting somewhat like an ordinary child (at least in regard to bodily requirements vs. 40), the parents would treat Him as such during the next twelve years that rolled by. The lapse of this period may have somewhat weakened the impressions made by the circumstances of Christ's conception and birth, but not necessarily weakened the faith of the parents.[1] Their conduct during the memorable incident of the twelfth year clearly shows that the facts stored away in their minds were not kept vividly in view. They acted like ordinary parents on this occasion. They set out for home without making sure that Jesus was with them, thinking that He was acting as usual, thinking that like an ordinary boy He was in the company. They expected nothing, and when they missed Him they became nervous and sought for Him with sorrow and anxiety. They thought of themselves only as ordinary parents, whose rights were to be respected. They did not reflect on the knowledge which they possessed, they did not consider that their Son tarried behind because of something which they already knew, His great relationship to God and His special work for His Heavenly Father in which He was not subject to their jurisdiction. Indeed the last place where they looked to find Him was the Temple, searching a whole day through the Holy City before

[1] Explaining why Mary did not "understand" Plumptre (Comment., 952), and Wilkinson (Concerning Jesus Christ the Son of Man, 45, 46), say that the lapse of years dulled the impressions of the annunciation and weakened Mary's faith.

going there. Thus expecting nothing, they were greatly surprised on discovering Him "sitting in the midst of the doctors." Yet Mary's "trouble overpowered her amazement."[1] Being Jesus' true mother, her motherly heart had experienced the keenest affliction during the three days of searching, and she could not quickly forget this intense sorrow; she refers to it, asking her Son why He had done this, feeling He must have a valid reason. She heard the Boy giving a great reason; she heard Him mentioning His true and only Father, and citing His obligation to be taken up with God's business or to be in God's house. She understood every one of the words that He uttered, but in these words there was enunciated a policy of Jesus suiting not only the present but also the future, and this policy neither she nor the foster-father realized. They did not see in the perspective the words and the occasion that drew them forth, and thus did not understand them as the first fulfillment of Simeon's prophecy, as having themselves a prophetic signification — the sword of sorrow was to go deeper into the mother's heart, all owing to the obligation and mission to which He referred.

Jesus' subjecting Himself to the "parents," His living as "one of the many,"[2] although it accustomed the mother to the rôle of an ordinary mother, yet did not make her lose sight of the memorable events of the twelfth year. These were added to the circumstances of Jesus' early childhood in the storehouse of Mary's heart. Frequently she took care to revolve in her mind all that she knew; once (it is recorded) she made use of the information she possessed, when, to save the bridal couple of Cana from embarrassment, her charity moved her to point out to her Son, "they have no wine" (John ii. 3). Taking the natural attitude of mother, she asked the miracle, irrespective of His "hour" or Divine obligation. The natural attitude of "mother" is again taken, when with "brethren" of the Lord she came to interrupt Him in His preaching, in His performing the Father's business, and finally she takes a true mother's place standing at the foot of the cross; the "Son" was fulfilling the obligations of His mission and the "mother" was again a sufferer. What had been

[1] Farmer, HDG I. 227.
[2] Words of St. Chrysostom, Hom. XXI., on St. John, N.P-NF XIV. 74.

hinted at and referred to, not only to the Apostles but also to the mother, not only during the Public Ministry but also during the Hidden Life, was now accomplished. It was not only the Apostles who heeded not the prophetic warnings of the Master that He must go the Way of the Cross, but also Mary herself acted as a mother generally does act, paying little or no attention to warnings or forebodings, overlooking prophetic utterances which could have prepared her for what the sad future had in store for herself and her Son. In spite of His pronouncements of the obligations of His nature and mission, she persistently assumed the attitude of an ordinary mother. Chrysostom, giving the reason why Jesus said "Who is My mother and who are My brethren?" writes, "because they did not yet think rightly of Him, and she, because she had borne Him, claimed according to the custom of other mothers, to direct Him in all things, when she ought to have reverenced and worshiped Him." [1] Mary's action bears about it all the marks of naturalness and historicity.[2]

Indeed when we compare the mutual attitude of the "Son" and the "parents" we are struck both at the natural mode of action of the "parents" and the preternatural mode of action of the "Son," at the natural attitude of the "parents" and the preternatural attitude of the "Son." Especially verse 50, "they did not understand . . ." reflects the preternaturalness of Jesus as well as the naturalness of the "parents." It was necessary for the "Son" to have acted as He did, for to quote Chrysostom again, "otherwise He could not have led up her thoughts from His present lowliness to His future exaltation had she expected that she should always be honored by Him as by a son and not that He should come as her Master." [3]

What an appropriate setting for the first recorded words as herein interpreted is the Evangelical account of the mutual attitude of the "Son" and the "parents." It was not they who in-

[1] Loc. cit. Christ greatly respected His mother, for as Chrysostom (op. cit.) says, "He was subject to her and had forethought of her at the very season of the crucifixion." Although He honored her, yet "He cared more for her soul, and for the doing good to the many, for which He took upon Him the flesh."
[2] Sweet (Birth and Infancy of Jesus Christ, 192) says of Mary, "The uniqueness of her experience only serves to emphasize the naturalness of the portraiture of her character."
[3] Loc. cit.

stilled into Him His idea of Himself or His mission; they did not even understand Him. What a contrast between Him and them; and they were those nearest to Him in all human respects, they were those from whom He received most, who should have known Him best. How inexplicable, then, appears His mental attitude, in other words, His self-consciousness.

CHAPTER XIII

THE CHRIST CHILD'S "WISDOM" AND "GRACE"

1. STUDY OF LUKE ii. 40 AND 52

St. LUKE envelops the narrative of the Boy Christ in the Temple with two somewhat similar verses, each containing a reference to physical growth, wisdom and grace; in fact these verses belong to the episode, being connected with it by Καί. It is claimed that here Christ is represented as undergoing not only a bodily but also "a normal psychical development"[1] and hence there is a serious objection to our conclusion above.

Verse 40 reads, τὸ δὲ παιδίον ηὔξανεν καὶ ἐκραταιοῦτο πληρούμενον σοφίᾳ, καὶ χάρις θεοῦ ἦν ἐπ' αὐτό. First, as τὸ παιδίον. In the preceding verse, St. Luke finishes the account of the Presentation in the Temple, "according to the law of the Lord." Jesus then was forty days old and this is why He is referred to as τὸ παιδίον, "the child."

Concerning this child, the Evangelist says "He grew" and "he got strong,"[2] bringing out the fact that He got taller and stronger physically.

St. Luke next gives a phrase in opposition, πληρούμενον σοφίᾳ.[3] The last word is taken in a general sense of wisdom.[4] What is the meaning of πληρούμενον? Plummer gives the meaning "being filled day by day";[5] this has in its favor the fact

---

[1] Harris, Wisdom of Christ, HDG II. 830. Others make similar statements.

[2] πνεύματι is added by Codex Alexandrinus and Codex Purpureus, but crept in probably on account of the resemblance of our verse with I. 80.

[3] Weymouth and Tischendorf have the genitive.

[4] Between his Gospel and his Acts, Luke used the word in all ten times. It is personified in Lk. vii. 35, and it seems it is used in the same manner in xi. 49. In a restricted sense it is used in Ac. vii. 10, "wisdom in the eyes of Pharao," in Ac. vii. 22, "wisdom of the Egyptians," and in Lk. xi. 31, "wisdom of Solomon"; while in Ac. vi. 3, 10, it is used in a general but good or spiritual sense; and in a like sense in Lk. ii. 40, 52.

[5] Comment. ad loc., p. 74; Farmer also says the words "imply a gradual progressive filling" (HDG I. 225).

that the present participle is used and is closely connected with two imperfects. On the other hand the Vulgate has the rendering "plenus," followed by the Douay "full of"; and the revised has much the same meaning, "filled with."

There are instances where this same present participle is used in a completed sense, that is with the meaning "filled" or "kept full" and not "being filled." In Ephes. i. 23 — the only other New Testament passage which has this present participle, we read: τὸ πλήρωμα τοῦ πάντα ἐν πᾶσιν πληρουμένου, "the fullness of Him who is filled all in all," the literal translation (as Douay), or according to meaning (as Rev.) "the fullness of Him that filleth all in all." Here on account of the word "fullness" the participle must have a completed sense. A completed sense is also found in Dan. viii. 23, πληρουμένων τῶν ἁμαρτῶν αὐτῶν, "after their iniquities are completed" or "are come to the full," and in Martyr. S. Polycarpi 15, 2: "Like a sail of a ship filled by the wind ὑπὸ πνεύματος πληρουμένη.[1] In Justin's Dialogue 87, 2 πληροῦται[2] is to be rendered "is filled," not "is being filled," and in 93.2 πληροῦσθαι[3] "to sum up," "to fulfil."

From these examples, it is clear that there is a foundation for the rendering of the present participle πληρούμενον in Luke ii. 40, by "filled." In its favor, too, is the fact that the word is placed in opposition, and also the fact that it is connected with the following statement, "and the Grace of God was in Him," expressive of state. But apart from the tense used, this word πληροῦν of itself has a completed sense; to quote Farmer, it means "to fill a thing full, so that it lacks nothing."[4] And even if the translation here be "being filled with wisdom," the meaning of the text is that the Child Jesus did become full of wisdom, — that is according to the strict letter of the text.

In the concluding phrase of this verse 40, χάρις has the signification, good-will, favor, grace, and ἐπ' αὐτό, "in Him." It is not said that the Child found favor in the eyes of God, as is said

---

[1] M.PG IV. 1040. The pres. part. πληρουμένην is also found in Athenagoras' Legatio pro Christianis 5, 2, M.PG VI. 900, but here the meaning of the passage is disputed.
[2] M.PG VI. 684.
[3] M.PG VI. 697. The use here is analogous to Gal. v. 14, where D E ms. have the present tense.
[4] HDG I. 226.

of Mary (Luke i. 30), and of David (Acts vii. 46), nor that the Child was full of grace, but absolutely and with a note of finality "the Grace of God was in Him."

The meaning, then, of verse 40 is: The Child (referring to Jesus who was previously mentioned as forty days old) grew and got strong, filled with wisdom (or being filled with wisdom) and the grace of God was in Him. It is ordinary to say of a child that he grew and got strong; but is it ordinary to say of a child that he was filled with wisdom (or became filled with wisdom) and the grace of God was in him? Was this said of any other child? Compare verse 40 with a somewhat similar statement made by the same writer concerning the growth of the Baptist, Luke i. 66, 80. It is said of both John and Jesus that they grew. It is stated that John got strong in spirit, while Jesus got strong, filled with wisdom or being filled with wisdom. That the hand of God was with him is asserted of John, while of Jesus, that the Grace of God was in Him. Strong in spiritual zeal, — this characterizes the early years of John's life as well as the later; as a Child, Jesus is filled with wisdom and has in Him the Grace of God. Luke brings out a marked contrast between the two, indicating the superiority of Christ.

St. Paul states that in Christ are "all the treasures of wisdom and knowledge," Col. ii. 3, and (Col. ii. 9) in Him "dwelleth all the fulness of the Godhead corporally." And St. John declares the word made Flesh to be "full of grace and truth" (i. 14). Closely corresponding to these,[1] is the statement of Luke that Jesus as a Child was "filled with wisdom and the Grace of God was in Him." This is by no means an ordinary thing to say of a child. Whether we read "filled with wisdom" or "being filled with wisdom" in this verse, it is a most extraordinary thing, and cannot be explained naturally, for men have to spend years of hard study before they can hope to be filled with wisdom. As Origen says, "Aliud est partem habere sapientiae aliud est sapientia esse completum. Non ambigimus ergo divinum aliquid in carne Jesu apparuisse . . . 'et gratia Dei erat super eum.' Non quando venit ad adolescentiam, non quando manifeste docebat, sed cum adhuc esset parvulus habebat gratiam Dei; et quo-

[1] As was early pointed out by Bede, M.PL XCII. 247.

modo omnia in illo mirabilia fuerant, ita et pueritia mirabilis fuit ut Dei sapientia compleretur."[1]

This verse 40, delineating the Christ Child as very extraordinary in regard to "wisdom" and "grace," is in perfect harmony with the representation a few verses further, that Jesus at twelve years manifested preternatural knowledge before the doctors (47), and expressed real Divine Sonship in His answer to His parents (49).

At the end of the episode of the "lost" Boy, after telling how He went down to Nazareth and was subject to Mary and Joseph, Luke adds: Καὶ Ἰησοῦς προέκοπτεν ἐν τῇ σοφίᾳ καὶ ἡλικίᾳ καὶ χάριτι παρὰ θεῷ καὶ ἀνθρώποις. The Evangelist mentions Jesus by name, whom he had called a Boy (Ἰησοῦς ὁ παῖς) in vs. 43, a child (παιδίον) in vs. 40, and a Babe (βρέφος) in vs. 16 of this same chapter. Concerning Jesus at twelve years, the inspired writer predicates, προέκοπτεν, "He advanced." The important question is, here, does this word necessarily include the idea of internal increase or acquisition to the subject?

The metaphor expressed by this word, προκόπτω, is taken either from pioneers cutting in front — felling trees to enable an army to advance, or from lengthening by hammering — the beating out of metals.[2] In either case this word would have the idea of advancing, going forward, but in neither, the idea of internal acquisition of the subject.

As to the usage of the word (found elsewhere in the New Testament, only five times in St. Paul), it sometimes has the idea of real internal acquisition and it sometimes has not. It has the meaning of internal increase in Gal. i. 14, where St. Paul uses it to express his advance in Jewish tradition and observance, προέκοπτο ἐν τῷ Ἰουδαϊσμῷ. It seems to have this idea too in 2 Tim. ii. 16; iii. 8, where the apostles use the verb with ἐπὶ πλεῖον, "more," and in iii. 13, where he uses it with ἐπὶ τὸ χεῖρον, "worse."

On the other hand St. Paul uses προκόπτω to denote the night is passed, Rom. xiii. 12, ἡ νὺξ προέκοψεν, ἡ δὲ ἡμέρα ἤγγικεν. We find a similar usage in Josephus' Jewish Wars, IV. iv, 6, τῆς νυκτὸς προκοπτούσης [3] (the context indicating that it was near morning),

[1] Homil. in Loc. ad loc. in M.PG XIII. 1849.
[2] Cf. Liddell and Scott, Greek Lexicon; Carr: Gospel accord. Luke, 97.
[3] Edit. Bekkero I.–IV., p. 318. In another place (Vita, 2) Josephus uses it with the idea of internal increase.

and in Justin's Dialogue, 56, 16, ἡ τε ἡμέρα προκόπτει.[1] But now the day or night does not really increase in itself; in fact during the last half of the day or night they wane away. So that from this use of προκόπτω it can be argued that this verb expresses the advance or proceeding of something, without necessarily including real internal increase or positive acquisition. The justice of this inference is confirmed by the fact that we find προβαίνω used to express the same idea; in the Septuagint we find in Jud. xix. 11, ἡ ἡμέρα προβεβήκει and in Job ii. 9, χρόνου δὲ πολλοῦ προβεβηκότος. A somewhat similar usage is that of Justin, Dial. II. 5, προκοπτόντων ἡμῖν τῶν λόγων, "as the words proceed for us";[2] II. Clement 17, 3, προκόπτειν ἐν ταῖς ἐντολαῖς, "to go forward in the commandments";[3] Symmachus, προκόπτε (where the LXX has κατευοδοῦ) to render הלצ "proceed prosperously" of Ps. xliv. (xlv.) 5.[4] There are cases therefore where προκόπτω means simply "to go forward," being used synonymously with προβαίνω, and increase of the subject is not implied.

Coming back to Luke ii. 52, before we decide what is the force of προκόπτω here, we shall have to consider in what was the advance and what is required by the context. We shall first take up ἡλικίᾳ. This word was used to signify both "age" and "stature," "in classical Greek more frequently age, in biblical, stature";[5] in the Greek of the Papyri always age.[6] It certainly means "stature" in Luke xix. 3, and it certainly means "age" in John ix. 21, 23; Heb. xi. 11. Scholars do not agree as to which meaning is signified in Matthew vi. 27, Luke xii. 25, and Ephes.

[1] M.PG VI. 601.
[2] M.PG VI. 500. In Dial. 2, 6, Justin also uses this verb to describe his advance in Platonic philosophy, but he uses another verb with it, so that we cannot make a definite decision as to his usage.
[3] Lightfoot: Apostolic Fathers, 51.
[4] Cf. Field, Origines Hexaplorum, II. 162 (Oxonis, 1875). In a papyrus from Fayûm (mentioned by Deissmann, Light from the Ancient East, transl. by Strachan, New York, 1911, p. 170, note 13), προκόψαι is used in the sense "to be promoted." A non-committal example of the first century B.C. is Syll. 325, 18 edit. Dittenberger, ὑπεστήσατό τε ἡλικίᾳ προκόπτων καὶ προαγόμενος εἰς τὸ θεοσεβεῖν (Moulton and Milligan, Texical Notes from the Papyri, Exp. vol. VII., ser. 7 (1909) 470. The noun προκοπή is used a few times in Scripture. In Phil. i. 12, "furtherance (of the Gospel)," and in verse 25 "furtherance (of faith)," it has the idea of progress without increase; but in 1 Tim. iv. 15, the idea of increase is included and the meaning is "profiting." The same idea seems to be expressed in Sir. li. 17; it would seem to have the meaning of success or goal in 2 Mac. viii. 8.
[5] Field: Notes on Transl. of New Test., 6.
[6] Moulton and Milligan, Texical Notes from the Papyri Exp., vol. VII., ser. 7 (1909) 470.

iv. 13; neither do they agree in regard to the meaning in Luke ii. 52. Plummer holds it is not "age" which "would be rather an empty truism here." [1] Yet to express "advanced in life" St. Luke uses the perfect participle of προβαίνω, "to go forward" (i. 7, 18; ii. 36). Indeed we find προβαίνω used with ἡλικίᾳ where the latter word certainly has the meaning of "age," namely, 2 Mac. iv. 40, also vi. 18. On account of this last mentioned fact, and on account of the imperfect προέκοπτεν signifying continual advance, I would take ἡλικίᾳ in Luke ii. 52, to mean "age." An incident of Christ's twelfth year had just been recorded; when He is next mentioned He is about thirty, in the meantime He was advancing in "age" but not in "stature." [2] But whether "age" or "stature" be understood, the Evangelist wishes to express the idea that Christ was advancing physically, He was continuing to be the subject of physical development. St. Luke does not use the word "increase"; the force of προκόπτω is: He continued to make advance or headway along the road of age or stature.

Next, as to the concluding phrase, χάρις is used in the same sense as it was in vs. 40; παρά with the dative signifies place where and is best rendered in English by "with." "He advanced in grace with God and men;" *i.e.* His good and beneficent actions won the esteem and good will of those around Him; each good act also was meritorious or had merit with God.

Lastly we come to what is more to our concern, προέκοπτεν ἐν τῇ σοφίᾳ. Here σοφίᾳ is taken in the same sense as it was in vs. 40, "wisdom." Advance in wisdom would ordinarily imply the acquiring of new wisdom. Does it here? What is the force of the word "advanced" here?

In the first place, as we have said, it is clear that this verse 52 is intimately connected with the immediately preceding Temple episode, which in its turn is connected with verse 40. The imperfects running through the principal verses from 40 to 52 mark them off from what precedes and what follows; besides, the καί at the beginning of both 41 and 52 serves as a connecting link, so that this very difficult verse 52 is not to be taken out of

---

[1] Comment. ad loc., 79.
[2] Farmer agrees with this (HDG I. 229).

CHRIST CHILD'S "WISDOM" AND "GRACE" 157

its context but should be understood in the light of what precedes.

What St. Luke has previously written in verses 40, 47 and 49 seems clear enough. He states that Jesus as a little Child was filled with wisdom, or was being filled with wisdom, and the grace of God was in Him. He says that Jesus as a Boy of twelve by His answers and His understanding exceedingly astonished all who heard Him and created a scene which struck His own parents with amazement. He records the first words of Jesus, mentioning God as His metaphysical Father, and referring to His mission. He utters a reply to His mother which was of so far-reaching a significance that it was understood only in the light of after years. With this context we must understand verse 52, which literally means: And Jesus continued to advance in (or proceed in or make headway in) wisdom and age and favor with God and men.

Now the Evangelist does not use the word to "increase" or "develop" but employs a word which means to advance, to proceed, and which in itself does not imply intrinsic increase to the subject. Then it should be remarked that he does not say "in His wisdom, in His age, in His favor with God and men," but he uses these words generically suiting the idea expressed by προκόπτω. An incident of Jesus' twelfth year had just been described and St. Luke, wishing to span eighteen years of Christ's life, writes that He advanced in age. "He continued along the road of age" is the concept brought out by this verb, "to advance," and this concept of continuing along is brought out whether ἡλικίᾳ be taken for "age" or "stature."

Χάρις is also used generically, no possessive pronoun being employed. On the occasion of the visit to the Temple, Jesus had responded to the obligation He felt to be in His Father's house or about His Father's business even to the sacrifice of His earthly parents; how great was His favor with God; even as a little Child the favor or grace of God was in Him. Does "advance in the favor of God" mean that the amount was added to every day? Evidently not,[1] nor does it mean that as His age or stat-

[1] All Catholic theologians are agreed that Christ did not intrinsically increase in grace, v. g. Pohle-Preuss (Christology, 237); and the Fathers and theologians explain Lk. ii. 52, "merely as an outward manifestation of sanctifying grace." Christ yet unborn was "holy" according Lk. i. 35.

ure increased, so His favor with God and men increased. He already possessed the favor of God (40); the verb employed, meaning simply to advance, expresses this idea (and need not express any more), that as Jesus continued along the way of age or stature, so He continued along the way of favor with God and men; He continued to perform acts which won the approval of God and men.

Coming to "wisdom," we again remark that in this case too, a possessive pronoun is not used, and whether we read the article or not, a generic sense is expressed as in verse 40. It should be borne in mind that "wisdom" is not synonymous with "knowledge" but includes it. In His first recorded words Jesus had uttered a saying which the parents "did not understand." He revealed the knowledge of His Divine Sonship and His mission. In the scene before the Doctors He displayed most extraordinary (indeed we were led to believe preternatural) understanding. Even as a little child Christ was filled with (or was being filled with) wisdom. Does, then, the expression "advanced in wisdom," in verse 52, signify that Christ continued to increase His amount of wisdom? Since Jesus already displayed wonderful understanding and knowledge, to hold that His wisdom increased daily would necessarily require one to hold that He became more wonderful every day — a view which is rejected by all. St. Luke does not write "Jesus increased in wisdom," but "Jesus proceeded in wisdom." He continued along the road of wisdom, in other words, He continued to do wise acts.

Very many writers interpret verse 52 to mean that Christ increased in wisdom and age pari passu; as His age increased so His wisdom.[1] These writers make the mistake of considering this text in itself apart from its context; they should take up the whole text, not only wisdom and age, but wisdom, age, and grace with God and men, and consider it in the light of verses 40, 47 and 49. From His twelfth year just mentioned, Christ continued along in age, He continued to win the favor of God (possessing it as a little child), and to win the favor of men. He continued

---

[1] Many conservative writers say this, and some even understand verse 52 to mean that Christ just had the wisdom appropriate for His age at each step. How then explain the great wisdom of the Public Life?

along in wisdom with which even as a little Child He was filled and of which He gave a wonderful example in His twelfth year. Briefly, verse 52 means, as Christ grew up He performed wise and gracious acts, He grew up in wisdom and grace.

Employing the figure of speech known as zeugma, St. Luke could use a verb signifying real increase in age or stature, yet not entailing this in regard to wisdom and grace.[1] The verb that he uses means simply "going forward" and does not in itself include increase to the subject.

Another point that is deserving of consideration: In vs. 52, the Evangelist spans a number of years of Christ's life as he did in vs. 40. When we allow for his love of variation of wording and style, it will be seen that he expresses the same ideas in both verses: Christ grew physically, He advanced in age or stature; He was filled with wisdom, He continued according to wisdom; the Grace of God was in Him, He continued to do gracious acts. If one contends that a different condition existing in the term after Christ's twelfth year explains St. Luke's change of wording, still one cannot oppose our method of explaining vs. 52 in the light of vs. 40 without accusing St. Luke of inconsistency. To say that real increase in wisdom and grace is expressed in vs. 52 is to say that the Evangelist contradicts what he had already written.

The imperfect of the verb "to proceed" does not require the meaning that Christ continued to display wonderful wisdom. But this imperfect connected with the Temple episode might imply that He continued to show wisdom. Doubtless He could advance in wisdom without showing it, but Luke's authority for the early chapters, Mary, could relate only what she saw or knew. He showed that He was proceeding in age and in favor with God and men, and He showed that He was proceeding in wisdom. St. Cyril of Alexandria writes concerning Christ's display of knowledge before the Doctors, "see how He advanced in wisdom through His becoming known to many to be such."[2] We also hear such

[1] Luke does use Zeugma in i. 64, "His mouth and tongue were opened," probably because he was translating from a Hebrew original. Cf. Torrey, Translation made from Aramaic Gosp., 293.
[2] M.PG LXXII. 508. In another place (Quod unus est Christus, 760 M.PG LXXV. 1352) Cyril well says, "He economically allowed the measures of humanity

explanations of vs. 52 as that of Ward, who says that "advanced" means "not that His knowledge intrinsically increased, but that it gradually declared itself more and more to those among whom He lived." [1] In this quotation exception may be taken to the "more and more," as is clear from what has been stated above, for Christ had already shown wonderful knowledge; we would confine ourselves to the meaning that His wisdom continued to declare itself, or rather, He continued to act wisely.

The purpose here is not to formulate or prove any theory in regard to Christ's increase in knowledge, but to endeavor to reach the exact meaning of the texts with which we are concerned. Certainly we hold that Jesus' experimental knowledge [2] increased since He was truly man and had human faculties, but we wish to point out that this is not stated in Luke ii. 52. An account of any of Christ's experiences or actions which represents Him as using His mental faculties would be as serviceable for indicating His increase in experimental knowledge, as this text which merely says that He proceeded in wisdom.[3]

---

to have power over Himself." Some of the Fathers (perhaps on account of the conflict with Arianism) explain Lk. ii. 52, that Christ advanced according to human nature. Theodoret, one of the latter explaining Christ's advance in wisdom, uses Lk. ii. 49, as we have done. (De Incarnatione, M.PG LXXIV. 73.)

[1] Saint Luke, 36.

[2] Christ possessed a threefold knowledge: (1) that derived from the Beatific Vision of God, (2) infused knowledge, and (3) acquired or experimental knowledge. Concerning the first two kinds it has always been held that there was no increase, concerning the last theologians have not been unanimous. St. Thomas at first (III. Sent. Dist. XIV.) held there was no increase, but afterwards he changed his mind and explained the matter thus: "Both the infused knowledge and the beatific knowledge of Christ's soul were the effect of an agent of infinite power which could produce the whole at once; and thus in neither knowledge did Christ advance, since from the beginning He had them perfectly. But the acquired knowledge of Christ is caused by the active intellect which does not produce the whole at once, but successively; and hence by this knowledge Christ did not know everything from the beginning, but step by step and after a time, i.e. in His perfect age: and this is plain from what the Evangelist says, viz., that He increased in knowledge and age together" (Sum. III. Q. xii, Art. 2 ad 1). This view is taken by many present-day writers: Janssens (Tractatus de Deo Homine, I. 473), Hurter (Theologiae dogmaticae Compendium, II. 461, Maas (Knowledge of J. C., Cath.Enc.), Vonier (Personality of Christ, 95 ff.), Pohle-Preuss (Christology, 247–277), Coughlan (De Incarnatione, 146–167), Lepicier (De Incarnatione Verbi, 395–472).

[3] This verse, Lk. ii. 52, was the main reason for the explanation of Jesus' increase in human knowledge by some of the Fathers, and for the explanation of the increase in experimental knowledge by later theologians. If our interpretation of the passage be accepted, it would seem that these explanations are not required; especially no pari passu explanation is needed.

2. A SIGNIFICANT SILENCE IN THESE VERSES

The twelve verses, Luke ii. 40-52, which we have examined were intended by the Evangelist to cover thirty years of Christ's life. He first spans nearly twelve years in one verse in which he refers to the Child's physical growth, remarking in opposition that He was filled with wisdom (or being filled with wisdom), and that the Grace of God was in Him. Then he gives an incident of the twelfth year, in which the Boy gave evidence of preternatural insight and consciousness of His mission and real Divine Sonship. He ends the account of the episode and the account of Jesus' early years by the reference to His proceeding or advancing in wisdom, age and favor with God and men, — in one verse bridging over eighteen years.

These twelve verses contain the only evangelical account of nearly thirty years of the Master's Life. It must be said that they are far from being an ordinary way of describing the growth of a child to manhood; there is not the slightest attempt to account for the Great Person Who, in so short a time, left such an impression on the world; there is not even an attempt to account for His great knowledge and divine self-consciousness either of His public life or His twelfth year. Whence came this knowledge and self-consciousness? One should be able to account for it if Christ was merely human. How is it that Luke does not tell us that Jesus received his knowledge under the guidance of some great philosopher? In this regard Luke is not silent concerning other men about whom he wrote; for example, about the wise Joseph, who from being a slave became the governor of all Egypt; "and (God) gave him favor and wisdom in the sight of Pharao," Acts vii. 10; about the great Lawgiver, Moses, "and Moses was instructed in all the wisdom of the Egyptians" (Acts vii. 22); about Paul the orator and apostle to the Gentiles, "brought up in this City, at the feet of Gamaliel, taught according to the truth of the law of the fathers," Acts xxii. 3. Christ is never mentioned as having received instructions at the feet of any Gamaliel; it is not mentioned in the Gospels that He even went to any school.

The Synoptics seem to imply that Christ did not receive His great knowledge in any school. They tell us that the people of the town "where He was brought up" could not account for His wisdom, Mtt. xiii. 54; Mk. vi. 2, 3; Lk. iv. 22; nor can Lk. iv. 16 be cited as proving that Jesus had attended school, for as Plummer (Comment. ad loc. p. 118) states, "it is best to confine κατὰ τὸ εἰωθός to the clause in which it is imbedded and not carry it on to ἀνέστη ἀναγνῶναι." In any case it only refers to Christ's custom on Sabbath days. The Fourth Evangelist makes Christ's hearers state that He was unschooled πῶς οὗτος γράμματα οἶδεν μὴ μεμαθηκώς (vii. 15), and makes Christ Himself explain in the following verse (16), "My doctrine is not Mine, but His that sent Me"; again viii. 28: "as the Father hath taught Me, these things I speak" (cf. also viii. 19, 20, 26). This same Evangelist who has it that Christ was unschooled, mentions His writing on the ground, viii. 6, 8; and twice (xvi. 30; xxi. 17) represents an apostle as saying that He knew all things. Cf. also Jn. iii. 2; xviii. 37. The Messiah was to know all things, cf. Jn. iv. 25; Is. lv. 4. In all tradition there is not the slightest implication that Jesus learned from any human being; the Apocryphal Gospels contain curious stories about His being brought to school, but they always make it clear that on the first day He knew more than His teacher. St. Thomas holds that Christ's human knowledge came by discovery, not by teaching, for he writes, "it was more fitting for Christ to possess a knowledge acquired by discovery than by teaching" (Summa, Part III. Q. ix, Art. 4 ad i), and in Q. xii. art. 3, he shows that Christ did not learn anything from men. An objection may be brought from Heb. ii. 17, "it behooved Him in all things (κατὰ πάντα) to be made like unto His brethren . . ." We know from St. Paul himself that sin is excepted (v.g. Heb. iv. 15); from the Gospel narrative, we know that miraculous power is excepted, and we know too that there is excepted a miraculous knowledge and a peculiar self-consciousness; could not the manner of receiving His knowledge be excepted also? It is not required by the context of the passage of Hebrews; it would suffice that Christ merely take our flesh "that He might become a merciful and faithful high priest before God, that He might be a propitiation for the sins of the people." In this same epistle, v. 8, "He learned obedience by the things which He suffered" is not a serious objection; it signifies He practiced obedience, and is much similar to the thought, "He was obedient unto death even unto the death of the cross" (Philipp. ii. 8). Most Protestant theologians in explaining the Kenosis think it necessary to admit Christ's ignorance and His need of learning like an ordinary child, but as

CHRIST CHILD'S "WISDOM" AND "GRACE" 163

Vonier says, "it is a very strange phase of thought in our own days to look for moral progress to ignorance instead of to knowledge, as does the older theology" (Personality of Christ, 105).

As has previously been stated, there probably existed at the time of Our Lord, a primary school at Nazareth; Edersheim [1] and others say that Jesus probably attended it. There is not the slightest reference to this in historical documents, which rather create a presumption against this view. But whatever view one may take of this matter, it is certain that Jesus did not attend any higher school. All evidence shows that He "never studied at any of the scribal colleges."[2] It is important to note that Christ, who afterwards (v.g. Matthew xix. 1–12; Luke xx. 20–47) showed His superiority over those trained in rabbinical discussion, who as a Boy of twelve in the midst of the Doctors astounded all by His understanding and His answers, did not receive any rabbinical education; He did not live in a theological atmosphere; He was not an inhabitant of the land famed for its Rabbis, Judea, nor of Jerusalem, the City of the Chief Priests and Doctors. He belonged to Galilee, a by-word among the Southerners for ignorance and uncouthness (cf. John vii. 52), and was a citizen of the town of Nazareth, from which nothing good was expected (John i. 46). St. Luke explicitly stated He was brought up there (ἦν τεθραμμένος, iv. 16), and all historical evidence bears this out.[3]

How then shall we account for Christ's great knowledge and self-consciousness? Since no teacher is responsible, the only other natural explanation that could be offered is Jesus' surroundings, His own meditations on nature and Sacred Scripture, and this is the explanation which is offered by many modern writers. Stapfer[4] and others go through several pages describing the natural beauties of Nazareth, the historical surroundings, the im-

[1] Life and Times of J., I. 233.
[2] Smith, Education, HDC I. 508. Even Harnack says, "It is improbable that He went through any rabbinical school" (What is Christianity, 31).
[3] Lk. ii. 39, 51; Mtt. ii. 23; iv. 13; Mk. i. 9; vi. 1; Jn. i. 45, 46; Ac. x. 38. As to His profession Christ was a carpenter, Mk. vi. 3; Justin (Dialogue, 88), and "Gospel of Thomas" (1st Gr. Form, XIII.) add "making ploughs and yokes" — but these were then made of wood.
[4] J. C. before His Ministry, see especially 35–7. Mere possible influences occupy Farquhar, The Schools and Schoolmasters of Christ, London, 1901.

pressive Jewish ceremonial, the inspirations likely to be awakened from familiarity with the Old Testament writings, contending that these externals gave birth to and developed in Christ His peculiar self-consciousness. But represent these as one will, were they not at the disposal of every Israelite? And how answer the pointed question: Why did a cause so common and so general produce in Christ and in Him alone a result altogether exceptional and special? If the causes were sufficient to produce such knowledge and self-consciousness in Jesus, why did they not produce the like in other children of Israel? Why was Christ an exception to His contemporaries and the companions of His youth? These questions come to one's mind and require to be answered by those who put forward Christ's historical surroundings and His Jewish bringing up as an explanation of His great knowledge and self-consciousness. Besides, the explanations brought forward are devoid of historical foundation, they are even excluded by historical evidence. St. Luke preserves a strange and significant silence, recording only the facts; but these facts exclude any natural explanation, for the Evangelist represents Christ as having exceptional knowledge and self-consciousness, not only in His thirtieth year, but also in His twelfth, and records that as a Child He was filled with (or kept full or being filled with) wisdom, and that the grace of God was in Him. There was no time or room for natural causes to produce naturally an effect in Him. St. Luke gives no explanation; he does not state any cause for or record any origin of Christ's knowledge and self-consciousness. The argument of silence is of value here, the silence is highly significant; it implies that the origin of Christ's knowledge and self-consciousness is to be sought in Christ's own origin and nature, which had previously been described by the Evangelist.

From the above considerations we can easily see that scholars who wish to follow the Gospel records can find no natural explanation for Christ's knowledge and self-consciousness. Even Wendt in his explanation has to postulate "a miraculous Divine endowment." [1] After describing the training of Jewish boys, Brough confesses that "the growth, in such an atmosphere, of an individual so unique is the work of something that is more than

[1] The Teaching of J., 94.

CHRIST CHILD'S "WISDOM" AND "GRACE" 165

human."[1] Ewald explicitly states that "Jesus would never have become what He subsequently became in the light of the great public history of His life, if His mind had not from the first received the Divine designation and power needful for it,"[2] and he refers to the matter as "superhistorical," and after saying that he could not find anywhere any signs of the origin of Christ's self-consciousness, Dalman rightly argues that "if Jesus was conscious of no beginning in His peculiar relationship to God, it must, of course, have had its genesis with His birth; and further, God must have so participated in assigning that position, that the human factors concerned fell entirely into the background."[3]

The silence then in these two verses, 40 and 52, which cover nearly thirty years of Christ's Life is fraught with significance implying that the origin and explanation of the wisdom with which Jesus was filled and in which He proceeded are to be sought in Christ's own origin and nature, and are supernatural; the fact that Jesus as a Child was filled with wisdom is itself supernatural; verse 52 offers no objection to the conclusion in our main chapter, as it can and should be explained in its context; and finally verse 40, far from opposing, rather strongly confirms our conclusion, — the fact that Jesus as a Child was filled with wisdom adds weight to the other arguments for the full and real meaning of the words "My Father" on His lips in His twelfth year.[4]

[1] Early Life of Our Lord, 46.
[2] History of Israel, VI. 189.
[3] Words of J., 86.
[4] Condemned propositions ex decr. S. Off. Lamentabile, 3 Julii 1907 (Denzinger, Encheridion, p. 541): XXII. Conciliari nequit sensus naturalis textuum evangelicorum cum eo quod nostri theologi docent de conscientia et scientia infallibili Jesu Christi, XXXIII. Criticus nequit asserere Christo scientiam nullo circumscriptam limite nisi facta hypothesi, quae historice haud concipi potest quaeque sensui morali repugnat, nempe Christum uti hominem habuisse scientiam Dei et nihilominus noluisse notitiam tot rerum communicare cum discipulis ac posteritate. XXXV. Christus non semper habuit conscientiam suae dignitatis messianicae.

SECTION VI

JESUS' FIRST RECORDED WORDS AND THE REMOTE CONTEXT

CHAPTER XIV

THE WHOLE LUCAN ACCOUNT OF CHRIST

1. THE INFANCY SECTION

THE Angel of the Annunciation foretells the great contrast that exists between Christ and John the Baptist. To Zachary he says, "Thy wife Elizabeth shall bear thee a son" (i. 13); but to Mary, "The Holy Ghost shall come upon thee and the power of the Most High shall overshadow thee" (i. 35). He prophesies that John "shall be great before the Lord" (i. 15), Jesus simply, "shall be great" (i. 32); John "shall be filled with the Holy Ghost" (i. 15); Jesus is to be conceived of the Holy Ghost (i. 35); and while John "shall convert many of the children of Israel to the Lord their God, and he shall go before Him in the spirit and power of Elias" (i. 16, 17), Jesus "shall be called[1] the Son of the Most High; and the Lord God shall give unto Him the throne of David His Father; and He shall reign in the house of Jacob forever, and of His Kingdom there shall be no end" (i. 32, 33). What a contrast between Jesus and John do these texts bring out! Jesus is far superior; He is even to be conceived of the Holy Ghost, hence the reason why He is to be in reality "the Son of the Most High" (i. 32), "the Son of God" (i. 35)!

Zachary himself said of his son, "Thou, child, shall be called the prophet of the highest, for thou shalt go before the face of the Lord and prepare His ways" (i. 76); while Mary sang, "From henceforth all generations shall call me blessed, because He that is mighty hath done great things to me" (i. 48, 49) — appropriate words on the lips of the mother of God. She is declared to be such in reality, by Elizabeth, for while the unborn Baptist did homage to the unborn Saviour (i. 41), she cried in joy and amaze-

---

[1] "Shall be called" is equivalent to "is," cf. Bardenhewer, Mariä Verkündigung, 113, 151.

ment, "Whence is this to me that the mother of my Lord, (ἡ μήτηρ τοῦ κυρίου μου) should come to me?" (i. 43). Christ is again called "Lord" by an "angel of the Lord" (ἄγγελος κυρίου, ii. 9), proclaiming to the shepherds that there was born to them a Saviour who is Christ the Lord (Χριστὸς Κύριος, ii. 11). It is to be noticed that the same word, κύριος, which is applied to Almighty God in ii. 9, is applied by the angel to the new-born Babe (ii. 11), and was applied by Elizabeth to the unborn Babe (i. 43). His birth, too, was signaled by a multitude of the heavenly army filling the air with their song, "Glory to God in the highest; and on earth peace to men of good will" (ii. 14). The Child was not many weeks old, when holy Simeon who had been informed by the Holy Ghost that he would not die till he should see the Christ of the Lord (Χριστὸν Κυρίου, ii. 26), blessing God for the fulfillment of the promise, said, "My eyes have seen Thy salvation . . . a light to the revelation of the Gentiles and the glory of thy people, Israel" (ii. 30, 31). Also the prophetess Anna acknowledged God[1] and "spoke of Him to all who looked for the redemption of Israel" (ii. 38).

In harmony with all this, and crowning it all, comes the next episode described by the Evangelist in which Christ as a Boy of twelve displayed supernatural understanding and referred to God as His true Father about whose concerns He must be (or in whose house He must be). Must not Jesus' words be interpreted in the light of the Virgin Birth previously described, of which it is a confirmation? The angel had foretold that Christ would be the Son of God because of His supernatural conception through the Holy Ghost (i. 32, 35), and as Dalman points out "the words of the angel, i. 35, explain for the readers the meaning of ὁ υἱὸς τοῦ θεοῦ by expressed reference to the unique nature of the birth of Jesus."[2] The words "My Father" on the lips of the Boy Jesus are co-relative to the angel's words "the Son of God" and are to be understood in accordance with the supernatural conception by the Holy Spirit, namely real Divine Sonship. Since the Evangelist had described this divine origin of Jesus, he felt no need of de-

---

[1] Some MSS. have κύριος here. Here as in ii. 50, is an example of St. Luke's use of a pronoun whose reference is ambiguous.

[2] Words of J., 288, cf. Sweet. The Birth and Infancy of Jesus Christ, 258–9, Felder, Jesus Christus, I. 286 ff. Box, Virgin Birth, 107.

THE WHOLE LUCAN ACCOUNT OF CHRIST

fining the meaning of the words "My Father" in ii. 49 and he felt no need of giving explanations of Christ's extraordinary wisdom and grace in ii. 40 and 52.

2. THE BEGINNING OF THE MINISTRY

The scene opens with John the Baptist, who prepares the way, "preaching the baptism of penance for the remission of sins" (iii. 3). He made such an impression on the people that they thought in their hearts "that perhaps he might be the Christ" (3.15). The great Forerunner, the greatest among those born of woman (vii. 28), who, with his thundering denunciations was making Israel tremble, unhesitatingly answered in the negative and generously pointed to another, to one far superior to himself, "There shall come one mightier than I, the latchet of whose shoes I am not worthy to loose; he shall baptize you with the Holy Ghost and with fire" (iii. 16). This other was to be so closely connected with God that He was to baptize with the Holy Ghost.

One day, among the crowds who flocked to the banks of the Jordan, Jesus Himself appeared and was baptized. This is how St. Luke describes the event (iii. 21, 22): "Jesus also being baptized and praying, heaven was opened; and the Holy Spirit descended in a bodily shape, as a dove upon Him; and a voice came from Heaven: "Thou art My beloved Son; in Thee I am well pleased" (σὺ εἶ ὁ υἱός μου ὁ ἀγαπητός, ἐν σοὶ εὐδόκησα).[1] This

[1] D a b c ff² l r Justin (Dial, 88, M.PG VI. 688), Clement of Alex. (Paed. I. 6, M.PG VIII. 279), and the Gospel of the Ebionites (cf. Epiphanius Adv. Haer. Lib. I. 5, ii. 30, n. 13, M.PG XLI. 429; three voices from heaven are here given: Thou art My beloved Son, etc. This is My beloved Son, etc., and I have this day begotten Thee) and others (cf. Sanday H D B IV. 572), in giving these words have a reflection of Ps. ii. 7, namely, υἱός μου εἶ σύ, ἐγὼ σήμερον γεγέννηκά σε. This is claimed to be the primitive reading by those who contend that Christ only became conscious of His Divine Sonship at His baptism. But as Dalman remarks, "This reading may equally well have arisen as an after-thought, because, apart from the doctrinal preconception, it was only too probable that the Divine words which recalled Ps. ii. 7, should be made to agree to the terms of the psalm" (Words of J., 277). Sanday (op. cit.) with other arguments points out the presumption against the originality of this reading. Justin, who uses this reading, explains it: Not that Christ became the Son of God then, but that "His generation would take place for men, at the time when they would become acquainted with Him" (Dial. 88 PG VI. 688). The Gospel of the Hebrews has it, "That the Holy Ghost resting upon Christ said to Him: Fili mi, in omnibus prophetis expectabam te, ut venires, et requiescerem in te. Tu es enim requies mea, tu es Filius meus primogenitus, qui

baptism account deserves our close attention on account of views and inferences, opposed to our conclusion from the study of Luke ii. 49, views held by certain early heretics who attached Christological importance to Christ's baptism, inferences drawn by nearly all modern non-conservative scholars, when they contend that the baptism marks the awakening of Christ's Messianic consciousness; that on the banks of the Jordan, Jesus first got the idea of His being the Son of God, — the heavenly voice being only the internal voice of His consciousness assuring Him of the fact.[1] Concerning the views of the early heretics, we need only to quote Irenaeus: "It certainly was in the power of the Apostles to declare that Christ descended upon Jesus, or that the so-called Superior Saviour (came down) upon the dispensational one, or He who is from the invisible places upon him from the Demiurge; but they neither knew nor said anything of the kind, for, had they known it, they would have also certainly stated it. But what really was the case, that did they record (namely) that the Spirit of God as a dove descended upon Him." [2]

Now as to the modern theories: In the first place, may the descent of the Holy Ghost and the heavenly voice be considered an internal experience? This is directly opposed to the representation of St. Luke, who explicitly states that the Holy Ghost came in bodily shape (σωματικῷ εἴδει) as a dove (iii. 22). And St. Luke's account is confirmed by the Fourth Gospel, according to which John says, "I saw the Spirit as a dove from heaven and He remained upon Him" (i. 32). It is true that neither Matthew

regnas in sempiternam (Jerome in Isa. xi. 4; in his Comment. Lib. IV. c. XI., M.PL XXIV. *D*. 145). This implies the contrary to the modern view. In the other quotation of this Gospel preserved by Jerome (Adv. Pelag. III. 2, M.PL XXIII. 570–571), when in answer to His parents, who asked Him to go up and be baptized by John, Jesus replied: "When have I sinned that I should go up and be baptized by Him, except perchance, this very thing which I have said is ignorance?" "Ignorantia" does not refer to self-consciousness. Augustine (Harmony of the Gospels II. 14, N.P–NF (1st ser.) VI. 120) refers to the fact that some codices of St. Luke have the reading: "This day have I begotten Thee," and he explains the matter on the ground that there was more than one voice from heaven. We may add that St. Paul applies Ps. ii. 7 to the Resurrection of Christ, Ac. xiii. 33; Heb. i. 5; v. 5.

[1] The modern view concerning the origin of Christ's self-consciousness at the baptism is not found among the views of the early heretics. The early views were all objective, with no reference to Christ's self-consciousness as such. Besides, unlike the modern view, they were not based on the heavenly voice, "This is My beloved Son."

[2] Adv. Haer. III. 17, 1, A–NF I. 444.

(iii. 16) nor Mark (i. 10) refer to the bodily form of the dove, but they both say that the Holy Ghost came "as a dove"; and while stating that Jesus saw the dove, they do not affirm that He alone saw it. As to the heavenly voice, if as radical scholars contend it is the all-important part of the account, symbolizing Jesus' consciousness arriving at assuredness, how is it that John does not give this at all? All the three Synoptics have "a voice from the heavens" (Luke writing "heaven"), implying that it was external; none of them mentions the fact that Christ heard it; indeed, Matthew intimates that it was intended for the bystanders, for he gives the words thus, "This is (not, 'Thou art') My Beloved Son in whom I am well pleased" (iii. 17). In the Fourth Gospel the Baptist states that the descending of the dove was a sign for him (i. 33, 34), "He who sent me to baptize with water said to me: He upon whom thou shalt see the Spirit descending . . . and I saw, etc." From all these indications it is clear that the descent of the Holy Ghost and the heavenly voice were external. To explain them by an internal experience is to argue subjectively and to disregard the text.[1]

We go on to the further question: Did the baptism mark a crisis in Christ's conscious life? Did it mark the awakening of His Divine self-consciousness, or its arrival at assuredness? Those who hold the affirmative point to the heavenly voice, "Thou art My beloved Son in whom I am well pleased" — the voice of His consciousness, they claim, telling Him He is God's Son. According to the Gospel narrative, as we have shown, the heavenly voice as well as the coming of the Holy Ghost in the form of a dove, must be understood as external manifestations. More than this, in none of the inspired accounts, is there a single reference to Christ's self-consciousness, much less a statement of any crisis or development. St. Matthew even implies that before the baptism Jesus was conscious of His dignity, for according to this Evangelist, to John who expostulated, "I have a need to be baptized by Thee, and comest Thou to me" (iii. 14), the Saviour acknowledging the truth of John's remark replied: "Suffer it now, for

[1] Cf. Irenaeus (Adv. Haer. III. 9, 3, A–NF I. 423); Origen (Adv. Celsus, I. xli ff. A–NF IV. 413 ff.), St. Thomas (Summa Theol. III., Q. XXIX. 8), Bornemann (Die Taufe Christi), Lepin (Christ and the Gospel, 251), Felder (Jesus Christus, I. 262, 275).

174 THE BOYHOOD CONSCIOUSNESS OF CHRIST

thus it becometh us to fulfil all justice" (iii. 15).[1] Finally, if the heavenly voice "Thou art My Beloved Son, in Thee I am well pleased" is only an indication of Christ's arrival at full self-consciousness, how is it that we again hear this voice uttering the same words on the Mount of Transfiguration (Matthew xvii. 5; Mark ix. 6; Luke ix. 9, 35; cf. 2 Peter i. 17)? In the theory of non-conservative writers, this cannot be explained. And this theory has not only to explain the voice, but also the coming of the Holy Ghost in the form of a dove, which could have no internal signification for Jesus, who is described as born of the Holy Spirit in the records of both Matthew and Luke. We may add that if for the Evangelists, the baptism witnessed Christ's awakening to self-consciousness, it is hard to explain how so important an event is not plainly described by them, how they do not refer to it, how they create the very opposite impression.[2]

Judging from the sacred narratives the incidents at the baptism were external, they marked no change in Christ's idea of His Messiahship and Divine Sonship, rather they were a confirmation of these intended not for Jesus Himself but for John and the bystanders, as is made clear in the accounts of Matthew ("This is," iii. 17), Luke ("In bodily shape" iii. 22), and John ("I saw and gave testimony" i. 34). As Dalman[3] rightly concludes, "the Evangelists give an account of the voice, not on account of any importance which the reception of such a divine voice might possibly have for Jesus, but in the sense of impressive testimonies that Jesus really was what His disciples before the world pro-

---

[1] Cf. D'Arcy (HDG I. 362). This is implied too by the Gospel according to the Hebrews, which represents Christ as saying to his mother and his brethren that He had not any need to be baptized (Jerome Adv. Pel. III. 2, M.PL XXIII. 570). An anonymous Tractatus de Rebaptismate (XVII), written by a contemporary of St. Cyprian, says that a book called the Pauli Praedicatio represents Christ "confessing His own sin — although He alone did not sin at all — and almost compelled by His mother Mary unwillingly to receive John's baptism" (A–NF V. 677).

[2] Against the modern view of Christ's baptism we have confined ourselves to the reasons drawn from the Gospel account; there are other reasons, for instance, the silence of St. Paul; as Sanday says, "There is not a single reference in the whole of his writings to our Lord's baptism, as a landmark or turning point in His career" (Life of Christ in Recent Research, 133). Besides the modern views cannot boast that they are according to the principles of psychology. Why should the baptism have the effect they claim, on Jesus, and not on anybody else? Was not Christ just emerging from private life, having no experience as a teacher or preacher? What was the relation of the coming of the Holy Ghost to Christ's self-consciousness?

[3] Words of J., 280.

claimed Him to be." So that instead of containing anything derogatory to the result in Section IV, the baptism account brings a confirmatory argument; the resting on Jesus of the Holy Spirit, and the Heavenly Father intervening so far in Jesus' behalf as loudly to proclaim Him as His beloved Son, are a further confirmation of the view that when the latter in His twelfth year called God, "My Father," He signified metaphysical relation.

St. Luke goes on to remark that when Jesus began His ministry He was about thirty years of age and was supposed (ὡς ἐνομίζετο, iii. 23) to be the son of Joseph; the Evangelist thus indicating that he bears in mind the Virgin Birth which he had previously described. In the genealogy which he subjoins the disciple of St. Paul mentions seventy-two members, — the symbol of universality;[1] and contrary to the previously universal custom, he enumerates the members backwards, placing Jesus the Saviour of all at the head and ending with the climax, τοῦ θεοῦ (iii. 38). This expression, coming after the proclamation of the Heavenly Father, coming after the episode in the Temple, after the account of the Virgin Birth, is truly the keystone proclamation of Divine Sonship. It is in perfect harmony with what precedes, tracing as it does Jesus' human lineage back to God.

The sacred historian then resumes the account of Christ's life which he had brought to the baptism, and tells us that Jesus returned from the Jordan "full of the Holy Ghost" (iv. 1). This same Holy Spirit leads Him into the desert where He was tempted by the devil (iv. 2, 13). Three temptations are described,[2] and in two of them Satan addresses Christ thus, "If Thou art the Son of God" (Luke iv. 3, 9; cf. Matthew iv. 3, 6).

In the first place, these temptations are not mere internal experiences. To hold this one must entirely disregard the Gospel narrative, which contains accurate references to places — a real desert (Luke iv. 1; Matthew iv. 1; Mark i. 12), a real mountain (Luke iv. 5, which supposes Matthew iv. 8), a real temple (Luke iv. 9; Matthew iv. 5) — and which describes real actions, e.g.,

[1] Cf. Heer, Die Stammbaume Jesu, 53 ff.
[2] The order of the last two is different in St. Matthew (iv. 5-10). Although Luke is generally more careful in chronological details, yet Matthew's order is preferable. Cf. Gigot, Studies in the Synoptics, NYR I (1905) 3, pp. 365-366; Harnack, The Sayings of J., 43-44.

Satan conducting Him (Luke iv. 5, 9; Matthew iv. 5, 8), the dialogue with the Old Testament quotations (e.g., Luke iv. 4; Matthew iv. 4).

And secondly: Since these temptations are not internal, by no means do they signify that Christ was struggling in His self-consciousness, and that the voice of the tempter, "If thou be the Son of God" indicated that He had not yet the full conviction of His Messiahship and Divine Sonship. The Second Gospel, which the negative school gives the credit for being the most primitive, allows only one verse for the account of the temptation, omitting altogether the dialogue with Satan. In none of the sacred accounts is there mention of His self-consciousness, nor are any of the temptations bearing directly on His nature or mission; in fact, His replies to the devil show assertiveness and conviction, — the contrary of doubt or hesitation.[1]

The temptation was a real occurrence, in which a personal tempter appearing in bodily form made outward suggestions to Jesus. Placed at the beginning of His Public Life it is meant to emphasize the fact that He discarded human means and the worldly Messiah (along which lines the temptations run) and to show that His manner of life was deliberately willed by Him. How appropriate this self-conscious way of acting is for one who realizes He is the Son of God! It is to be remarked that while Satan in two of his suggestions says, "If Thou art the Son of God," referring back to the words of the heavenly voice at the baptism,[2] Christ does not answer "No" to this part of the tempter's question. His mode of procedure implies that He knew He was the Son of God.

When all the temptation had been ended, Jesus began His Public Ministry. He "returned in the power of the spirit into Galilee and the fame of Him went out through the whole country" (Luke iv. 14). We see that immediately on His first appearance, He makes a deep impression, winning widespread fame and receiving the applause of all for His teaching, as the next verse tells us: "And He taught in their Synagogues, and was magnified by all" (iv. 15). As examples, Luke describes His first

[1] Cf. D'Arcy, Consciousness, HDG I. 362.
[2] Cf. Dalman, Words of J., 275; Robertson: Epochs in the Life of J., 20.

visit to Nazareth where He was brought up (iv. 16–30), and an early visit to Capharnaum, the city which He afterwards so much loved (iv. 31–44). In the former place Christ applied to Himself a Messianic prophecy; in the latter place He spoke "with power" and cured diverse diseases, and said to those who wanted to detain Him there "to other cities also I must preach the Kingdom of God, since for this end am I sent" (Luke iv. 43).

The account of the opening of Christ's Public Ministry, therefore, does not inform us that, during it, He got the idea either of His divine mission or nature. There is not the slightest hint to that effect. There is here asserted that the Heavenly Father proclaimed Him as His "beloved Son," that Satan addressed Him, "If thou art the Son of God," that devils recognized Him as the "Son of God," and there is given no denial on His part, nor is there given even an intimation that He doubted about His mission or nature. On the contrary, there are brought out His unwavering conviction and His full realization of His calling, during His first appearance at Nazareth, where He applied to Himself the Messianic prophecy of Isaias, and in His early visit to Capharnaum, where He announced that He must preach the kingdom of God. It is to be remarked that there is nowhere described, nor is there even any reference to, any beginning of His Divine self-consciousness. The impression directly and indirectly created by the Gospel record is that Christ came to His public career fully self-conscious.

3. THE PUBLIC LIFE

According to the Third Gospel, Christ, in His Public Life, both directly and indirectly declared He was the real Son of God. St. Luke not only represents Christ as reading the very hearts of men (e.g., v. 21, 22; vii. 39, 40; xi. 39), as foretelling future events (e.g., ix. 22, 44; x. 14, 15; xxi. 20–24) and as performing many and great miracles (cf. vi. 19); but he also represents Christ as acting the part of God, for he describes how He worked miracles in His own name and authority (e.g., vii. 14; viii. 24, 54; ix. 43), how He imparted to His disciples the power of working miracles by His authority and in His name (ix. 1, 2, 6; x. 9,

17; cf. Acts iii. 6, 16; iv. 10, 30; ix. 34; xvi. 18), and how He claimed the power of forgiving sins (v. 20, 24; vii. 48; xix. 10). St. Luke represents Christ as taking the place of God, for he informs us that He set Himself up in the place of Jahweh as the spouse of immortal souls (v. 34), that He declared that for His sake one must hate one's relatives and even one's life (xiv. 26), and assured His fellowmen that "he that shall lose his life for My sake, shall save it" (ix. 24).

The Third Evangelist represents Christ as assuming prerogatives which presuppose Him to be God, for he depicts Him as announcing He is "Lord also of the Sabbath" (vi. 5), as claiming to be the Great Judge of all men at the last day (ix. 26; xii. 8, 9; xxi. 27; xxii. 69), as possessing authority to send the Holy Ghost (xxiv. 49; cf. Acts i. 4, 8), as allowing Himself to be adored (προσκυνήσαντες) by His apostles and disciples (xxiv. 52), as rising from the dead and manifesting Himself to His disciples during a period of forty days (xxiv. 26, 31, 34, 36 ff; Acts i. 3), and as ascending into heaven (xxiv. 51; Acts i. 9).

In this Gospel, by His pointed question as to how David should call His son Lord (xx. 41, 44; cf. Matthew xxii. 41, 46; Mark xii. 35, 37) Christ adverts to the fact that the Messiah is in reality Son of One more exalted than David, that is, the Son of God.[1] According to this same evangelical record, Jesus frequently calls God His Father (ix. 26; x. 21, 22; xxii. 29, 42; xxiii. 34, 46; xxiv. 49),[2] thus distinguishing His own Sonship from the sonship of all others (cf. xi. 2); and in the parable of the wicked husbandmen (xx. 9, 19; cf. Matthew xxi. 33, 46; Mark xii. 1, 12), sharply distinguishing from the whole series of servants the "beloved son" as the sole heir, He indirectly says He is the true and only Son of God. In this Gospel, too, we find the famous declaration "All things are delivered to Me by My Father; and no one knoweth Who the Son is, but the Father; and Who the Father is, but the Son, and he to whom the Son

[1] Cf. Dalman, Words of J., 286.
[2] It makes no difference whether the Greek has πατήρ or ὁ πατήρ "for in each case the word to be presupposed on the testimony of Mark xiv. 36 (cf. Rom. viii. 15; Gal. iv. 6) is ἀββᾶ (אבא). This is just the definite form and means strictly the Father; but during the obsolescence of the form with the pronominal suffix (אבי still to be seen in Dan. v. 13) it became the regular form for "my Father." Dalman, op. cit., 191, 192. Cf. Burkitt, Evangelion Da-Mepharresha, p. 47.

will reveal Him" (x. 22; cf. Matthew xi. 27). Here Christ claims to be the only revealer of the Father and, besides, explicitly states that no one can know Him but the Father; by thus signifying that His nature is such that it can be known only by God, He unmistakably expresses that His nature is truly Divine, as everyone who accepts this passage must admit.[1] Finally according to this same inspired writer, Jesus openly declared both His Messiahship and His Divine Sonship on the very solemn occasions of His trial, when, His very life being at stake, He was questioned by the official representatives of Israel, "the ancients of the people and the chief priests and scribes" (xxii. 66). The latter first asked Him if He was the Messiah, "If thou be the Christ, tell us." As in His answer, "hereafter the Son of Man shall be sitting on the right hand of the power of God" (xxii. 69), He directly associated Himself with God, they immediately asked Him the further question, "Art thou then the Son of God?" and He said, "You say that I am" (xxii. 70), — which is the way of saying: You speak the truth; I am in very deed.[2]

4. THE ACTS OF THE APOSTLES

In the Acts of the Apostles St. Luke continues to represent Christ on the lines found in the Third Gospel. The Risen Saviour has the same name for God on His lips, "the Father" (i. 4, 7), as the Boy Jesus had in the first recorded words. And Christ too is conscious of His great dignity and His great value for mankind, for He declares that the disciples shall be witnesses unto Him, even to the uttermost part of the earth (i. 8). Beginning this witnessing, in the first sermon St. Peter mentions Christ in the same sentence as "the Father" and "the Holy Ghost" (ii. 33), and declares emphatically, "Let all the house of Israel know most certainly that God hath made both Lord and Christ, this same Jesus whom you have crucified" (ii. 36). On other occasions St. Peter called Christ "Lord of All" (x. 36), "Author of

---

[1] See the confession of Harnack (The Sayings of Jesus, 302). Some critics try to cast doubts on the genuineness and integrity of passage; concerning these points see Schumacher, Die Selbstoffenbarung Jesu, 33–100.

[2] Cf. Dalman, Words of J., 314 ff. Luke xviii. 19 offers no objection; it can be explained that Christ would not accept the title of "good" unless He were recognized as God.

Life" (iii. 15), "Judge of the living and the dead" (x. 42). His words "Jesus of Nazareth; how God anointed Him with the Holy Ghost and with power" (x. 38), offer no serious objection to our conclusion in this study. If these words have reference to the scene at Christ's baptism they do not attach any Christological importance to it, given as they are by the same historian, Luke, who represents Christ as conceived through the operation of the Holy Ghost. Likewise St. Paul's words at Antioch ". . . raising up Jesus, as in the second psalm also is written: Thou art My Son, this day have I begotten thee" (xiii. 33), do not offer any objection, do not imply that Christ was not Son of God before His resurrection, which was a great approval and confirmation of Christ's Divinity. According to this chronicle, shortly after his miraculous conversion St. Paul preached that Christ "is the Son of God" (ix. 20). Indeed the Christ depicted in the Acts is "the Christ — Son of God, intimately sharing the powers and privileges of God, the wholly Divine Christ of the Synoptics." [1]

The whole Lucan account of Christ confirms the conclusion from the study of the first recorded words. Christ was conceived through the power of the Holy Ghost, hence He was in reality and truth the Son of God. He clearly expresses this in His Public Life; He never betrays the least indication that He had doubts about Himself and His mission, much less that there was a time when He was ignorant of these facts. Reading the Gospel in which are found the words of the Boy Jesus, seeing the words "My Father" in such a context, one is naturally led to accept them in the light of the supernatural conception of the Holy Ghost, in the same sense as that in which they were used in later life. In so doing, everything in the whole Lucan account falls into place, — everything harmonizes. As the true Son of God it was perfectly natural that in His first words Jesus should refer to His great relation to God, calling Him "My Father," as He did in His last words on the Cross, "Father into Thy hands I commend My Spirit" (Luke xxiii. 46), as He does in His last words before the Ascension, "And I send the promise of My Father upon you" (Luke xxiv. 49; cf. Acts i. 7).

[1] Lepin, Christ and the Gospel, 383.

CHAPTER XV

THE WHOLE NEW TESTAMENT ACCOUNT OF CHRIST

St. Luke is the only writer of the New Testament who records the episode of the twelve-year-old Christ in the Temple. This fact can be easily explained for the reason that the Gospels were not intended to be complete biographies of Christ, but simply a brief account of the "good news"; they preserve "only a few stray flowers thrown over the wall of an ample garden." [1] St. Luke is the only sacred writer who professes to present facts in order, and to make investigations concerning all things from the beginning (Luke i. 2, 3); most of the matter preserved in the Infancy Section is peculiar to the Third Evangelist and can be attributed to his special sources.

If the point be pressed that the other writers of the New Testament must not have known of the episode of Christ's twelfth year, since if they had known His words, which, we claim, express real Divine Sonship, they would surely have given them as too important to be omitted, we say in answer that since modern writers have raised the problem of Christ's self-consciousness the first words are very important, but in the early years of Christianity this problem was hardly raised. Jesus had been put to death on account of what He said He was; His claims seem to be clearly known. The first preachers of Christianity had only to emphasize the fact that Christ was "approved of God" by "miracles and wonders and signs" (Acts ii. 22) — the principal one of these being His fulfilling the Old Testament prophecies and adumbrations. Although St. Luke alone gives Christ's first words, the other inspired writers do not exclude the fact that Christ expressed real Divine Sonship in His twelfth year; they are in harmony with our conclusion in the main chapter of this work.

[1] Stalker, Son of God, HDG II. 656.

1. ST. MATTHEW

St. Matthew does not refer to the episode of Christ's twelfth year, yet he too, like St. Luke, has an Infancy section. He begins his Gospel with a genealogy whose purpose is to show that Christ is the Messiah (i. 1–17). He represents Christ as conceived by the Holy Ghost (i. 18, 20). He gives the angel's announcement that Jesus "shall save His people from their sins," and that He shall be called "Emanuel" which the Evangelist himself interprets as "God with us" (i. 21, 23), implying that Jesus is God Incarnate.[1] He also narrates other miraculous apparitions of an angel in the interests of the Child (ii. 13, 19); and he describes a very strange and miraculous event, that wise men were miraculously led by a star to the crib of the Child Jesus, that they adored Him (ii. 2, 11) and offered Him gold, frankincense[2] and myrrh (ii. 11). This adoration of the Magi offered to Jesus as a little Babe would help to strengthen the conclusion previously reached; so would the applying to Christ in Egypt of the words of Osee xi. 1, "out of Egypt have I called My Son" (ii. 15); all the miraculous accounts in the first two chapters of St. Matthew do likewise, but especially the account of Christ's Virgin Birth and conception by the Holy Ghost. As we said regarding this point in St. Luke, the supernatural and divine origin of Jesus is a very strong argument in favor of the opinion that when He called God His Father He meant this word in the real true sense.

According to St. Matthew, when Christ came to St. John to be baptized the latter "stayed Him, saying, "I ought to be baptized by Thee, and comest Thou to me?" And Jesus answering said to Him: "Suffer it to be so now . . ." (iii. 14, 15). Here Christ's consciousness of His own sinlessness and His superiority is clearly reflected, and this, it is to be noted, is done prior to the baptism scene, prior to the Public Ministry. St. Matthew's account of the Public Life coincides substantially with that of St. Luke. He, too, has the so-called Johannine passage, xi. 27, upon which so much emphasis has been laid. A saying of Christ, given by this Evangelist alone, "where there are two or three gathered

[1] Cf. Box, The Gospel Narrative of the Nativity, ZntW VII (1905) 87.
[2] The frankincense is said by the Fathers to be offered "because Christ was God."

together in My name, there am I in the midst of them" (xviii. 20),[1] is said to show the "most exalted Christology" and to supply "a well attested basis for the doctrine of the abiding Christ as given in John."[2] Christ expressed exalted Christology, too, according to the closing verses of the First Gospel in which is given the command to baptize "in the name of the Father, and of the Son, and of the Holy Ghost" (xxviii. 19). We can safely conclude, therefore, that in the light of St. Matthew's Gospel, there is implied our conclusion from Christ's use of the words "My Father" in His twelfth year.

2. ST. MARK

In St. Mark's Gospel there is no account of the Boy Christ, nor is there any Infancy section at all; yet these would seem to be presupposed. The first reference[3] to Christ is the prophecy of John that there cometh one mightier than himself, one who shall baptize with the Holy Ghost (i. 7, 8). Immediately follows Christ's baptism which we have previously examined, and we can sum up our results in the words of Sweet, "the miraculous birth, and the story of the youthful visit at Jerusalem are necessary to any intelligible explanation of the baptism."[4]

At Capharnaum Jesus teaches "as one having power" (i. 22). He shows His power over spirits (i. 26, 34), and divers diseases (i. 34), and He said to His followers, "Let us go into the neighboring towns and cities that I may preach there also; for to this purpose am I come" (i. 38). This last saying corresponds to Luke iv. 43 and at least suggests Christ's preëxistence. This seems also to be done in i. 24; ii. 17; ix. 36; x. 45.[5] These intimations that Christ was aware of His preëxistence would confirm the conclusion that He expressed real Divine Sonship in His twelfth year, for would it not be natural for a person who was so extraordinary as to have preëxisted to be always aware of this fact?

[1] Cf. Mtt. xxviii. 20, "behold I am with you all days, even to the consummation of the world."
[2] Stokes, What Jesus Christ Thought of Himself, 101.
[3] According to many texts the Gospel of Mark commences thus: The beginning of the Gospel of Jesus Christ, the Son of God.
[4] Birth and Infancy of J. C., 83.
[5] These have parallel passages in the other two Synoptics.

184 THE BOYHOOD CONSCIOUSNESS OF CHRIST

This result from the study of Christ's first words would be confirmed by St. Mark's account of the Public Life, where substantially the same claims are made for Jesus[1] as those found in the Third Gospel. Although Mark does not give the Johannine passage, he gives a saying which even radical scholars declare to be certainly authentic, "of that day or hour no man knoweth, neither the angels in heaven nor the Son, but the Father" (xiii. 32).[2] If this saying signifies a deficiency in Christ's knowledge with regard to the last day, it certainly does not signify a deficiency or limitation in His knowledge with regard to Himself as "Son" and God as "the Father"; and this placing Himself as "Son" above the angels is admitted even by certain negative scholars[3] to imply metaphysical relation to God. Christ speaks along similar lines again in viii. 38, "he that shall be ashamed of Me . . . , the Son of man shall be ashamed of Him, when He shall come in the glory of His Father with the holy angels." But particularly in iii. 31, 35, we have an attitude assumed by our Lord which is parallel to the attitude He took towards His parents in Luke ii. 49. Here as in the first words Jesus emphasizes the spiritual; here as there, He states that it is God's Will that counts for Him, that it is God that determines the time and place of His work for mankind, that other authorities even those of flesh and blood He considers not.[4] The same principle was stated and followed in the Public Life as well as in the twelfth year, so that there is in Mark a text to a great extent parallel to Luke ii. 49, and there is an indirect confirmation of our conclusion therefrom.[5]

[1] Christ puts Himself in the place of God for the individual soul, ii. 19, 20; viii. 35, 38; xiii. 13; xvi. 15, 16.

[2] Basing their view on this text and Jn. xi. 34, the Agnoëtae (6th–8th century) put a limit to Christ's knowledge. Gregory the Great argues against them, "For with what meaning can one that confesses that the very Wisdom of God was incarnate say that there is anything that the Wisdom of God is ignorant of?" Ep. x. xxix. N.P–NF (2d Ser.) XIII. 48. See the answers to three propositions given by the Holy office June 5, 1918 (Acta Apostolicae Sedis, 1 Jul. (1918) 282).

[3] Concerning this passage Holtzmann writes, "This is the single passage in which the Son while opposed along with the angels to the Father, appears to become a metaphysical magnitude" (Lehrbuch der ntl. Theol. I. 268, note 2).

[4] Cf. Bartmann: Christus ein Gegner des Marienkultus? 104.

[5] In Mark iii. 21, it is said that Christ's friends wanted to lay hold on Him saying He was mad. This shows that they could not account for His miracles and wisdom, and that neither His education, nor meditation, nor the natural means which they know, accounted for them. Thus it agrees with Lk. ii. 50.

3. ST. JOHN

Like St. Mark, the Fourth Gospel has no Infancy section, but it begins with a profession of Christ's preëxistence and Divinity: "In the beginning was the Word and the Word was with God, and the Word was God [1] . . . and the Word was made flesh . . . the only begotten of the Father" (i. 1, 14). According to this Gospel Christ in clear and explicit terms makes reference to the fact of His preëxistence (vi. 63; viii. 58; xvi. 28; xvii. 5, 24, etc.), and in clear and explicit terms (terms which were not mistaken by the Jews) He teaches His Divinity and expresses real Divine Sonship, — a fact universally recognized.

But St. John says that the changing of water into wine at the marriage feast of Cana was "the beginning" of Jesus' miracles (ii. 11). At first sight this might seem to imply that either the scene in the Temple (Luke ii. 41–51) did not really occur or that, if it did occur, it was not outside the natural order. But logically St. John's statement does not demand either of these conclusions. In the first place, this miracle at Cana is not the first miracle described by the Fourth Evangelist; He narrates others previously; for instance, he previously gives Christ's recognition and characterization of Nathaniel, with Nathaniel's confession (i. 47, 51), and the miraculous coming of the Holy Spirit in the form of a dove at the baptism (i. 32), etc. If these miraculous occurrences are not excluded by St. John's statement in ii. 11, surely the saying of the Boy Christ and His preternatural display of knowledge are not excluded.

Now as to the meaning of this verse of the Fourth Gospel (ii. 11), Christ had told His mother that His hour — the time of His manifesting Himself had not yet come. He had probably intended to begin His public manifestation of Himself in the Temple of Jerusalem at the feast of the Pasch which He attended a few days later (ii. 12 ff); [2] but at the mother's request He performed the great miracle, and thereby He "manifested His glory and His disciples believed in Him" (ii. 11). The meaning of ii. 11, is then, that it emphasizes the fact that it was at Cana of Galilee

---

[1] Here Christ is called "God" as in Jn. xx. 28; Apoc. xix. 10; xxii. 9.
[2] Schaefer, The Mother of Jesus in S., 241, 242. Bartmann, Christus ein Gegner des Marienkultus? 73 ff.

and not elsewhere that Jesus began the public manifestation of Himself.

This account of the miracle at Cana does not, therefore, exclude St. Luke's narrative of the Boy Christ (as we have explained it); rather a close examination would suggest that one implies the other. What put it into the mother's head to ask a great miracle of her Son? St. John Chrysostom answers that it was suggested to her by the witness of John the Baptist and especially "the conception itself and all its attending circumstances."[1] And St. Ambrose rightly says that Mary, being astonished at the miraculous occurrence of Christ's twelfth year, learned thereby to ask a favor from her Son when He was grown up.[2] Not only this, but as previously referred to, in the words in which Jesus replies to His mother at Cana, the same stand is taken as in the first recorded saying at twelve. Replying to her appeal, He said, "Woman what is it to Me, and to thee? (τί ἐμοὶ καὶ σοί, γύναι); My hour is not yet come" (ii. 4). The expression "what is it to Me and to thee" signifies that ties of flesh and blood did not count in regard to a public manifestation of His power, in regard to His Messianic work. For this reason He does not call her, Mother, but Lady (γύναι), both here and at the foot of the cross (xix. 26).

Immediately after the narrative of the feast of Cana, St. John gives another account of Christ (ii. 13 ff.) which is in harmony with the episode of the twelfth year. The scene was again the Temple, and again it was the feast of the Pasch, the very next one the sacred records inform us that Christ attended. He was not the same; He was now grown to man's attire and being angered at the sight of dealers and money changers within the sacred precincts, He lashed them out of the Temple, making havoc among their wares. And to the dove sellers He said, "Take these things hence, and make not the house of My Father a house of traffic" (ii. 16). Here, as in Luke ii. 49, Jesus calls God "My Father." He calls the Temple the house of His Father; He may have done the same in the first recorded words (ἐν τοῖς). Then He felt His relation to God to be so close that

---

[1] In Joann. Hom. XXI. N.P-NF (1st. Ser.) XIV. 74.
[2] In Luc. II. Corp. Script. Lat., XXIV. 18.

THE WHOLE N. T. ACCOUNT OF CHRIST 187

He must remain in the Temple; now He feels that the relation obliges Him to incur the anger and hatred of these profaners of the Temple. He certainly is about His Father's business now. He was carrying on the same policy that He followed as a boy; He "took up the thread where He had dropped it on His first recorded appearance in the Temple."[1]

4. ST. PAUL

Although St. Paul's epistles are only occasional letters written for specific purposes, yet it is clear that the Christ that is referred to there is the Christ of the Synoptics. It is expressly stated that Christ was "made under the law" (Gal. iv. 4), which is said to have reference to Jesus' circumcision, presentation in the Temple, and attendance at the feasts, as St. Luke records in the second chapter of his Gospel.[2]

St. Paul's Christology would imply our conclusion from Luke ii. 49. His most frequent name for Christ is "the Son" and "Lord," and he makes mention of Him as the only Son (τὸν ἑαυτοῦ υἱὸν) Rom. viii. 3, (τοῦ ἰδίου υἱοῦ) Rom. viii. 32. He refers to Him as "the one Lord Jesus Christ, through whom are all things and we through Him" (1 Cor. viii. 6); he calls Him "the image of God" (2 Cor. iv. 4; Col. i. 15); indeed He seems to call Him "God blessed for ever" (Rom. ix. 5).[3]

St. Paul implies that Christ was always conscious of His Divinity and Divine Sonship, teaching as he does that He preëxisted. Thus he writes to Timothy that "Christ Jesus came into the world to save sinners" (1 Tim. i. 15), and in other places he speaks of God sending His Son in the likeness of flesh (Rom. viii. 3; Gal. iv. 4). This doctrine is taught more clearly in 2 Cor. viii. 9, where the Apostle says that Christ who was rich became poor for men's sake, and most clearly in Philip ii. 5–8, where St. Paul expressly states that Christ preëxisted "in the form of God" and "considered it no injustice to be equal to God." The

---

[1] Edersheim, Life and Times of J., I. 373.
[2] V. g. Streatfeild: The Self-interpretation of J. C., 24.
[3] According to the construction of the sentence that most readily suggests itself. Cf. Bruce, St. Paul's Conception of Christianity, 340.

doctrine of preëxistence and Divine self-consciousness is clearly expressed here.[1]

The Apostle (in this last mentioned passage) goes on to say that Christ "emptied Himself, taking the form of a servant, being made to the likeness of man." This expression would not require the meaning that Jesus emptied Himself of His Divine self-consciousness. St. Paul is merely referring to Christ's assuming human nature and does not touch the question of Jesus' knowledge of Himself; that this is so is seen from another place where he says that in Christ are "all the treasures of wisdom and knowledge" (Col. ii. 3). The Pauline references to Christ's self-humiliation, to His taking the form of man, to His assuming the likeness of sinful flesh, do not include Christ's knowledge and self-consciousness.

5. CHRIST'S SONSHIP IN THE NEW TESTAMENT

At twelve years of age Jesus referred to God as "My Father." This name "Father" was His most frequent name for God. It occurs 45 times in Matthew, 5 times in Mark, 17 times in Luke, and about 90 times in John. As Sanday says, "no name of God was more constantly on the lips of Christ; and no name so dominated the whole thought of God, as He not only cherished it for Himself, but bequeathed it to His disciples." [2] Jesus teaches a threefold grade in God's Fatherhood: He is Father of all men, He is especially Father of the disciples, He is in a very special manner Father of Jesus Himself.[3]

In regard to the Synoptics, there is no doubt that Jesus reserved a peculiar use of the word "Father," as a name of God, for His own case. Nowhere does He include Himself along with His disciples under the title "Our Father" — the Lord's Prayer not being an exception since it was prescribed and constructed for them. Many times (over a score of times in Matthew, thrice

[1] Cf. Schumacher, Christus in seiner Präexistenz und Kenose nach Phil. ii. 5–8. Drum interprets from passage, "He was conscious that He was God by nature, and not by usurpation, — not by a Modernistic evolution of the Messianic consciousness." Homil. and Pastoral Rev. XXI. (1920) 13.
[2] Art. God, HDB II. 209.
[3] Cf. Stephens, Theol. of New Test., 54, Robertson, The Teaching of Jesus concerning God the Father, 43–69.

THE WHOLE N. T. ACCOUNT OF CHRIST 189

in Mark, nine times in Luke), Christ referred to God as His Father; on several occasions (six times in Matthew, once in Mark, thrice in Luke), He denominates Himself "the Son" in such a way as to prove unmistakably that He regards Himself as "the Son of God."[1] On many other occasions where the title "Son of God" is applied to Him, He treats the title in such a manner as to show He adopts it.

As in the Synoptics, so in St. John, Christ refers to His Special Divine Sonship; the same stand is taken, the difference being that in St. John it is taken more explicitly and more frequently. Very frequently He calls Himself "the Son," and very frequently He calls God "My Father." Indeed in St. John, Christ refers to Himself as "the Son of God" (v. 25; ix. 35, 37; x. 36; xi. 4). He teaches He preëxisted in Heaven with the Father before the foundation of the world (xvii. 5, 24); He indicates the great uniqueness of His Sonship by declaring Himself to be the only begotten (μονογένης)[2] Son of God (iii. 16, 18; cf. i. 14, 18); the climax is when He claims His Sonship involves equality with the Father: I and the Father are one (x. 30; cf. v. 17; x. 38).

Not only did Christ Himself claim to be Son of God, but we find this title accorded to Him by others. Announcing His miraculous conception of the Holy Ghost (thus giving a physical basis for the title) the angel Gabriel foretold He would be called "Son of the Most High," "Son of God" (Luke i. 32, 35). From Heaven the Eternal Father proclaimed Him His beloved Son at the baptism (Matthew iii. 17; Mark i. 11; Luke iii. 22) and at the Transfiguration (Matthew xvii. 5; Mark ix. 6; Luke ix. 35; cf. 2 Peter i. 17). Demoniacs addressed Him as Son of God (e.g. Mark iii. 12; v. 7); Satan, too, mentions the title (Matthew iv. 3, 6); St. John the Baptist testified He was the Son of God (John i. 34); Peter (Matthew xvi. 16; John vi. 70), Nathaniel (John i. 49), and the disciples (Matthew xiv. 33) are on record as confessing this fact; so did Martha (John xi. 27); so did the centurion at the foot of the cross (Matthew xxvii. 54; Mark xv. 39). Christ's enemies, who had Him put to death, claimed that He said He was the Son of God (Matthew xxvii. 40, 43; John xix. 7).

[1] Cf. Stalker, Son of God, HDG II. 654. Christology of J., 86.
[2] According to Mark xii. 6, the Son, the sole heir distinguished from the whole series of servants is called ἕνα υἱὸν ἀγαπητόν. As Dalman (op. cit. 281) says, there is no difference between this and St. John's "only begotten Son."

190   THE BOYHOOD CONSCIOUSNESS OF CHRIST

As to the evidence for the period after Christ's death, the Acts tells us that the Ethiopian eunuch professed before being baptized "I believe that Jesus Christ is the Son of God" (viii. 37; cf. 16), and that immediately after his conversion St. Paul preached that Jesus is the "Son of God" (ix. 20). Writing in his epistles only a few decades afterwards, St. Paul very frequently gives to Christ the name "the Son," at once contrasting and associating Him with God "the Father," and he mentions Him as "the Son of God" (Rom. i. 4; v. 10; 1 Cor. i. 9; Gal. iv. 4).

As Christ had distinguished, so St. Paul too distinguishes between Christ's Sonship and the sonship of others; indeed (Rom. viii. 3, 32) he calls Jesus God's own Son sent into the world on man's behalf. This use of the word "own" corresponds to Christ's usage of the expression "My Father" and the word "only-begotten,"[1] and thus there is expressed a Christology equivalent to that of the explicit pronouncements of the Fourth Gospel. Especially is this the case in Hebrews which frequently applies to Christ the title "Son of God" (e.g. iv. 14; v. 8; vi. 6; vii. 3; x. 29), which while referring to Moses as "a faithful servant" calls Christ "a Son over the household" (iii. 5, 6), and which begins by saying that God never applied Ps. ii. 7, "Thou art My Son," etc. to anyone else, not even to the angels, but reserved it for Christ (i. 5; v. 5). The first Epistle of St. John follows these same lines, with its frequent use of titles "Son," "the Son of God," its use of the expression "only begotten Son," and its clear pronouncements on Christ's preëxistence (e.g. 1 Jn. iii. 8; iv. 9, 14, 15; v. 5, 7, 13).[2] This epistle of St. John bears testimony that the confession of Jesus as the Son of God was the cardinal point in the Christian Faith.

[1] As Bruce (op. cit. 338) explains the expression "His own Son," "not merely the first begotten in a large family, but the only-begotten in some sense."

[2] We find in the Apoc. iii. 5, "My Father"; God is called "Father of our Lord Jesus Christ," 1 Pet. i. 3; He is mentioned as "Father" 1 Pet. i. 17; Jam. i. 17, 27; Jude i. 1. This Testimony to Christ's Divine Sonship and preëxistence can be continued through the Apostolic and sub-Apostolic Fathers, see p. 13. About the middle of 2nd century the Marcosians (whom Irenaeus mentions) were using Christ's first words (Lk. ii. 49) in support of their contention that the Father whom Jesus announced was not the God of the Old Testament and was till then unknown. Irenaeus implies that he understood the Boy Jesus' reference to His Father in the metaphysical sense. In the following generation, Origen clearly interprets real Divine Sonship, and this view has been held all down the ages to the present day, almost exclusively so till the rise of modern Rationalism.

THE WHOLE N. T. ACCOUNT OF CHRIST

From the facts presented, it is clear that the attributing to Christ of a unique Divine Sonship can be traced back (almost through every decade) to St. Paul. As Sanday says, "if the use of 'the Father' and 'the Son' as theological terms belongs to the early Church, it at least goes back to the very first moment at which we possess contemporary evidence for the vocabulary of that Church, and indeed to a date which is not more than twenty-three years from the ascension (see 1 Th. i. 1)." [1] From that time on the Christian writings abound in references to God as the Father of Jesus and to Him as "the Son," "the Son of God," "God's own Son," "God's only begotten Son," "The Logos Who was with the Father before Creation." What is the origin of this vocabulary? How are we to account for "the rapid growth within some twenty-three years of a usage already so fixed and stereotyped?" [2] Knowing the Jewish conception of God and the expressions employed for it in the time of Christ, we cannot account for it if Christ Himself is not its cause and author. Yes Jesus Himself was the authority for this vocabulary. He frequently announced He was the most special Son of God. He announced this even in His first recorded words.

[1] Son of God, HDB IV. 573.
[2] Sanday, op. cit.

CONCLUSION

The frequent use of the name "Father" as applied to God goes back to the Saviour. It was His most frequent epithet for God. He speaks of Him to His followers, "your heavenly Father"; He bade them repeat "Our Father." Terms for God such as, "the blessed One," "the Holy One," "the Place" — common to the synagogue of His day, He does not use at all. He sparingly uses the title "Lord." Christ strictly followed the religious custom among the Jews in respect to the use and avoidance of the name God, but, "in such a manner that, in conforming to it, He preserved a peculiar position of His own by His marked preference for the appellation of God as Father." [1] He breaks with contemporary usage and with all previous usage in His employment of this name Father, sparingly used before the time of Christ, and hardly ever in an individualistic sense by an ordinary individual. But the great difference between the usage ushered in by Our Lord and what had previously been in vogue consists not alone in the frequency of the title but also, and especially, in the content. In comparison with that of the Old Testament, it is well said that Christ's doctrine of God's Fatherhood "assumes such proportions as to amount to a new revelation." [2] The history of the question warrants our saying that St. Paul (Rom. viii. 14–17; Gal. iv. 4–7; cf. John i. 12) also is witness that "it was Jesus who first introduced into the world the religious spirit whose characteristic cry Godwards is Father." [3] Christ uttered the last word on the question of God's Fatherhood to men; this conception is a salient characteristic of His teaching; some even consider it the essence of Christianity.

In this special doctrine of Christ, God's Fatherhood to mankind, there is something still greater, still more characteristic,

---

[1] Dalman, Words of J., 233.
[2] Sanday, God, HDB II. 208.
[3] Bruce, St. Paul's Conception of Christianity, 199.

still more special, namely God's special Fatherhood to Jesus Himself. Christ teaches He is a very special Son of God, according to many of His recorded sayings, and it is clear that real Divine Sonship is meant. To use the words of Sanday, "a scientific examination of the Gospels, whatever else it brings out, brings out this, that the root element in the consciousness of Jesus was a sense of Sonship to the Divine Father, deeper, clearer, more intimate, more all embracing and all absorbing, than ever was vouchsafed to a child of man."[1] Christ's followers have always considered and called Him "the Son of God" because He expressed a consciousness of being such, because not putting Himself under the same grade of God's Fatherhood that He taught for others, not including Himself under the "Our Father" that He bade His disciples use, He appropriated a very special degree of God's Fatherhood for Himself, calling Himself "the Son," "the Son of God" and using the phrase "My Father."

In regard to Himself, Christ always used the word "My" and never "our" when calling God "Father." It is a fact worth noting that although in the writings of the Synoptics the Saviour does not appear as laying claim to the actual title of Son of God in the same direct way as is recorded in the Fourth Gospel, yet according to the former the title "Son of God" was applied to Christ and Christ's enemies alleged He said He was the Son of God. We find in the Synoptics no basis for such a charge other than Christ's use of the phrase "My Father" which the Jews took to imply His Divine Sonship. In the eyes of His contemporaries therefore, Christ's use of the words "My Father" for God was equivalent to His applying to Himself the title "Son of God." The word "My" signifies the distinctive quality of His Sonship and "it would be difficult to exaggerate its importance as an expression of the Messianic consciousness and as implying a transcendental origin."[2] The "My" in Christ's expression for God, "My Father," stands for what is special in God's Fatherhood to Him, it represents His special real Divine Sonship, it corresponds to the words "well beloved," "own," "only begotten," in the terms of this Sonship. And this expression "My Father" is fre-

[1] Son of God, HDB IV. 575.
[2] Streatfeild, The Self-interpretation of Jesus Christ, 84.

quently on Christ's lips both in the Synoptics and in St. John, it appears among the last words and it appears among the first recorded words.

The first saying of Jesus does not merely enunciate the doctrine of God's Fatherhood to man — a doctrine which originated an epoch in the religious thought of the world, and which at once marked Christ as the great religious teacher of the human race — but over and above this, the saying contains an expression of God's special Fatherhood to Jesus Himself. He says "My Father," words which correspond to His applying to Himself the title of "Son of God," words which express all that is special in His Sonship. As D'Arcy says, "Jesus from His youth possessed a consciousness of God as His Father, which was utterly different from the faith to which others attain through teaching and the influence of religious surroundings." [1] That Jesus at the age of twelve when yet only a mere Boy should thus already reach the highest point, the climax of His teaching, should announce what is distinctive in His special characteristic teaching of God's Fatherhood, this cannot be explained naturally, but clearly shows that Christ was not the subject of merely natural development and growth.[2]

In His youth Jesus referred to His special Divine Sonship in the same way as He did in after life. The words "My Father" in the first recorded saying are uttered as a matter of course and in as emphatic a manner as He ever did utter them; indeed here they are in contrast to the closest of human ties, that of parents to children, and are reinforced with the sacred "Must." Christ's expression of His Sonship in His twelfth year corresponds to all His references to His Sonship as found in the New Testament. Nowhere is it said that at any time Christ was not aware of Divine Sonship, nowhere is it intimated that He grew in the knowledge of His Sonship, rather the contrary opinion is everywhere implied. After examining Christ's sayings and not being able to find anywhere what idea He entertained in regard to the genesis

---

[1] Consciousness, HDG I. 363.
[2] As Reinhard asks, "Tell me how a common indigent lad of Galilee who had never enjoyed any of those advantages calculated to fill the mind with great conceptions and mighty resolutions could have struck upon a thought to which the greatest men before Him had never approached?" Plan of the Founder of Christ. 263.

of His Divine Sonship, Dalman confesses that the utterances "appear to imply that Jesus had shown no cognizance of any beginning to this relationship. It seems to be an innate property of His Personality." [1] The meaning of the words "My Father" did not change for Jesus; they are given by St. Luke in ii. 49 without comment, and there is no reason why one should not attach the same meaning to them here as in other places of the sacred record, because one should consider them in the context of this Third Gospel, and in the context of the New Testament,—it being a foremost canon of interpretation that a matter be decided according to the context and according to the spirit of the whole work.

The main arguments for the interpretation of real Divine Sonship from Jesus' first recorded words are: (1) The Virgin Birth previously described, suggesting that the words "My Father" in Luke ii. 49 are fraught with metaphysical meaning. (2) Christ's later preaching describing the nature of His Divine Sonship as real Divine Sonship. (3) Unbroken tradition that Jesus' declaration of Divine Sonship in His twelfth year and His later declarations express real Divine Sonship. These arguments require that Jesus expressed in His first recorded words more than mere Messianic consciousness. They require that the Sonship he announced was more than a mere ethical relationship to God.[2] The view of "ordinary Israelitic consciousness" is rejected even by the very facts of the Temple episode itself, the Boy's overriding ordinary duties to parents, His word "must" and His word "My." There is no historical evidence whatsoever for any view of "dawning consciousness." There is no hesitation or self-limitation in Christ's words. He is as emphatic and matter-of-course about His Sonship as He ever was. His special term for God "My Father" is fully uttered. Entire conviction, complete consciousness of Divine Sonship is expressed. In the light of the whole New Testament, in the light of Christ's own expressions in

[1] Words of J., 285.
[2] Dalman writes: "Nowhere do we find that Jesus called Himself the Son of God in such a sense as to suggest a mere religious and ethical relation to God." (Words of J., 287.) Besides, as Stalker (Son of God, HDG II. 654) says: "The closeness of the ethico-religious relation may be such as to demand a metaphysical relationship of an intimate and peculiar kind between Father and Son." If this is true anywhere, it is true in the text in hand.

regard to His Divine Sonship, in the light of the tradition of this Sonship going back to St. Paul, in the light of the history of the exegesis of Luke ii. 49, the only consistent view is that of real Divine Sonship.

This is why the first recorded saying, Luke ii. 49, is of great importance for modern scholars, namely on account of its bearing on the modern problem of tracing the growth and development of Jesus' self-consciousness. The view and theories that are not based on the first words are not according to the historical documents. The theories widely held in the non-Catholic world of a gradual and as it were natural development of Christ's self-consciousness, of the awakening of His Messianic consciousness at the baptism, of doubts and crises in His self-consciousness that existed even during the Public Life, these views are entirely excluded by the Gospel text. At least according to Luke ii. 49, Christ at the age of twelve was fully aware of His real Divine Sonship. His expression of this fact is made with such calmness and indeed emphasis that there is left no ground or basis for any view that His self-consciousness was then awakening. Jesus was fully self-consciousness then, and there are no signs or hints in His saying or in any text of the Scripture of any dawning consciousness or of any time when His self-consciousness of Divine Sonship was wanting to Him. The inspired records thus imply, what is handed down in tradition, that there never was a moment when Christ did not know exactly the nature of His filial relation to God.[1]

Christ's self-consciousness or, to speak more correctly, His own testimony to Himself, is one of the chief supports of the belief in His Divinity — the other being the performance of miracles in confirmation of what He said. Hence for this question also the words of the Boy Jesus are important. Indeed the mere fact that contrary to all ordinary laws of development and ex-

---

[1] Tradition has it that Christ's knowledge had its source and principle in the Hypostatic Union and dated from the first moment of this Union, i.e., His conception. Owen (Comment. on Gospel of Luke, 44) had already argued with force against Olshausen's theory of a gradual development of Christ's consciousness. See the able statement of Dalman: Words of J., 286. Du Bose says, "There was never a time in the history of His consciousness when His divinity was wholly latent or lay completely beneath the activities of His human mind." (The Consciousness of Jesus, 29.)

clusive of every natural explanation Christ at a tender age should declare His real Divine Sonship, is in itself a strong argument for His Divinity. There can be no question here of His not being in His proper senses, of His being deceived, or of His wishing to deceive; such theories are excluded by the preternatural knowledge previously displayed, by the sincerity of the reply, by the occasion which drew it forth, and by its reverential acceptance on the part of the parents.

Certainly He could not be deceiving; at His age one could hardly be capable of such a deception; to be deluded into the belief in His own Divine Sonship would presuppose years of thought and experience and would be wofully out of keeping with the character of a pious Jewish lad come from a country town on a pilgrimage to the Holy City to celebrate with beating heart and warm affection Jahweh's feast in Jahweh's house. That the most sincere, the most humble, the most saintly Person who ever lived, the "Man approved of God . . . by miracles and wonders and signs" (Acts ii. 22), should as a mere Boy, and in opposition to the claims of His earthly parents, declare that He was the Son of God, a claim unique in history, would seem to have only one explanation: that He was compelled to do so by the greatest of realities — the Divine Nature which was in Him and which must proclaim itself.

BIBLIOGRAPHY

I

LIST OF WORKS QUOTED [1]

ABBOTT, LYMAN, A Life of Christ, 2 ed. New York, 1882.
ADAMSON, THOMAS, Studies of the mind in Christ, Edinburgh, 1898.
ADENEY, W. F., The transcendental element in the consciousness of Christ, AmJTh III (1889) 99 ff.
———, St. Luke, in the New Century Bible, New York, 1914.
*AELREDUS, ABB. REVALLIS, Tractatus de Jesu Puero duodenni, M.PL CLXXXIV. 830–870.
*AIKEN, CHARLES F., The Dhamma of Gotama the Buddha and the Gospel of Jesus the Christ, Boston, 1900.
*ALBERTUS MAGNUS, In Evangelium Lucae, Opera omnia, ed. Borgnet, vol. 22, Parisiis, 1894.
*ALCUIN (or ALBINUS), B. F., Adversus Felicem, lib. VII. 1, n. 12. M.PL CI. 137.
*ALEXANDER, NATALIS, Expositio litteralis s. Evangelii Jesu Christi secundum Marcum, Lucam et Joannem, tom. 2, Venetiis, 1782.
*ALEXANDER OF HALES, Summae theologiae pars tertia, Venetiis, 1575.
ALFORD, HENRY, The Greek Testament, New York, 1859.
ANDERSON, FREDERICK L., The Man of Nazareth, New York, 1914.
ANDREWS, S., The Life of our Lord upon the earth, New York, 1892.
ANGUS, S., The environment of early Christianity, New York, 1915.
*ANSELM, SAINT, Homilia VII. in Evangelium secundum Lucam, Opera ed. D. G. Gerberon, 2 ed. Lutetiae Parisiorum, 1721.
Apocrypha and Pseudepigrapha of the Old Testament (ed. Charles), Oxford, 1913.

[1] Catholic authors are marked with an *, The Fathers are not given here.

*ARETIUS, BENEDICTUS, Commentarii in Domini nostri J. C. Nov. Testamentum cum indicibus locupletissimis, Parisii, 1607.

BACON, BENJAMIN W., Christianity old and new, New Haven, 1914.

BALDENSPERGER, WILHELM, Das Selbstbewusstsein Jesu im Lichte der messianischen Hoffnungen seiner Zeit, 2 ed. Strassburg, 1892.

BALJON, J. M. S., Commentaar op het Evangelie van Lukas, Utrecht, 1908.

*BARDENHEWER, OTTO, Patrology, the lives and works of the Fathers of the Church, 2 ed. transl. by T. J. Shahan, Freiburg im Breisgau, 1908.

———, Mariä Verkündigung, ein Kommentar zu Lukas I. 26-38, BSt X (1905).

BARNARD, D. MORDAUNT, Business, HDG I. 243.

BARNES, ALBERT, Notes, explanatory and practical on the Gospels, designed for Sunday school teachers and Bible classes, vol. 2, New York, 1851.

BARROWS, SAMUEL J., Mythical and legendary elements in the New Testament, NW VIII (1899) 272.

BARTH, FRITZ, Die Hauptprobleme des Lebens Jesu, Gütersloh, 1911.

*BARTMANN, BERNHARD, Das Himmelreich und sein König, Paderborn, 1904.

———, Christus ein Gegner des Marienkultus? Jesus und seine Mutter in den heiligen Evangelien, gemeinverständlich dargestellt, Freiburg, Breisgau, 1909.

BARTON, W. E., Jesus of Nazareth, Boston, 1904.

*BATIFFOL, P., Évangiles Apocryphes, VDB II. 2114.

BAUER, BRUNO, Kritik der Evangelien und Geschichte ihres Ursprungs, erster Theil, 2 ed. Berlin, 1851.

*BEDE, VENERABLE, In Lucae Evangelium expositio, lib. I., M.PL XCII. 348-350. Also Homil. XII. Dominica prima post Epiphaniam, M.PL XCIV. 65 ff.

BEECHER, HENRY WARD, The Life of Jesus the Christ, New York, 1871.

BEET, JOSEPH AGAR, The "Father's Business," Homiletic Rev. XXXIV (1897) 242-243.

———, Christology, HDB I. 386-389.

BENGEL, JOHN ALBERT, Gnomon of the New Testament, transl. by C. F. Lewis and M. P. Vincent, Philadelphia, 1860.

BERGH VAN EYSINGA, Indische Einflüsse auf evangelische Erzählungen, Göttingen, 1914.
*BERNARDINUS A PICINIO, Sanctus Lucas et sanctus Joannes, Opera omnia, tom. 2, Parisiis, 1872.
BERTHE, AUGUSTINE, Jesus Christ; His life, etc., transl. from the French by E. Girardy, St. Louis, 1914.
BESSER, M. F., Das Evangelium St. Lucä in Bibelstunden für die Gemeinde ausgelegt, 3 ed. Halle, 1854.
BEYSCHLAG, WILLIBALD, New Testament Theology, transl. by Neil Buchanan, Edinburgh, 1895.
BEZE, THEODOR, Jesu Christi D. N. Novum Testamentum . . . Londini, 1587.
*BILLOT, LUDOVICUS, De Verbo Incarnato, Comment. in III., S. Thomae, Romae, 1900.
*BISPING, AUG., Erklärung der Evangelien nach Markus und Lukas, 2 ed., Münster, 1863.
BLASS, FRIEDRICH, Evangelium secundum Lucam, sive Lucae ad Theophilum liber prior, Lipsiae, 1897.
———, Philology of the Gospels, London, 1898.
BLEEK, FREIDRICH, Synoptische Erklärung der drei ersten Evangelien herausgegeben von H. Holtzmann, vol. I., Leipzig, 1862.
BLOOMFIELD, S. T., The Greek Testament with English notes, critical, philological, and exegetical, IV., Philadelphia, 1854.
BLUNT, HENRY, Lectures upon the history of our Lord and Saviour J. C., Philadelphia, 1857.
BLUNT, JOHN HENRY, The annotated Bible, being a household commentary upon the Holy Scriptures, London, 1882.
BOARDMAN, GEORGE D., The Divine Man from the Nativity to the temptation, New York, 1887.
BOEHMER, JULIUS, Das Lukas Evangelium in religiösen Betrachtungen für das moderne Bedürfnis, Gütersloh, 1909.
*BOLO, HENRI, Histoire de L'Enfant Jésus, 2 ed., Paris, 1896.
*BONAVENTURA, S., Commentarius in Lucam, Opera omnia, tom. 7, ed. Collegio A. S. Bonaventura Quaracchi, ex Typographis Colleg. S. Bon.
BOND, JOHN, The Gospel according to St. Luke, London, 1900.
BORNEMANN, JOHANNES, Die Taufe Christi durch Johannes in der dogmatischen Beurteilung der christlichen Theologen der vier ersten Jahrhunderte, Leipzig, 1896.
BOSSUET, JACQUES, Élévationes sur les Mystères, oeuvres complètes, ed. J. Tachet, Paris, 1862.

BOUSSET, WILHELM, Jesus, transl. by J. Penrose Trevelyan, New York, 1908.
———, Die Religion des Judentums im neutestamentlichen Zeitalter, Berlin, 1903.
*BOURDALOUE, LOUIS, Sermon pour le premier dimanche après Epiphanie, oeuvres complètes, Lyon-Paris, 1906.
BOVON, JULES, Théologie du Nouveau Testament, 2 ed., tom. I., Lausanne, 1902.
Box, G. H., The Virgin Birth, HDG II. 804 ff.
———, The Gospel narratives of the Nativity and the alleged influence of Heathen ideas, ZntlW VI (1905) 80–101.
———, The Virgin Birth of Jesus, a critical examination of the Gospel narratives of the Nativity, London, 1916.
BRASSAC, A., Manuel Biblique, 3 ed., tom. 3, Paris, 1910.
———, The Gospels–Jesus Christ, transl. by J. Weidenham, London, 1913.
BRIGGS, C. A., The Messiah of the Gospels, New York, 1894.
———, New Light on the Life of Jesus, New York, 1904.
BROUGH, J., The early Life of Our Lord, London, 1897.
BROWN, DAVID, The Life of Jesus prior to His Public Ministry, ExpT VI (1894–5) 415.
BRUCE, ALEXANDER, St. Paul's conception of Christianity, New York, 1894.
*BRUNO, S., Episc. Signensis, Comment. in Lucam, M.PL CLXV. 365.
BUCER, M., Enarrationum in Evangelia Matthaei, Marci et Lucae, lib. I., Argeniorati, 1527.
BUDHAM, F. P., The integrity of Luke i. 5–11, ExpT VIII (1896–7) 116 ff.
BURKITT, WILLIAM, Exposition, notes and practical observations on the New Testament of Our Lord and Saviour J. C., vol. I., Philadelphia, 1849.
BURNSIDE, W. F., The Gospel according to St. Luke, Expositor's Bible, 3 ed. London, 1908.
*CAIETANUS, THOMAS DE VIO, Commentarii in Scripturam S., tom. III., Lugduni, 1639.
*CALMET, AUGUSTINUS, Commentarius litteralis in omnes libros Novi Testamenti, transl. by J. D. Mansi, tom. II., Wirceburgi, 1787.
CALOVIUS, ABRAHAM, Biblia illustrata Novi Testamenti, Dresdae et Lipsiae, 1710.

CALVIN, JOHN, Commentarius in harmoniam Evangelicam; also Sermons sur l'harmonie Évangélique, 38, 39. Opera quae supersunt omnia, vols. 45, 46. Edit. by Baum, E. Cunitz and E. Reuss (Corp. Reform), Brunsvigae, 1891.

CAMPBELL, GEORGE, The four Gospels, transl. from the Greek with preliminary dissertation and notes critical and explanatory, Philadelphia, 1796.

CAMPBELL, R. J., The new theology, New York, 1907.

CANDLISH, J. S., Children (sons, daughters) of God, HDB II. 215–221.

*CANISIUS, PETER, Commentariorum de Verbi Dei corruptelis, tom. 2, de sacrosancta Virgine Maria Deipara, Parisiis, 1584.

*CAPECELATRO, ALFONSO, La Vita di Gesu Cristo, vol. I., Roma, 1887.

CAPPELLUS, LUD., In Biblia Critica, vol. 6, 286.

CARMAN, AUGUSTINI, S., Philo's doctrine of the Divine Father and the Virgin Birth, AmJTh IX (1905) 491–518.

CARPENTER, S. C., Christianity according to S. Luke, London, 1919.

CARR, ARTHUR, The Gospel according to St. Luke, London, 1875.

CARTWRITUS, THOMAS, Commentaria practica in totam historiam evangelicam ex quatuor evangelistis harmonice con-cinnatam, Londonini, 1630.

*CATENAE GRAECORUM PATRUM, Edit. J. A. Cramer, tom. 2, Oxford, 1844.

CHARLES, R. H., Religious development between the Old and New Testament, New York, 1915.

*CHATEILLON, SEBASTIAN, Biblia interprete Sebastiano Castalione una cum ejusdem annotationibus, Basileae, 1551.

CLARKE, ADAM, The New Testament, text with comment., Baltimore, 1836.

CLEMENS, JOHN S., Childhood, the Childhood of Jesus, HDG I. 298 ff.

*COGHLAN, DANIEL, De Incarnatione, Dublini, 1910.

CONRADY, L., Die Quelle der kanonischen Kindheitsgeschichte Jesu, Ein wissenschaftlicher Versuch, Göttingen, 1900.

COOKE, R. J., The Incarnation and recent criticism, New York, 1907.

*CORDERIUS, BALTHASAR, Catena sexaginta quinque graecorum patrum in s. Lucam . . . et annotationibus illustrata, Antwerpiae, 1628–47.

CREMER, HERMANN, Biblisch-theologisches Wörterbuch der ntl. Gräcität, Gotha, 1902, transl. by W. Urwich, Edinburgh, 1892.
CRITICI SACRI, sive annotata doctissimorum virorum in Vet. et Nov. Test., Amstelodami, 1698.
*CURCI, CARLO M., Il Nuovo Testamento volgarizzato ed exposto in note esegetiche e morali, Roma, 1879.
DAAB, Jesus von Nazareth, wie wir ihn heute sehen, Leipzig, 1907.
DALMAN, GUSTAF, The Words of Jesus considered in the light of post-biblical writings and the Aramaic language, transl. by Kay, Edinburgh, 1909.
D'ARCY, CHARLES F., Consciousness, HDG I. 361 ff.
DAVIS, N., The Story of the Nazarene in annotated paraphrase, New York, 1903.
DELITZSCH, FRANZ, Hebrew New Testament, 13 ed., Berlin, 1904.
DENNEY, JAMES, Jesus and the Gospel, Christianity justified in the mind of Christ, New York, 1909.
*DENZINGER, HENRICUS, Enchiridion symbolorum definitionum et declarationum de rebus fidei et morum, 12 ed. Freiburgi, 1911.
DICKENSON, C. H., The perfecting of Jesus, in And R XVII (1892) 339–360.
DICKEY, SAMUEL, The significance of the baptism of Jesus for His conception of His authority, BW (N.S.) XXXVII (1911) 359–368.
*DIDON, REV. FATHER, Jesus Christ, Our Saviour's Person, mission and spirit, transl. by B. O'Reilly, New York, 1891.
*DIONYSIUS CARTUSIANUS, Opera Omnia, V., Monstrolii, 1898.
DODERLEIN, JUL., Das Lernen des Jesusknaben, NJdTh I (1892) 606–619; cf. Think. III (1893) 171–174.
DODS, MARCUS, Baptism, in HDG I. 170.
DOLLINGER, JOHN J., The Gentile and the Jew in the courts of the Temple of Christ, vol. 2, transl. by N. Dorrell, London, 1906.
DOREN, W. H. VAN, A suggestive commentary on St. Luke with critical and homiletic notes, vol. I., New York, 1868.
DORNER, J. A., History of the development of the doctrine of the Person of Christ, transl. by W. L. Alexander, Edinburgh, 1872.
*DRUM, WALTER, The Consciousness of the preëxisting Christ, a study of Philip. ii. 6, Homiletic and Past. Rev. XXI (1920) 11–15.

BIBLIOGRAPHY 205

Du Bose, Horace M., The consciousness of Jesus, New York, 1917.
*Duchesne, Mgr. Louis, Early history of the Church, from its foundation to the end of the third century, transl. from the 4th French ed., New York, 1909.
*Durand, A., The Childhood of Jesus Christ, according to the Canonical Gospels, transl. by J. Bruneau, Philadelphia, 1910.
Ebrard, J. H. A., The Gospel History, A Compendium of critical investigations in support of the historical character of the Four Gospels, transl. by A. Bruce, Edinburgh, 1876.
Edersheim, Alfred, The life and times of Jesus the Messiah, 8 ed., New York, 1912.
———, The Temple, its ministry and services as they were at the time of Christ, New York, n. d.
———, In the days of Christ, Sketches of Jewish social life, New York, n. d.
Ellicott, C. J., Historical lectures on the Life of Our Lord J. C., with notes critical, historical and explanatory, Boston, 1864.
Erasmus, D., Novum Testamentum . . . cum annotationibus . . . Basileae, 1541. Quoted in Biblia Critica, tom. VI., 275.
———, Paraphrase upon the Gospels and Acts, London, 1548.
*Estius, Guilielmus, Annotationes aureae in praecipua ac difficiliora Sacrae Scripturae loca. Coloniae Agrippinae, 1622.
*Euthymius, Zigabenus, Commentarius in Lucam, M.PG CXXIX. 897.
Evans, Daniel, The self-consciousness of Jesus, AndthSB II (1891) 16–19.
Ewald, Heinrich, Die drei ersten Evangelien und die Apostelgeschichte übersetzt und erklärt, 2 ed. Göttingen, 1871.
———, The History of Israel, vol. VI., transl. by J. F. Smith, London, 1883.
*Fabrus, Jacobus Stapulensus, Commentarium initiatorium in quatuor Evangelia, Coloniae, 1541.
Fairbain, A. M., Studies in the Life of Christ, New York, 1897.
Fairweather, William, Development of doctrine, HDB Ex. vol. 272–308.
———, The background of the Gospels; or Judaism in the period between the Old and New Testaments, Edinburgh, 1908.
Farmer, George, "Boyhood," "Boyhood of Jesus," HDG I. 221–230.
Farrar, Frederic W., The life of Christ, New York, 1888.

FARRAR, The Gospel according to St. Luke, Cambridge, 1912.
FAUT, S., Die Christologie seit Schleiermacher, ihre Geschichte und ihre Begründung, Tübingen, 1907.
FEINE, PAUL, Eine vorkanonische Überlieferung des Lukas in Evangelium und Apostelgeschichte, Eine Untersuchung, Gotha, 1891.
―――, Theologie des Neuen Testaments, Leipzig, 1912.
*FELDER, HILARIN, Jesus Christus, Apologie seiner Messianität und Gottheit gegenüber der neuesten ungläubigen Jesus-Forschung, vol. I., Das Bewusstsein Jesu, Paderborn, 1911.
FELDMAN, W. M., The Jewish Child, Its history, folklore, biology and sociology, London, 1917.
FELTON, JOSEPH, Neutestamentliche Zeitgeschichte oder Judentum und Heidentum zur Zeit Christi und der Apostel, Regensburg, 1910.
FIELD, FREDERICK, Notes on the translation of the New Testament, being the Otium Norvicense (Pars Tertia), Cambridge, 1899. See also a review in ExpT X (1898-9) 484.
*FILLION, CL., Évangile selon S. Luc. Introduction critique et Commentaires, Paris, 1882.
―――, Le développement intellectuel et moral de Jésus. In RcIfr, April 1 and April 15, 1914.
FINDLAY, A. F., Gospels (Apocryphal), HDB I. 671-685.
FLEETWOOD, JOHN, The Life of Our Lord and Saviour J. C., Philadelphia, 1855.
FOOTE, JAMES, Lectures on the Gospel according to St. Luke, vol. I., Edinburgh, 1858.
FOXELL, W. J., The Temptation of Jesus, a study, London, 1920.
*FOUARD, CONSTANT, The Christ the Son of God, 5 ed., transl. by Griffeth, New York, 1891.
FREDERICK, HENRY ALFRED, The self-consciousness of Jesus, AndthSB II (1891) 19-22.
FURRER, KONRAD, Das Leben Jesu Christi, 3 ed., Leipzig, 1905.
GARVIE, Alfred E., Studies in the Inner Life of Jesus, London, 1907.
―――, The Gospel accord. to St. Luke, Westminster New Test., vol. III.
GATES, HERBERT WRIGHT, The life of Jesus, A manual for teachers, Chicago, 1907.
GEIKIE, CUNNINGHAM, The life and words of Christ, New York, 1902.

GELPKE, ERNST FRIEDRICH, Die Jugendgeschichte des Herrn; ein Beitrag zur höheren Kritik und Exegese des neuen Testaments, Bern, 1841.
GEORGE, E. A., The Gospels of the Infancy, in OT–NTSt X (1890) 281 ff.
GESS, WOLFGANG E., Christi Person und Werk nach Christi Selbstzeugniss und den Zeugnissen der Apostel, Basel, 1887.
*GIGOT, FRANCIS, The Virgin Birth in St. Luke's Gospel, IthQ VIII (1913) 412–434.
———, Studies in the Synoptic Gospels, NYR I (91895) 3.
GILBERT, GEORGE HOLLEY, The student's life of Jesus, Chicago, 1896.
———, Father, Fatherhood, HDG I. 579–582.
GODET, F., A commentary on the Gospel of St. Luke, 2 ed., transl. by E. W. Shalders and W. D. Cousin, New York, 1881.
———, The Life of Jesus prior to His Ministry, Think. VII (1895) 390–404.
GORE, CHARLES, Dissertation on subjects connected with the Incarnation, New York, 1895.
GOULBURN, EDWARD M., The Gospel of the Childhood, a practical and devotional commentary on the simple recorded incident of O. B. L.'s Childhood, Lk. ii. 41–52, New York, 1873.
GOULD, EZRA P., The biblical theology of the New Testament, New York, 1900.
*GRIMM, JOSEPH, Das Leben Jesu nach den vier Evangelien. Geschichte der Kindheit Jesu, Regensburg, 1906.
GUIGNEBERT, CHARLES, Manuel d'histoire ancienne du Chrétianisme, les origines, Paris, 1906.
GUYSE, JOHN, The practical expositor, or an explanation of the New Testament in the form of a paraphrase, vol. 2, Glasgow, 1792.
HÄCKER, JOHANNES, Die Jungfrauen — Geburt und das neue Testament Exeg. Untersuchung, ZWTh XLIX (1906) 18–61.
HAHN, G. L., Das Evangelium des Lucas, vol. I., Breslau, 1892.
HALL, FRANCIS, The kenotic theory consid. with ref. to its anglican forms and arguments, New York, 1898.
———, The Incarnation, New York, 1915.
HALL, G. STANLEY, Jesus, the Christ in the light of psychology, New York, 1917.
HANNA, W., The earlier years of our Lord's life on earth, New York, 1870.
HARDEN, J. M., Mary, the Virgin, HDG II. 140.

HARNACK, ADOLF, What is Christianity? transl. by T. Saunders, London, 1901.
———, Luke the Physician, the author of the Third Gospel and the Acts of the Apostles, transl. by Wilkinson, New York, 1908.
———, The Sayings of Jesus, The second source of St. Matthew and St. Luke, transl. by Wilkinson, New York, 1908.
———, The Date of the Acts and of the Synoptic Gospels, transl. by Wilkinson, New York, 1911.
HARTMANN, JULIUS, Das Leben Jesu nach den Evangelien geschichtlich dargestellt für gebildete Leser, Stuttgart, 1839.
HASE, CARL, The Life of Jesus, a manual for academic study, 4 ed., transl. by J. F. Clarke, Boston, 1860.
———, Geschichte Jesu nach akademischen Vorlesungen, Leipzig, 1876.
HASE, KARL A., New Testament parallels in Buddhistic literature, New York, 1907.
HASTINGS, JAMES, The great texts of the Bible, St. Luke (edit. by J. Hastings), New York, 1913.
HAUSRATH, ADOLF, A History of the New Testament times, the time of Jesus, transl. by C. Poynting and P. Quenger, vol. I., London, 1878.
———, Jesus und die neutestamentlichen Schriftsteller, Band II., Berlin, 1909.
HAWKINS, J. C., Horae Synopticae, Oxford, 1909.
*HAYMONIS, HALBERSTAT, Episc., Homilia 17 Dominica prima post Epiphaniam, M.PL CXVIII. 120–126.
*HEER, M., Die Stammbäume Jesu nach Matthäus und Lukas, BSt XV Freiburg i. B., 1910.
HENRY, MATTHEW, An exposition of the Old and New Testament, vol. 8, London, 1866.
HERFORD, R. TRAVERS, Pharisaism, its aim and its method, New York, 1912.
HESS, WILH., Jesus von Nazareth, Tübinger, 1906.
HILGENFELD, ADOLF, Die Geburts — und Kindheitsgeschichte Jesu, Luc. i. 5–ii. 52. ZWTh XLIV (1901) 177–235.
HILLMANN, JOHANNES, Die Kindheitsgeschichte Jesu nach Lucas, JprTh XVII (1891) 192–261.
HITCHCOCK, ALBERT W., The self-consciousness of Jesus in its relation to the Messianic hope, OT–NTSt XIII (1891) 209 ff. and 270 ff.
———, The psychology of Jesus, A study of the development of His self-consciousness, Boston, 1907.

BIBLIOGRAPHY 209

HOBEN, ALLEN, The Virgin Birth, AmJTh VI (1902) 473 ff.
HOFMANN, CHR. K. V., Die heilige Schrift neuen Testaments zusammenhangend untersucht, vol. VIII., Nordlingen, 1878.
HOFMANN, R., art. Apocrypha of the New Testament, in Sch-HEnc I. 105-107.
HOFMEISTERUS, JOANNES, Commentarium in evangelium Lucae, Lovanii, 1562.
HOLLMANN, L. The Jewish Religion in the time of Jesus, transl. by E. W. Lummis, London, 1909.
HOLMES, PETER, Jesus Christ, Kit. EBL I. 541 ff.
HOLTZMANN, H. J., Hand-Commentar zum Neuen Testament, I., Freiburg i. B., 1892.
———, Lehrbuch der neutestamentlichen Theologie, Freiburg i. B., 1897.
———, Das messianische Bewusstsein Jesu, Ein Beitrag zur Leben-Jesu-Forschung, Tübingen, 1907.
HOLTZMANN, OSCAR, The life of Jesus, transl. by Bealby and Cenney, London, 1904.
———, Das Messiasbewusstsein Jesu und seine neuste Bestreitung (Vortrag), Giessen, 1902.
*HUGO, CARDINALIS DE SANCTO CARO, Postilla super IV. Evangelia, Basil, 1482.
HUMPHREY, W. G., A commentary on the Revised Version of the New Testament, London, 1882.
*HURTER, HUGO, Theologiae dogmaticae compendium, II. Oeniponte, 1891.
*ISAAC DE STELLA, Homilia (duo) in Dominica infra octavam Epiphaniae, M.PL CXCIV 1715-1719.
JACOBUS, MELANCTHON W., Notes on the Gospels, critical and explanatory, Mark and Luke, New York, 1867.
*JACQUIER, B., Histoire des livres du Nouveau Testament. 6 ed., vol. 2, Paris, 1910.
*JANSENIUS, CORNELIUS, Tetrateuchus sive commentarius in sancta Jesu Christi Evangelia, tom. 2, Avenione, 1835.
*JANSSENS, J., Tractatus de Deo Homine, I. Friburgi, 1901.
JEREMIAS, ALFRED, Babylonisches im Neuen Testament, Leipzig, 1905.
*JOHN SCOTUS ERIGENA, De divisione naturae, IV. 10, M.PL CXXII. 777.
JONES, MAURICE, The New Testament in the twentieth century. A survey of recent christological and historical criticism of the New Testament, London, 1914.

KEIL, C. F., Commentar über die Evangelien des Markus und Lukas, Leipzig, 1879.
KEIM, THEODOR, The history of Jesus of Nazara, transl. by G. Goldart, London, 1876.
KENNEDY, A. R. S., Education, HDB I. 346 ff.
KENT, CHARLES F., The Life and Teaching of Jesus according to the earliest records, New York, 1913.
———, Biblical geography and history, New York, 1911.
KILPATRICK, T. B., Character of Christ, HDG I. 281 ff.
———, Incarnation, HDG I. 796 ff.
KLOSTERMANN, ERICH, Lukas, Tübingen, 1919.
*KNABENBAUER, JOSEPH, Commentarius in Quatuor S. Evangelia Domini N. Jesu Christi., vol. 3, in Lucam, Paris, 1896.
KRENKEL, MAX, Josephus und Lucas, der schriftstellerische Einflus des jüdischen Geschichtschreibers auf den Christlichen Nachgewissen, Leipzig, 1894.
KÜHL, ERNST, Das Selbstbewusstsein Jesu, BZSF ser. III. nbr II (1907).
*LAGRANGE, M. J., Le récit de l'enfance de Jésus dans S. Luc., Rb IV (1895) 160 ff.
———, Les sources du Troisième Évangile, Rb IV (1895) 5 ff.
———, La Paternité de Dieu dans l'ancien Testament, Rb (N. S.) V (1908) 481 ff.
———, La Conception surnaturelle du Christ d'après Saint Luc., Rb (1914) 67–71 and 188–208.
———, Evangile selon Saint Luc, Paris, 1921.
*LAMY, BERNARDO, Commentarius in harmoniam sive concordiam quatuor Evangelistarum, Venetilis, 1869.
LANGE, J. P., The life of Christ, transl. by Taylor and Rylud, vol. I., Edinburgh, 1872.
*À LAPIDE, CORNELIUS, Commentaria in Sacram Scripturam, editio Xysto Riario Sfortiae, tom. 8, Niapoli, 1857. Transl. into English by Mossman and Ross, 1882.
*LEBRETON, JULES, Les origines du dogme de la Trinité, Paris, 1910.
*LE CAMUS, La Vie de N. S. Jésus Christ, vol. I., Paris, 1883.
*LEPICIER, ALEXIO M., Tractatus de Incarnatione Verbi, Parisiis, 1905.
*LEPIN, MARIUS, Christ and the Gospel, or Jesus the Messiah and Son of God, authorized English version, Philadelphia, 1910.
*LESÊTRE, H., La Vièrge Mère, RCLfr (1907) 113–130.
———, La methode historique de S. Luc, Rb I (1892) 171 ff.

*Lesêtre, H., Jésus Christ, VDB III. 1444.

———, Le Temple de Jerusalem, Paris, 1912.

Lester, C. S., The historical Jesus, a study of the synoptic Gospels, New York, 1912.

Lightfoot, John, Horae Hebraicae et Talmudicae or Hebrew and Talmudical exercitations upon the Gospel of St. Luke, edit. by R. Gaundel, Oxford, 1859.

Lightfoot, J. B., The Apostolic Fathers, ed. by Harmer, London, 1912.

Lobstein, Paul, The Virgin Birth of Christ, an historical essay transl. by V. Leutiett, London, 1903.

Loisy, Alfred, Les Évangiles Synoptiques, vol. I. 278–384. Ceffonds, 1907.

———, Les écrits de Saint Luc, a propos d' un livre récent, RHLr, N. S. IV (1913) 352–368.

Löw, Leopold, Die Lebensalter in der jüdischen Literatur von psychologischen rechts — sitten — u. religions — geschichtlichen Standpunkte betrachtet, Szegedin, 1875.

*Lucas, Franciscus Brugensis, Commentarius in Sanctum Jesu Christi Evangelium, tom. 2, Antuerpiae, 1619; found also in Migne, Cursus Completus, S. S.

*Ludolphus Saxonius, Vita Christi ex Evangeliis et scriptoribus orthodoxis, Paris, 1534.

Luther, Martin, Werke, vol. I.–III. and X.–XII. Edit. E. Ludwig Enders, Frankfurt am Main, 1862.

*Lyra, Nicolas de, Biblia latina compostillis, vol. 4. Wornberg, Koberger, 1487.

*Maas, A. J., The life of Jesus Christ according to Gospel history, St. Louis, 1891.

———, Jesus Christ, Cath. Enc. VIII. 374 ff.

———, A Day in the Temple, St. Louis, 1908.

MacDermott, G. M., The Gospel according to St. Luke, London, 1916.

*MacEvilly, Rev. Dr., An exposition of the Gospel of St. Luke, 3 ed., New York, 1888.

Machen, J. Gresnan, The New Testament account of the birth of Jesus, PrthR III (1905) 64 ff. and IV (1906) 38 ff.

———, The origin of the first two chapters of Luke, PrthR X (1912) 212–277.

Mackintosh, H. R., The doctrine of the Person of Jesus, New York, 1912.

MACKINTOSH, ROBERT, The dawn of the Messianic consciousness ExpT XVI (1905) 157–158 and 211–215.

MACLAREN, ALEXANDER, The Gospel of St. Luke, New York, 1894.

McLAUGHLIN, G. A., Commentary on the Gospel according to St. Luke, Chicago, 1912.

MACLEAN, ARTHUR J., God, HDB, sing. vol. 299–303.

*MACRORY, J., The authorship of the Third Gospel and the Acts, IthQ II (1907) April.

———, Professor Harnack and St. Luke's historical authority, IthQ II (1907) 223 ff.

MAHAFFY, JOHN P., The silver age of the Greek world, Chicago, 1906.

MALAN, C., L'avénément dans Jésus enfant de la conscience religieuse, RThQr V (1896) 269–283.

*MALDONATUS, JOANNIS, Commentarius in Quatuor Evangelistas, ed. J. M. Raich, tom. 2, Moguntiae, 1874.

*MANGENOT, E., L'Évangile de Saint Luc, two articles in RClfr, Sept. and Nov., 1910.

———, Les Évangiles Synoptiques, Conferences apologetiques, Paris, 1911.

MARTIN, ALFRED W., The life of Jesus in the light of the higher criticism, New York, 1913.

MASON, ARTHUR JAMES, The conditions of our Lord's life on earth, New York, 1896.

MATTHEWS, SHAILER, The Messianic hope in the New Testament, Chicago, 1905.

———, A history of New Testament times in Palestine, 175 B.C.–70 A.D., New York, 1914.

MELANCHTHONIS, PHILIPP, Opera quae supersunt omnia, Bretschneider, ed. by Bindseil, vol. 24, Brunsvigae, 1856.

*METAPHRASTES, SIMEON, Oratio de Sancta Maria, 13 and 14, M.PG CXV. 447–8.

MEYER, H. W. W., Critical and exegetical commentary on the New Testament, transl. rev. and ed. by Dickenson and Stewart, Edinburgh, 1880.

MICHAELIS, JOHANN DAVID, Uebersetzung des Neuen Testaments, vol. I., Göttingen, 1790.

MICHAELIS, JOHANNS GEORG, Exercitatio Philologico-theologica de Christo ONTI EN TOIΣ TOY ΠΑΤΡΟΣ ad Luc. ii. 49, in Miscellanea Groningona, in miscellaneorum Duisburgensium continuationem publicata, I. fasc. II. 262–282 (ed. D. Gerdes) tom. I, Amstelodami et Duisburgi, 1736.

MICHEL, CHARLES, Évangiles Apocryphes, Paris, 1911.
MILLER, LUCIUS HOPKINS, Our knowledge of Christ, an historical approach, New York, 1914.
———, The Life of Jesus in the light of modern criticism, BW XLIII (1914) 75–85.
MILNER, G. E. J., The Gospel according to St. Luke, ed. with introduction and notes, London, 1916.
MOFFATT, JAMES, An introduction to the literature of the New Testament, New York, 1911.
MONNIER, HENRI, La Mission historique de Jésus, 2 ed., Paris, 1914.
MONTEFIORE, C. G., The synoptic Gospels, ed. with introduction and a commentary, with a series of additional notes by I. Abrahams, vol. 2, London, 1909.
MOORE, CLIFFORD H., The Religious thought of the Greeks from Homer to the triumph of Christianity, Cambridge, Mass., 1916.
MORUS, SAM. FRIED, NATHAN, Praelectiones in Lucae Evangelium, ed. C. A. Donat, Lipsiae, 1795.
MOULTON, JAMES HOPE, A Grammar of New Testament Greek, I. Edinburgh, 1908.
MOULTON and MILLIGAN, Texical notes from the Papyri, Exp. vol. VII., ser. 7 (1909) 470.
MURRAY, POTTER, The Legendary Story of Christ's Childhood, NW VIII (1889) 648.
NEANDER, AUGUSTINE, The Life of Jesus Christ, 4 ed., transl. and ed. by J. Clintock and C. E. Blumanthal, New York, 1850.
NEBE, A., Die Kindheitsgeschichte unseres Herrn Jesu Christi nach Matthäus und Lukas ausgelegt, Stuttgart, 1893.
NEVIN, ALFRED, Popular Commentary on the Gospel according to Luke, Philadelphia, 1868.
NEUMANN, ARNO, Jesus, transl. by M. A. Canney, London, 1906.
NICOLL, W. R., The Incarnate Saviour, a Life of Christ, New York, 1882.
NOLLOTH, CHARLES F., The Person of our Lord and recent thought, London, 1908.
———, The rise of the Christian Religion, a study in origins, London, 1917.
NÖSGEN, E., Geschichte Jesu Christi, München, 1891.
OESTERLEY, WILLIAM, Judaism in the days of Christ, in "The Parting of the Roads," ed. by F. Jackson, London, 1912.

OLSHAUSEN, HERMANN, Biblical commentary on the Gospels, adapted especially for preachers and students, transl. by S. Lowe, Edinburgh, 1847.

OOSTERZEE, J. J. VAN, The Gospel according to Luke, 4 ed., transl. by Schaff and Starbuck, New York, 1867 (in Lange's Comment.).

ORR, JAMES, The Virgin Birth of Christ, London, 1908.

OWEN, JOHN J., A commentary, critical, expository and practical on the Gospel of St. Luke, New York, 1859.

PATERSON, W. P., Jesus Christ, HDB (sing. vol.).

*PATRITIUS, FRANCISCUS XAVERIUS, De Evangeliis, lib. 3, Fribourgi-Brisgoviae, 1853.

PAULUS, H. E. G., Philologisch-kritischer Commentar über die drei ersten Evangelien, vol. I., Lübeck, 1800–1802.

———, Das Leben Jesu, als Grundlage einer reinen Geschichte des Urchristentums, Heidelberg, 1828.

———, Exegetisches Handbuch über die drei ersten Evangelien, Heidelberg, 1842.

PAYNTER, A. W., The Holy Life, a contribution to the historical development of, and a critical exposition, Chicago, 1886.

PEABODY, FRANCIS, The Character of Jesus Christ, HJ Jul. (1903) 641 ff.

*PESCH, CHRISTIAN, Praelectiones dogmaticae, IV., De Verbo Incarnato, de B. V. Maria, de cultu sanctorum, 3 ed. Friburgi, 1909.

PFLEIDERER, OTTO, The early Christian conception of Christ, its significance and value in the history of religion, New York, 1905.

———, Christian Origins, transl. by Huebach, New York, 1906.

———, Primitive Christianity, its writings and teachings in their historical connections, transl. by W. Montgomery, New York, 1909.

PHELAN, WILLIAM, The remains of William Phelan, D.D., with a biographical memoir by John Bishop of Limerick, vol. I., London, 1832.

PHILO JUDAEUS, Works, transl. by C. D. Yonge, London, 1855.

*PHOTIUS, Constantinopolitani Patriarcha, Ad. Ampilochium, quest, 157, M.PG CI. 832; Contra Manichaeos, IV. 16 M.PG CII B. 233.

*PICARD, LOUIS, La transcendance de Jésus Christ, tom. I., La vie et la psychologie de Jésus Christ, Paris, 1905.

*PISCATOR, JOHN, Commentarii in omnes libros Novi Testamenti, ante hac separatim editi nunc vero in unum volumen collecti, 3 ed. Herbornae Nassoviorum, 1638.

PLUMMER, ALFRED, A critical and exegetical commentary on the Gospel according to St. Luke, 7 ed., NewYork, 1906.

———, The advance of Christ in Σοφία. In Exp. ser. 4, vol. IV. 1–14.

PLUMPTRE, E. H., The Gospel according to St. Luke (in Ellicott's New Test. Comment. I.), London, 1884.

*POHLE, JOSPEH, Christology, a dogmatic treatise on the Incarnation, transl. by A. Preuss, 2 ed., St. Louis, 1916.

*POWER, MATTHEW, Who were they who "understood not"? IthQ VII (1912) July and Oct.

DE PRESSENSÉ, EDMOND, Jesus Christ, His times, life and work, 2 ed., transl. by A. Harwood, New York, 1868.

———, The early years of Christianity, transl. by A. Harwood, New York, 1872.

PREUSCHEN, ERWIN, Vollständiges griechisch-deutsches Handwörterbuch zu den Schriften des Neuen Testaments und der übrigen urchristlichen Literatur, Giessen, 1910.

PRICAEUS, JOANNES, Commentarii in varios novi Testamenti Libros, Londini, 1681, also in Biblia Critica VI. 304.

PURVES, GEORGE T., The story of the Birth, BW VIII (1896) 423 ff.

RAMSAY, W. M., Was Christ born at Bethlehem? a study in the credibility of St. Luke, New York, 1898.

———, The education of Christ, 2 ed., New York, 1902.

———, Luke the Physician. And other studies in the history of religion, London, 1908.

———, The bearing of recent discovery on the trustworthiness of the New Testament, 2 ed., London, 1915.

REINHARD, F. V., Plan of the Founder of Christianity, transl. by Oliver Taylor, New York, 1831.

RENAN, ERNEST, The Life of Jesus, transl. by Brentano, New York, 1863.

———, Les Évangiles et la seconde génération chrétienne, 3 ed., Paris, 1877.

RESCH, A., Das Kindheits Evangelium nach Lucas und Matthaeus T. U. Leipzig, 1897.

REUBELT, J. A., The Scripture doctrine of the Person of Christ, based on the German of W. F. Gess, 2 ed., Andover, 1871.

REUSS, EDOUARD, Histoire Évangélique, synopse des trois premières évangiles, Paris, 1876.
RÉVILLE, ALBERT, Jésus de Nazareth, études critiques sur les antecedents de l'histoire évangélique et la vie de Jesus, vol. I., Paris, 1897.
———, The Birth and Infancy of Jesus, NW I (1892) 695–723.
RHEES, RUSH, The Life of Jesus of Nazareth, a study, New York, 1900.
RICE, EDWIN, Popular commentary on the Gospel according to St. Luke, 4 ed., Philadelphia, 1894.
RIDDLE, M. B., The Gospel according to Luke, New York, 1822.
ROBERTSON, A. T., The teaching of Jesus concerning God the Father, New York, 1904.
———, Keywords in the teaching of Jesus, Philadelphia, 1906.
———, Epochs in the life of Christ. A study of development and struggle in the Messiah's work, New York, 1908.
———, A grammar of the Greek New Testament in the light of historical research, London, 1914.
———, The romance of the census in Luke's Gospel. Bib. Rev. V (1920) 491.
———, Luke the historian in the light of research, New York, 1920.
ROBINSON, FORBES, The self-limitation of the Word of God as manifested in the Incarnation, London, 1914.
*RYAN, CORNELIUS, The Gospels of the Sundays and Feasts, 2 ed., vol. 2, New York, 1906.
RYLE, J. C., Expository thoughts on the Gospels for family and private use, St. Luke, vol. 1, New York, 1867.
SADLER, M. F., The Gospel according to St. Luke with notes critical and practical, London, 1888.
*SALMERON, ALPHONSUS, Commentarii in Evangelicam historiam et in Acta Apostolorum, Coloniae Agrippinae, 1612.
SANDAY, WILLIAM, The Virgin Birth, ExpT XIV (1902–3) 296–303.
———, God (in New Test.), HDB II. 205–215.
———, Son of God, HDB IV. 570–579.
———, The Life of Christ in recent research, Oxford, 1907.
———, Outlines of the Life of Christ, 2 ed., New York, 1908.
*SCHAEFER, ALOYS., The Mother of Jesus in Holy Scripture, biblical theological addresses, 2 ed., transl. by F. Brossart, New York, 1913.

SCHAFF, PHILIP, A popular commentary of the New Testament, by English and American scholars of various evangelical denominations, Edinburgh, 1879.
*SCHANZ, PAUL, Commentar über der Evangelium des heiligen Lucas, Tübingen, 1883.
*SCHEGG, PETER, Evangelium nach Lukas, I. München, 1861.
SCHENKEL, DANIEL, Das Charakterbild Jesu, Weesbaden, 1879, transl. by W. H. Furness, Boston, 1866.
SCHLATTER, D. A., Die Theologie des neuen Testaments, vol. I., Das Wort Jesu, Stuttgart, 1909.
SCHLEUSNER, JOH. FRIED., Novum Lexicon Graeco-Latinum in N. T. cum variis observationibus philologicis, London, 1829.
SCHLEIERMACHER, FREDERICK, Ueber die Schriften des Lukas, Berlin, 1817.
———, A critical essay on the Gospel of St. Luke, transl. from German, London, 1825.
———, Das Leben Jesu (ed. K. A. Rutenik), Berlin, 1864.
SCHMIDT, HERMANN, Bildung und Gehalt des messianischen Bewusstseins Jesu, StKr LXII (1889) 423–507.
SCHMIDT, NATHANIEL, The Prophet of Nazareth, New York, 1905.
SCHMIDT, P. WILH., Die Geschichte Jesu I. erzählt II. erläutert, Tübingen and Leipzig, 1900–1904.
SCHMIEDEL, P. W., Arts., Mary and Luke in E. B.
———, Jesus in modern criticism,—A lecture transl. by M. A. Canney, London, 1907.
SCHOETTGENIUS, CHRISTIANUS, Horae Hebraicae et Talmudicae in theologiam Judaeorum dogmaticam antiquam et orthodoxam, tom. 2, Dresdae, 1742.
Scholia Vetera in Lucam, M.PG CVI. 1189.
*SCHULTE, P. ELZEAR, Die Entwickelung der Lehre vom menschlichen Wissen Christi bis zum Beginn der Scholastik, Paderborn, 1914.
*SCHUMACHER, HEINRICH, Die Selbstoffenbarung Jesu bei Mat. 11, 27 (Luc. 10, 22), ein kritisch-exegetische Untersuchung, Freiburg i. B., 1912.
———, Christus in seiner Präexistenz und Kenose nach Phil. 2, 5–8 Rom., 1914.
SCHÜRER, EMIL, Geschichte des jüdischen Volkes im Zeitalter Jesu Christi, 4 ed., Leipzig, 1907; English transl. by S. Taylor and P. Christie, New York, 1891.
———, Das messianische Selbstbewusstsein Jesu Christi, Göttingen, 1903.

*Schwäiger, J., Leben Jesu, Innsbruch, 1860.
Schweitzer, Albert, The quest of the historical Jesus, a critical study of its progress from Reimarus to Wrede, transl. by Montgomery, London, 1910.
Scott, E. F., Father's house, HDG I. 582.
*Seitz, A., Das Evangelium vom Gottessohn, Freiburg i. Br. 1908.
*Shanahan, Edmund T., Was the Son of Man brusque to His mother? Catholic World CIV (1916) 342 ff.
Sheldon, Henry C., New Testament theology, New York, 1911.
Sickenberger, Joa., Titus von Bostra, Studien zu dessen Lukashomilien, Leipzig, 1901.
Smith, David, Education, HDG I. 507 ff.
――, The days of His Flesh, the earthly life of our Lord and Saviour J. C., New York, 1905.
Sodon, Hermann von., Die wichtigsten Fragen im Leben Jesu (Vortrag), Berlin, 1904.
Soltau, Wilhelm, The Birth of Jesus Christ, transl. by M. A. Canney, London, 1903.
Spaeth, H., Die Entwickelung Jesu (Vortrag), Berlin, 1872.
Spitta, Friedrich, Die chronologischen Notizen und die Hymnen in Lc. i. u. 2, ZntlW VII (1906) 281–317.
Stalker, James, The Life of Jesus Christ, New York, 1909.
――, Son of God, HDG II. 654 ff.
――, The Christology of Jesus, being His teaching concerning Himself according to the Synop. Gosp., London, 1899.
Stapfer, Edmond, Jésus Christ avant son Ministère, Paris, 1896, transl. by S. G. Houghton, New York, 1900.
Steinbeck, Joh., Das göttliche Selbstbewusstsein Jesu nach dem Zeugnis der Synoptiker, eine Untersuchung zur Christologie, Leipzig, 1908.
*Steinmetzer, Franz, Die Geschichte der Geburt und Kindheit Christi und ihr Verhältnis zur babylonischen Mythe, Münster i. E., 1910.
Steinmeyer, F. L., Die Geschichte der Geburt des Herrn und seiner ersten Schritte im Leben, in Bezug auf die neueste Kritik, Berlin, 1873.
*Stella, Didachus, De Observantia in Sanctum Jesu Christi Evangelium secundum Lucam doctissima pariter et purissima commentaria, I., Lugduni, 1592.
Stephens, George Barker, The theology of the New Testament, New York, 1903.

BIBLIOGRAPHY 219

STEWART, A. MORRIS, The temptation of Jesus, a study of our Lord's trial in the wilderness, 2 ed., New York, 1903.

STIER, RUDOLF, The Words of the Lord Jesus, 2 ed., transl. by W. Pope, I., Edinburgh, 1894.

STOKES, ANSON PHELPS, What Jesus Christ thought of Himself, another outline study and interpretation of His self-revelation in the Gospels, New York, 1916.

STRAUSS, DAVID FRIEDRICH, The Life of Jesus, critically examined, 4 ed., transl. by M. Evans, New York, 1855.

STREATFEILD, G. S., The Self-interpretation of Jesus Christ, a study of the messianic consciousness as reflected in the Synoptics, New York, 1906.

*SUAREZ, R. D. FRANCISCUS, De myst. disp. iv. quaest. 27., art. 6, Opera omnia, tom. 19, Paris, 1860.

SWEET, LOUIS M., The birth and infancy of Jesus Christ according to the Gospel narrative, Philadelphia, 1907.

*SYLVEIRA, JOANNIS, Commentariorum in textum evangelicum, tom. I, Lugduni, 1655.

TASKER, JOHN G., Apocryphal Gospels, HDB Ex. vol. 431 ff.

*TERRIEN, T. B., La Mère de Dieu et la Mère des hommes d'après les pères et la theologie, Paris, 1900–2.

*THEOPHYLACTUS, BULGARIAE ARCHIEP., Ennaratio in Evangelium Lucae, M.PG CXXIII. 733.

THILO, Codex apocryphus Novi Testamenti, Leipzig, 1832.

THIRIET, TH. M., L'évangile médité avec les pères, I., Paris, 1905.

THOLUCK, A., Die Glaubwürdigkeit der evangelischen Geschichte, zugleich eine Kritik des Lebens Jesu von Strauss für theologische und nicht theologische Leser dargestellt, Hamburg, 1858.

*THOMAS AQUINAS, ST., Summa Theologica, literally transl. by the Fathers of the English Dominican Province, New York, 1913.

THOMSON, WILLIAM, Jesus Christ, SDB I. 1039 ff.

*TIRINUS, JACOBUS, In universam S. Scripturam commentarius, tom. 4, Taurini, 1883.

*TOLETUS, FRANCISCUS, Commentarii in sacrosanctum Jesu Christi D. N. evangelium secundum Lucam, Parisiis, 1600.

TORREY, CHARLES C., The transl. made from the original Aramaic Gospels (in Studies in the hist. of relig. pres. to C. H. Toy), New York, 1912.

TOY, C. H., Judaism and Christianity, a sketch of the progress of thought from Old Testament to New Testament, Boston, 1801.

USENER, H., Nativity, EB III. 3340–3352.

VALLINGS, J. F., Jesus Christ, the Divine Man, His life and times, New York, 1889.

*VEUILLOT, LOUIS, La vie de notre Seigneur Jésus-Christ, 14 ed., Paris, 1900.

VINCENT, MARVIN R., Word studies in the New Testament, vol. I., New York, 1887.

VOGEL, THEODOR, Zur Charakteristik des Lukas nach Sprach und Stil, Leipzig, 1899.

*VOGLES, H. F., Die "Eltern" Jesu, BZ XI (1913) 33 ff.

VÖLTER, DANIEL, Die evangelischen Erzählungen von der Geburt und Kindheit Jesu kritisch untersucht, Strassburg 1911.

——, Jesus der Menschensohn oder das Berufsbewusstsein Jesu, Strassburg, 1914.

*VONIER, DOM ANSCAR, The Personality of Christ, London, 1915.

WALLIS, ROBERT E., "About My Father's Business," a plea for a neglected transl., Luke ii. 49, Exp. ser. 2, vol. VIII. 17–23.

WALPOLE, A. S., The Gospel according to St. Luke in the revised version with introduction and notes, London, 1910.

*WARD, MGR., The Holy Gospel according to St. Luke, with introduction and notes, London, 1905.

WARFIELD, BENJAMIN B., Amazement, HDG I. 47 ff.

——, Astonishment, HDG I. 131.

WEINEL, HEINRICH, and A. E. WIDGERY, Jesus in the nineteenth century and after, Edinburgh, 1914.

WEISS, BERNARD, The life of Christ, transl. by J. W. Hope, vol. I., Edinburgh, 1883.

——, Biblical theology of the New Testament, 3 ed., transl. by E. Dugnid, vol. 2, Edinburgh, 1893.

——, A commentary on the New Testament, transl. by Schodde and Wilson, New York, 1906.

WEISS, JOHANNES, Die Schriften des Neuen Testaments, I. die drei älteren Evangelien, die Apostolgeschichte, Göttingen, 1907.

WELLHAUSEN, JULIUS, Das Evangelium Lucae, Berlin, 1904.

——, Einleitung in die drei ersten Evangelien, Berlin, 1905.

WENDT, HANS HEINRICH, The teaching of Jesus, transl. by J. Wilson, vol. I., Edinburgh, 1892.

WERNLE, PAUL, The beginnings of Christianity, transl. by G. A. Beinemann and edit. by W. D. Morrison, London, 1903.

——, The sources of our knowledge of the life of Jesus, transl. by E. Lummis, London, 1907.

WETTE, W. M. L. DE, Kurze Erklärung der Evangelien des Lukas und Markus, Leipzig, 1846.
WETTSTENIUS, JOANNIS J., Novum Testamentum Graecum, tom. I., Amstelaedami, 1751.
WHITEFOORD, B., Christ and popularity, a study of St. Luke ii. 52. Exp. ser. 5, vol. II., pp. 69-76.
WILKINSON, WILLIAM C., Concerning Jesus Christ the Son of Man, Philadelphia, 1918.
WOLFIUS, JO. CHRISTOPHORUS, Curae philogicae et criticae in quatuor S. Evangelia et Acta Apostolorum, 3 ed., Hamburgi, 1739.
WRIGHT, ARTHUR, The Gospel according to St. Luke in Greek, London, 1900.
———, A Synopsis of the Gospels in Greek, with various readings and critical notes, 3 ed., London, 1906.
*ZACHARIAS, CHRYSOPOLITANUS, In unum ex quatuor seu de concord, Evang., M.PL CLXXXVI. 88.
ZAHN, THEODOR, Introduction to the New Testament, 3 ed., transl. under direction of M. E. Jacobus, Edinburgh, 1909.
———, Das Evangelium des Lucas, vol. I., Leipzig, 1913.
ZIMMERMANN, HELLMUTH, Evangelium des Lukas Kap. 1 und 2, ein Versuch der Vermittlung zwischen Hilgenfeld und Harnack, StKr LXXVI (1903) 247-290.
ZÖCKLER, OTTO, Jesus Christ, SchHEnc II. 1170.

II

SELECTED LIST ON CHRIST'S CONSCIOUSNESS IN BOYHOOD

ST. EPIPHANIUS, Adv. haer. lib. I. tom. 2, haer. 30, M.PG XLI. 456-457.
ST. CYRIL OF ALEXANDRIA, Explanation of St. Luke's Gospel ad loc., M.PG LXXII. 509; also De recta fide, M.PG LXXVI. 1320.
ST. AUGUSTINE, Serm. LI. De concord Evang., Matt. et Luc. in generationibus Dom. C. II., M.PL XXXVIII. 342-343.
———, Also de nuptiis et concup. Corp. Script. Lat. (edit. Vrba and Zycha) XLII. 225.
SIMEON METAPHRASTES, Vita sanctorum, oratio de S. Maria, M.PG CXV. 548.

MALDONATUS, IOA, Comment. ad loc.
SYLVEIRA, JO., Comment. in text. evang. I. 352–354.
STIER, RUDOLF, Words of the Lord Jesus, 23 ff.
GOULBURN, E. M., The Gospel of the Childhood, 162–171.
STEINMEYER, F., Geschichte der Geburt des Herrn, 167 ff.
SCHMIDT, H., Bildung und Gehalt des messianischen Bewusstseins Jesu, StKr LXII (1889) 429–430.
NEBE, A., Die Kindheitsgeschichte J. C., 417.
MALAN, C., L'avénement dans Jésus enfant de la conscience religieuse, RThQr V. (1896) 269–283.
FURRER, K., Das Leben J. C., 51–58.
GARVIE, A., Studies in the inner Life of Jesus, 110–114.
BARTMANN, N. B., Christus ein Gegner des Marienkultus?, 43–61.
SEITZ, A., Das Evangelium vom Gottessohn, 194–209.
FILLION, CL., Le développement intellectuel et moral de Jésus, RCIfr (April 1, 1914), 15 ff.
FELDER, H., Jesus Christus, I. 278–280, 328–331.

III

TREATISES ON THE INFANCY AND BOYHOOD OF CHRIST

AELREDUS, ABB. REVALLIS, Tractatus de Jesu Puero duodenni, M.PL CLXXXIV. 830–870.
Chiefly of a moral and religious value.
BEDE, VENERABILIS, Homil. XII. in Dominica prima post Epiphaniam, M.PL XCIV. 65 ff.
A sermon dwelling mostly on the moral aspect.
BEET, JOSEPH A., The "Father's Business," Homiletic Rev. XXXIV. (1897) 242–243.
Brief and in the homiletic line.
BERG, EMIL P., Our Lord's preparation for the Messiahship, a study on the early life of Jesus Christ, London, 1909.
Rather odd, certainly not composed on the Gospel records.
BERNARD, THOMAS D., The Songs of the Holy Nativity, London, 1895.
BOARDMAN, GEORGE D., The Divine Man from the Nativity to the Temptation, New York, 1887.
From the negative standpoint.
BOLO, HENRI, Histoire de l' Enfant Jésus, 2 ed., Paris, 1896.
Simple explanatory exposition of the Gospel account.

BOUGH, J., The early life of Our Lord, London, 1897.
BOX, G. H., The Gospel narratives of the Nativity and the alleged influence of heathen ideas, ZntlW VI (1905) 80–101. Afterwards enlarged into his work: The Virgin Birth, London, 1916.
: A good critical presentment of the arguments for the historical trustworthiness.

BROOKE, S. A., The early life of Jesus, London, 1870.
BROUGH, J., The early life of Our Lord, London, 1897.
: A good treatment of the historical background.

BROWN, DAVID, The life of Jesus prior to his public ministry. (Exp. T VI (1894–5) 415 ff.)
: An answer to points raised by Godet.

BUDHAM, F. P., The integrity of Lk. i. 5–ii, Exp. T VIII. (1896–7) 116 ff.
: A critical study of the question.

CALTHROP, GORDON, On Lk. ii. 49 in Quiver, Dec. 1889.
CARTER, T. T., Our Lord's early life, London, 1887.
——, Meditations on the hidden life of Our Lord.
CHAUVIN, C., L'Enfance du Christ, Paris, 1901.
CLEMENS, JOHN S., Art. The Childhood of Jesus, HDG I. 298 ff.
: Good from the historical point of view.

CONRADY, L., Die Quelle der kanonischen Kindheitsgeschichte Jesu, ein wissenschaftlicher Versuch, Göttingen, 1900.
: Phantastic and with results rejected by all.

DURAND, A., The Childhood of Jesus Christ according to the can. Gospels, transl. by J. Bruneau, Philadelphia, 1910.
: Good answer to the criticisms of the negative school.

FARMER, GEORGE, Art. Boyhood, Boyhood of Jesus, HDG I. 221–230.
: Good historical background and literal meaning of the Gospel text.

FILLION, CL., Le développement intellectuel et moral de Jésus. RCIfr April 1 and 15, 1914.
: A good exposition of this question.

GELPKE, ERNST F. Die Jugendgeschichte des Herrn, ein Beitrag zur höheren Kritik und Exegese des neuen Testaments. Bern, 1841.
: Good conservative exposition of the Gospel narratives.

GEORGE, E. A., The Gospels of the Infancy, OT–NTSt X (1890) 281 ff.
: Weighing the arguments for and against the historicity.

GODEFRIDUS, VEN ABB. ADMONTENSIS, Homilia 14–15 in Dominica infra Oct. Epiphaniae, M.PL CLXXIV. 95–108.
: He occupies himself mostly with the accommodative sense.

GODET, F., The Life of Jesus prior to his ministry, Think VII. (1895) 390–404.
: A brief account, not conservative.

GOULBURN, EDWARD M., The Gospel of the Childhood. A practical commentary on St. Luke ii. 41 to the end, New York, 1873.
: An excellent sympathetic exposition.

GRAY, JAMES, A sketch of the life of J. C. from His Birth to the commencement of His public ministry (in dissertation on the concordance between the priesthoods of J. C. and Melchisedeck, 123–158) Philadelphia, 1845.
: A good exposition following the Gospel lines.

GREG, DAVID, The Boy Christ. In the Treasury of Religious thought (New York) XIII (1896) 839–850.
: Mostly concerned with Christ amidst the Doctors.

GRESSMANN, HUGO, Die Weihnachts — Evangelium auf Ursprung und Geschichte untersucht, Göttingen, 1914.
: A negative explanation of the Gospel account of Christ's Birth.

HANNA, W., The earlier years of our Lord's Life on earth, New York, 1870.
: A fairly conservative presentment.

HANSEN, T., Aus d. Jugendjahren Jesu. Transl. into Ger. by Gleis, 1896.

HAYMO, BISHOP OF HABBERSTAT, Homilia XVII. in Dominica prima post Epiphaniam M.PL CXVIII. 120–126.
: A good sermon, keeping mostly to the literal sense.

HESS, JOHAN JAKOB, Erste Jugendgeschichte Jesu, Frankfurt, M. 1773. Published as vol. I. in work, Geschichte der drey letzten Lebensjahre Jesu.
: Just an exposition of the Gospel text.

HILGENFELD, ADOLF, Die Geburts — und Kindheitsgeschichte Jesu, Luc. i. 5–ii, 52, ZWTh XLIV (1901) 177–235.
: A good critical exposition of the section, yet evidencing a negative tendency in many points.

HILLMANN, JOHANNES, Die Kindheitsgeschichte Jesu nach Lucas, JprTh XVII (1891) 193–261.
: A critical treatment from the negative standpoint.

IRONS, W. J., The first recorded words of Christ, an epiphany to the Blessed Virgin and to us. Epiph I. in Sermons (1844).

ISAAC OF STELLA, Homilia (duo) in Dominica infra Oct. Epiphaniae. M.PL CXCIV. 1715–1719.
: Mostly concerned with the accommodative sense.

KITTO's MAG., Vol. XII. 351 ff. and XIII. 420 ff. Birth and Infancy of Christ.

KNOWLES, ARCHIBALD C., The holy Christ-Child, a devotional study of the Incarnation of the Son of God, New York, 1905.
> A reverential treatment of the Gospel account.

KOHLER, Zu den kanonischen Geburts — und Jugendgeschichte Jesu in Schweiserische theologische Zeitschrift, VI. (1902) 221 ff.

LAGRANGE, M. J., Le récit de l'Enfance de Jésus dans S. Luc. Rb IV (1895) 160 ff.
> A forcible vindication of the conservative side.

MACHEN, J. GRESHAM, The New Testament account of the birth of Jesus, PrthR III (1905) 64 ff. and IV (1906) 38 ff.

———, The origin of the first two chapters of Luke, PrthR X 91912) 212–277.
> Good conservative treatises, the latter especially critical and scholarly.

MALAN, C., L'Avénement, dans Jésus Enfant, de la conscience religieuse, RThQr V (1896) 269–283.
> A discussion of Christ's religious consciousness in development.

MAYERUS, B., Disp. de Jesu 12.

MICHAELIS, J. G., Exercitatio philol. theol. de Christo . . . ad Luc. ii. 49.
> A very conservative treatise of this passage, mostly dealing with the question of ἐν τοῖς.

MONOD, ADOLPHE, Enfance de Jésus, ou l'éducation chrétienne, Paris, 1860.
> More a treatise on method.

MORGEN, G. CAMPBELL, The hidden Jesus at Nazareth, New York, 1898.
> Short and popular, dealing mostly with term from 12th to 30th year.

MULLEADY, BERTHOLD, Devotion to the Divine Infant, Am. Ecclesiastical, Rev. lxii. (1917) 593–606.
> The author deals mostly with the history of this subject.

MURRAY, POTTER, The legendary story of Christ's Childhood, NW VIII (1889) 648 ff.
> Contrasting the apocryphal with the gospel account.

NEBE, A., Die Kindheitsgeschichte unseres Herrn Jesu Christi nach Mattäus und Lukas ausgelegt, Stuttgart, 1893.
> A good explanatory treatise of the Gospel accounts.

PHELAN, WILLIAM, Christ in the Temple in "Remains" I., London, 1832.
> A good sermon from the theological standpoint.

PRIDEAUX, BP., De Christi Adolescentia in Lectiones; consciones, II.

PURVES, GEORGE I., The story of the Birth, BW VIII (1896) 423 ff.
Defending the historical trustworthiness of narrative.

RAMSAY, W. M., Was Christ born at Bethlehem? A study in the credibility of St. Luke, London, 1898.

———, Luke's narrative of the Birth of Jesus, Exp. ser., 8 vol. IV. (1912) 481–507.
Excellent vindication of St. Luke's historical trustworthiness.

RESCH, A., Das Kindheits Evangelium nach Lucas und Matthaeus, TU Leipzig (1897).
An unsuccessful attempt to reconstruct the Hebrew basis of the accounts.

REUTERDAHL, Observationes criticae in priora duo Evang. Lucae capita, London, 1823.

RÉVILLE, ALBERT, The Birth and Infancy of Jesus, NW I(1892) 695–723.
Sweeping and negative in results.

ROBERTSON, A. T., The romance of the census in Luke's Gospel, Bib. Rev. V (1920) 491 ff.
A summary of Ramsay's arguments.

SANDAY, WILLIAM, A paper on the origin and character of the first two chapters of St. Luke.

SCHUBERT VON, De Infantiae J. C., historiae a Matt. et Luc. exhibitae authentia et indole, Gripeswald 1815.

SIMEON, C., Christ's early habits, in "Works," XII. 268.

SMITH, THORNLEY, The holy Child Jesus, the early life of Christ viewed in connection with the hist. chronol. and archaeol. of the times, London, 1868.

SPITTA, FRIEDRICH, Die chronologischen Notizen und die Hymnen in Luc. i. u. 2, ZntlW VII (1908) 281–317.
Negative in its conclusions.

STAPFER, EDMOND, Jésus Christ avant son Ministère, Paris, 1896. Eng. transl. by S. G. Houghton, New York, 1900.
Much of it is imaginative.

STEINMETZER, FRANZ, Die Geschichte der Geburt und Kindheit Christi und ihr Verhältnis zur babylonischen Mythe, Münster, I E., 1910.
A good treatment of this question from the conservative point of view.

STEINMEYER, F. L., Die Geschichte der Geburt des Herrn und seiner ersten Schritte im Leben, in Bezug auf die neueste Kritik, Berlin, 1873.
A good complete critical treatise.

BIBLIOGRAPHY

SWEET, LOUIS M., The Birth and Infancy of Jesus Christ according to the Gospel Narrative, Philadelphia, 1907.
> A thorough and scholarly book, answering all objections to the Virgin Birth.

USENER, H., Art. Nativity, E. B. III. 3340–3352.

———, Geburt und Kindheit Christi, ZntlW IV (1903) 1–21.
> Both radical and destructive.

VAN DYKE, HENRY, The Childhood of Jesus, Harpers New Monthly Mag. LXXXVII. (1893) 723–730.

———, The Childhood of Jesus Christ with 20 illustrations from paintings of great masters, New York, 1905.
> Both from the art point of view.

VÖLTER, DANIEL, Die evangelischen Erzählungen von der Geburt und Kindheit Jesu kritisch untersucht, Strassburg, 1911.
> Negative and sweeping in its conclusions.

WALLACE, LEW, The Boyhood of Christ, illustrated, New York, 1888.
> Popular treatment, very well done.

WALLIS, ROBERT E., "About My Father's business," A plea for a neglected translation, Lk. ii. 49, Exp. ser. 2, vol. VIII. 17–23.
> Dealing mostly with the question in hand.

WANDEL, Die Kindheitsgeschichte Jesu Christi nach Nösgen und Nebe, in Neue Kirchliche Zeitschrift V. (1894) 286–315, 449–465.

ZENOS, A. C., The Birth and Childhood of Jesus, BW VI (1895) 433–443.
> An account of the Gospel narrative to the flight into Egypt.

ZIMMERMANN, HELLMUTH, Evangelium des Lukas, Kap. I. u. 2, ein Versuch der Vermittlung zwischen Hilgenfeld und Harnack. StKr LXXVI (1903) 247–290.
> A good critical treatment.

See also the excellent list in S. G. Ayres': Jesus Christ our Lord, an English bibliography of Christology. New York, 1906, pp. 124–128, and the early sections of the Lives of Christ, Commentaries on first two chapters of St. Matthew and St. Luke, etc.

LIST OF ABBREVIATIONS FOR PERIODICALS AND COLLECTIONS

AmJTh.....American Journal of Theology.
AndR......Andover Review.
AndthSB...Andover Theological Seminary Bulletin.
A–NF......Ante-Nicene Fathers.

BSt........Biblische Studien.
BW........Biblical World.
BZ........Biblische Zeitschrift.
BZSF...... Biblische Zeit- und Streit-Fragen.

Cath. Enc..Catholic Encyclopedia.

EB........Encyclopedia Bibliotheca.
Exp........Expositor.
ExpT......Expository Times.

HDB......Hastings' Dictionary of the Bible.
HDG......Hastings' Dictionary of Christ and the Gospels.
HJ........ Hibbert Journal.

IthQ.......Irish Theological Quarterly.

JewEnc....Jewish Encyclopedia.

JprTh......Jahrbücher für Protestantische Theologie.

Kit.EBL....Kitto's Encyclopedia of Biblical Literature.

M.PG PL...Migne, Patrologia Graeca, Patrologia Latina.

NJdTh.....Neue Jahrbücher für Deutsche Theologie.
N.P–NF....Nicene and Post-Nicene Fathers.
NW........New World.
NYR......New York Review.

OT-NTSt...Old and New Testament Student.

PrthR......Princeton Theological Review.
Rb.........Revue Biblique.
RClfr......Revue du Clergé Française.
RHLr......Revue d'Histoire et de Litérature Religieuse.
RThQr.....Revue de Théologie et des Questions Religieuses.

Sch-HEnc..Schaff-Herzog, Encyclopedia of Religious Knowledge.
SDB.......Smith's Dictionary of the Bible.
StKr......Theologische Studien und Kritiken.

Think......The Thinker.
TU........Texte und Untersuchungen.

VDB.......Vigouroux's Dictionnaire de la Bible.

ZntlW.....Zeitschrift für Neutestamentliche Wissenschaft.
ZwTh......Zeitschrift für Wissenschaftliche Theologie.

SCRIPTURAL INDEX

OLD TESTAMENT

Genesis —
  vi. 1–4 83

Leviticus —
  xxiii. 4–22 75

Exodus —
  iv. 22 81
  xiii. 8 75
  xxiii. 14, 17 75
  xxxiv. 23, 24 75

Numbers —
  xxi. 29 81

Deuteronomy —
  i. 31 81
  vi. 20 75
  viii. 5 81
  xxxii. 5, 6, 18, 19 81
  xiv. 1, 2 81
  xvi. 16 75
  xxi. 18–21 144

Judges —
  xix. 11 155

1 Kings —
  i. 3, 4, 7, 21 76
  i. 22 68–71
  i. 28 68–71
  ii. 1–10 67
  ii. 26 67
  iii. 4–14 68
  iii. 10 68–91
  iii. 19 67

2 Kings —
  vii. 14 83
  vii. 18, 19, 25 91

3 Kings —
  viii. 13 99
  ix. 3 99

1 Paralipomenon —
  xxix. 10 81

2 Paralipomenon —
  vii. 16 99
  xxxiv. 3 66

Tobias —
  xiii. 4 82

Job —
  i. 6 83
  ii. 1 83
  ii. 9 155
  xxxviii. 7 83

Psalms —
  ii. 7 .... 83, 114, 171, 172, 190
  xv. (xvi.) 2 85
  xxii. (xxiii.) 1 85
  xxviii. (xxix.) 1 83
  xliv. (xlv.) 5 155
  liii. 3 122
  lxxxviii. (lxxxix.) 7 83
  lxxxviii. (lxxxix.) 27, 28 ... 83
  lxxxi. (lxxxii.) 1–6 83
  cii. (ciii.) 13 85
  cvi. (cvii.) 41 85
  lxviii. (lxviii.) 5 85
  cxix.–cxxxiii 78
  cxii.–cxviii 78
  cxxxi. 7, 8 78
  cxxxv 78

Proverbs —
  xxx. 17 144

Wisdom —
  ii. 18 82
  v. 5 82
  ii. 13, 16 82–85
  xiv. 3 82

Ecclesiasticus —
  xxiv. 1, 4 82–85
  li. 14 85
  li. 17 155

Isaias —
  i. 2, 4 81
  iii. 7 15
  vi. 9, 10 122
  xxx. 9 81
  xlii. 1 ff 91
  xliii. 6 82
  lxiii. 8, 16 82
  xlv. 11 81
  lii. 15 122

INDEX

Isaias —
  lv. 4 162
  lxii. 5 81
  liv. 6 81

Jeremiah —
  i. 6 16
  ii. 2 81
  iii. 1, 4 81
  iii. 7 15
  iii. 14, 19, 20, 22 81
  xxxi. 9, 20 82
  xxxi. 32, 34 82

Ezechiel —
  xvi. 8, 20 81
  xviii. 4 82

Daniel —
  v. 13 178
  viii. 23 152

Osee —
  ii. 2, 19, 20 81
  xi. 1 .... 81, 182
  xi. 3 81

Malachi —
  iii. 1 37
  i. 6 81
  ii. 10, 11 81

2 Maccabees —
  iv. 40 156
  vi. 18 156
  viii. 8 155

OLD TESTAMENT APOCRYPHA

3 Maccabees —
  v. 7 82
  vi. 4, 8 82
  vii. 6 83

Jubilus —
  i. 23–25 83

Testament of Levi —
  xviii. 6, 8 83

Testament of Juda —
  xxiv. 2 83

Psalms of Solomon —
  xvii. 29 83

1 Enoch —
  lxii. 11 83
  cv. 2 .... 83, 114

4 Esdras —
  vii. 28 114
  vii. 28, 29 83
  xiii. 32, 37 83
  xiv. 9 83

Sibylline Books —
  v. 360, 480, 560 83

NEW TESTAMENT

Matthew —
  i.–ii. 62
  i. 1–17 182
  i. 18 .... 146, 182
  i. 20 .... 146, 182
  i. 21 .... 146, 182
  i. 23 .... 146, 182
  i. 25 146
  ii. 2 182
  ii. 4–6 133
  ii. 11 .... 14, 26, 182
  ii. 13–18 .... 73, 182
  ii. 19 182
  ii. 22 .... 73, 77
  ii. 23 .... 73, 74, 163
  iii. 14 .... 173, 183

Matthew —
  iii. 15 .... 173, 183
  iii. 16 173
  iii. 17 .... 174, 189
  iv. 1 175
  iv. 3 .... 175, 189
  iv. 4 .... 175, 176
  iv. 5 .... 175, 176
  iv. 6 .... 175, 189
  iv. 8 .... 175, 176
  iv. 13 163
  vi. 27 155
  vii. 28 .... 126, 133
  vii. 29 133
  ix. 14 138
  xi. 27 179

INDEX

Matthew —
- xi. 25.................. 122
- xii. 10.................. 129
- xii. 23.................. 124
- xii. 46–50............... 110
- xiii. 14................. 122
- xiii. 15................. 122
- xiii. 19............121, 140
- xiii. 23................. 121
- xiii. 51................. 121
- xiii. 54........126, 133, 162
- xiv. 33.................. 189
- xv. 10................... 122
- xv. 16................... 122
- xv. 26.................... 87
- xvi. 12.................. 122
- xvi. 16.................. 189
- xvii. 5..............174, 189
- xvii. 13................. 122
- xviii. 20................ 183
- xix. 1–12............99, 163
- xix. 13................... 99
- xix. 23.................. 127
- xix. 25.................. 126
- xi. 27................... 183
- xxi. 33–46............... 178
- xxii. 33................. 126
- xxii. 35................. 129
- xxii. 41–46.............. 178
- xxvii. 40................ 189
- xxvii. 43................ 189
- xxvii. 54................ 189
- xxvii. 63................. 79
- xxviii. 19............... 183
- xxviii. 20................ 83

Mark —
- i. 7..................... 183
- i. 8..................... 183
- i. 9..................... 163
- i. 10.................... 173
- i. 11.................... 189
- i. 12.................... 175
- i. 22............126, 133, 183
- i. 24.................... 183
- i. 26.................... 183
- i. 34.................... 183
- i. 38.................... 183
- ii. 12................... 124
- ii. 17................... 183
- ii. 19................... 184
- ii. 20................... 184
- iii. 12.................. 189
- iii. 21........71, 124, 125, 184
- iii. 31–35........71, 110, 184
- iv. 12................... 122
- v. 7..................... 189

Mark —
- v. 42.................... 124
- vi. 1.................... 163
- vi. 2..............126, 133, 162
- vi. 3................162, 163
- vi. 51................... 125
- vi. 52..............122, 140
- vii. 14.............122, 140
- vii. 18.................. 122
- vii. 27................... 87
- vii. 37.............126, 127
- viii. 17................. 122
- viii. 31.................. 79
- viii. 35................. 184
- viii. 38................. 184
- ix. 6...............174, 189
- ix. 11................... 133
- ix. 13–17................. 99
- ix. 18................... 126
- ix. 31.................... 79
- ix. 36................... 183
- x. 26..............126, 127
- x. 45.................... 183
- xii. 1–12...........178, 189
- xii. 33.................. 122
- xii. 35–37............... 178
- xiii. 13................. 184
- xiii. 32................. 184
- xiv. 36.................. 178
- xv. 39................... 189
- xvi. 15.................. 184
- xvi. 16.................. 184

Luke —
- i. 1–4.................... 61
- i. 2, 3.................. 181
- i. 7, 18................. 156
- i. 13.................... 169
- i. 15 twice.............. 169
- i. 32.................... 169
- i. 35 twice.............. 169
- i. 16–17................. 169
- i. 32.................... 169
- i. 32, 33................ 169
- i. 35.................... 169
- i. 26.............74, 76, 108
- i. 29..................... 64
- i. 30.................... 153
- i. 31.................... 146
- i. 32...........146, 170, 189
- i. 34..................... 62
- i. 35. 62, 93, 108, 146, 157, 170, 189
- i. 38.................... 108
- i. 43.................... 170
- i. 46–55.................. 67
- i. 48.................... 146
- i. 59..................... 76

Luke —
i, ii. .... 60, 65, *passim*
i. 64. 159
i. 66. .... 67, 153
i. 68. .... 67, 92
i. 76. 169
i. 48, 49. 169
i. 41. 169
i. 79. 67
i. 80. .... 67, 153
ii. 4. 74
ii. 5. 135
ii. 7. 64
ii. 7 ff. 73
ii. 9 twice. 170
ii. 11. .... 26, 170
ii. 14. 170
ii. 16. 154
ii. 18. 147
ii. 19. .... 64, 147
ii. 21. .... 73, 76
ii. 22 ff. 73
ii. 25–33. 147
ii. 26. 170
ii. 29. 92
ii. 30, 32. 170
ii. 33. .... 16, 17, 64
ii. 34, 35. 147
ii. 36. .... 76, 156
ii. 38. 170
ii. 39. .... 68, 73, 74, 163
ii. 40. .... 65, 67, 70, 94, 123, 147,
            151, 154, 156, 157
ii. 41–51. 185
ii. 41. ... 16, 17, 18, 69, 76, 135, 185
ii. 42. .... 68, 69, 76, 77
ii. 43. .. 17, 18, 69, 79, 124, 135, 136,
            154
ii. 44. .... 69, 79, 136
ii. 45. 79
ii. 46. .... 69, 79, 124, 128ff.
ii. 46–48. .... 7–9, 14
ii. 47. ... 68, 94, 103, 137, 153, 157
ii. 47–48(a). .... 121ff.
ii. 48. ..... 8, 16, 17, 18, 31, 54, 69,
            80, 92
ii. 48. .... 104ff.
ii. 48. .... 137ff.
ii. 49. .... *passim*
ii. 50. . 5, 64, 69, 72, 94, 116, 121,
          139ff., 149, 170
ii. 51. . 64, 72, 80, 94, 108, 137,
          142ff., 143, 163
ii. 52. . 15, 65, 67, 123, 154ff., 158,
          161, 165, 171
iii. 1. 76
iii. 3. 170

Luke —
iii. 15. 171
iii. 16. 171
iii. 21, 22. .... 171ff.
iii. 22. .... 115, 174, 189
iii. 23ff. 76, 175
iii. 32. 116
iii. 38. 175
iv. 1. 175
iv. 2–13. .... 98, 100, 115, 175, 176
iv. 14. .... 25, 175, 176
iv. 15. .... 175, 176
iv. 16. .... 75, 162, 163
iv. 17–20. 75
iv. 22. 162
iv. 31–44. .... 126, 133, 177
iv. 39. 74
iv. 43. .... 177, 183
v. 20. 178
v. 21. 177
v. 22. 177
v. 24. 178
v. 34. 178
vi. 5. 178
vi. 9. 131
vi. 19. 177
vii. 14. 177
vii. 28. 171
vii. 35. 151
vii. 39. 177
vii. 40. 177
vii. 48. 178
viii. 10. 122
viii. 19–21. 110
viii. 24. 177
viii. 42. 76
viii. 54. 177
viii. 55. 124
ix. 1. 177
ix. 2. 177
ix. 5. 100
ix. 6. 177
ix. 22. 100
ix. 22, 44. 177
ix. 24. 178
ix. 26. 178
ix. 35. .... 174, 189
ix. 43. 177
x. 9, 17. 177
x. 14, 15. 177
x. 21, 22. .... 96, 122, 178, 179
xi. 2. 178
xi. 27. 111
xi. 28. 111
xi. 31. 151
xi. 39. 177
xi. 49. 151

INDEX

Luke —
- xii. 6, 9.................. 178
- xii. 25................... 155
- xiii. 33.................. 100
- xiv. 26................... 178
- xvi. 24, 25............... 80
- xvii. 25.................. 100
- xviii. 19................. 179
- xviii. 34............122, 141
- xix. 3.................... 155
- xix. 10................... 178
- xix. 45–46................ 99
- xx. 9–19.................. 178
- xx. 20–47............133, 163
- xx. 40.................... 129
- xx. 41–44................. 178
- xxi. 20–24................ 177
- xxi. 27................... 178
- xxii. 22.................. 100
- xxii. 27.................. 128
- xxii. 29.................. 178
- xxii. 37.................. 100
- xxii. 42.................. 178
- xxii. 66.................. 179
- xxii. 69.............178, 179
- xxii. 70.................. 179
- xxiv. 21.................. 141
- xxiv. 22.................. 124
- xxiv. 26.................. 101
- xxiii. 34................. 178
- xxiv. 44.................. 101
- xxiv. 45.................. 122
- xxiii. 46..........101, 178, 179
- xxiv. 49..............178–180
- xxiv. 51.................. 178
- xxiv. 52.................. 178

John —
- i. 1...................... 185
- i. 12..................... 192
- i. 14............153, 185, 189
- i. 18..................... 189
- i. 32................172, 185
- i. 33..................... 173
- i. 34..............173, 174, 189
- i. 45..................... 163
- i. 46..................... 163
- i. 47..................... 185
- i. 49..................... 189
- i. 51..................... 185
- ii. 3..................... 148
- ii. 4.................110, 186
- ii. 11.................... 185ff.
- ii. 12ff.................. 185
- ii. 13ff.................. 186
- ii. 16.................6, 186
- ii. 17.................... 99

John —
- iii. 2.................... 162
- iii. 16, 18................ 189
- iv. 25.................... 162
- v. 17.................85, 189
- v. 25..................... 188
- vi. 38.................... 35
- vi. 63.................... 185
- vi. 70.................... 189
- vii. 15, 16................ 162
- vii. 42................... 133
- vii. 52................... 163
- viii. 6, 8................. 162
- viii. 19, 20, 26........... 162
- viii. 27.................. 139
- viii. 28.................. 162
- viii. 41.................. 87
- viii. 58.................. 185
- ix. 21, 23................. 155
- ix. 35, 37................. 189
- x. 20..................... 124
- x. 30................138, 189
- x. 34..................... 83
- x. 36..................... 189
- x. 38..................... 189
- xi. 4..................... 189
- xi. 27.................... 189
- xi. 34.................... 184
- xii. 40................... 122
- xiv. 22................... 59
- xvi. 16................... 139
- xvi. 28................... 185
- xvi. 30...............129, 162
- xvii. 5, 24...........185, 189
- xviii. 37................. 162
- xix. 7.................... 189
- xix. 26...............111, 186
- xx. 28.................... 185
- xxi. 17................... 162

Acts —
- i. 4..................178–179
- i. 7..................178–179
- i. 8..................178–179
- i. 9...................... 178
- ii. 7, 12................. 125
- ii. 22................181–197
- ii. 33.................... 179
- ii. 36.................... 179
- iii. 6, 16................. 178
- iii. 15................... 179
- iii. 21................... 101
- iv. 10, 30................. 178
- iv. 7..................... 128
- vi. 3, 10................. 151
- vii. 22...............161–181
- viii. 16, 37,.............. 190

INDEX

Acts —
vii. 10 151
vii. 10 151–161
vii. 22 151–161
vii. 25 122–140
vii. 46 153
viii. 9, 11 124
viii. 13 125
ix. 20 179–190
ix. 21 125
ix. 34 178
x. 36, 42 179
x. 38 163–178
x. 45 124
xii. 16 124
xiii. 3 172
xiii. 7 122
xiii. 12 126
xiii. 15 75
xiii. 33 179
xv. 21 75
xvi. 18 178
xvii. 3 101
xvii. 14 136
xxi. 17ff. 64
xxii. 3 161
xxviii. 27, 29 122

Romans —
i. 4 190
i. 14, 22, 31 122
iii. 11 122
v. 10 190
viii. 3 187–190
viii. 32 187–190
viii. 14–17 192
viii. 15 178
ix. 5 187
x. 19 122
xii. 7 98
xiii. 12 154
xv. 21 122

1 Corinthians —
i. 9 190
i. 19 122
iii. 16 102
viii. 6 187
ix. 6 138
ix. 24 102
xv. 25 102

2 Corinthians —
iv. 4 187
v. 13 124–125
viii. 9 187
x. 12 122

Galatians —
i. 14 154
iv. 4 .... 187, 190, 192
iv. 6 178
iv. 7 192
v. 14 152–154

Ephesians —
i. 23 152
iii. 4 122
iv. 13 155
v. 17 122

Philippians —
i. 12 155
ii. 5 187
ii. 8 162–187
iv. 11 98

Colossians —
i. 9 122
i. 15 187
ii. 2 122
ii. 3 153–188
ii. 9 153
iv. 14 60

1 Thessalonians —
i. 1 191

1 Timothy —
i. 15 187
iv. 15 98–155

2 Timothy —
ii. 7 122
ii. 16 154
iii. 8 154
iii. 13 154

Philemon —
24 60

Hebrews —
i. 5 172–190
ii. 17 162
iii. 5 190
iii. 6 99–190
iv. 15 162
iv. 14 190
v. 5 172–190
v. 8 162–190
vii. 3 190
x. 29 190
xi. 11 155

James —
i. 17, 27 190

INDEX

Jude —
  i. 1 190

1 Peter —
  i. 3, 17 190

2 Peter —
  i. 17 .... 174, 189

1 John —
  iii. 8 190
  iv. 9, 14, 15 190
  v. 5, 7, 13 190

Apocalypse —
  iii. 5 190
  xix. 10 185
  xxii. 9 185

NEW TESTAMENT APOCRYPHA

Protevangelium of James —
  xix 19

Childhood Gospel of Ps. Matthew —
  xiii 19
  xxi 20
  xxiv 20

Childhood Gospel of Thomas —
  iii 20
  iv 19
  vi. 20
  vii. 20
  viii 21
  xiii 163

Childhood Gospel of Thomas —
  xix 20, 21, 80
  xix 53, 56, 58

Arabic Gospel of Infancy —
  i 20
  x 20
  l.–liii 20, 21, 22
  liii 57, 80

Apocryphal Gospel of the
  Hebrews 171, 174

Gospel of Ebionites 23

Gospel of Marcosians 3–4

GENERAL INDEX

Abbott, 41
Abelard, 33
Adamson, 46, 103
Adeney, 47, 129
Aelredus, 32, 139
Agnöetae, 184
Aiken, 67
Albert the Great, 11, 33
Alcuin, 17, 30
Alexander of Hales, 32
Alexander the Great, 66
Alford, 47, 139
Ambrose, 10, 11, 14, 15, 56, 106, 107, 137, 143, 186
Anderson, 41
Angus, 84
Annas, 77
Anselm, 32
Aoculus, 15
Apocryphal: Gospel of the Childhood, 18 ff., 162; Protevangelium of James, 18–19; Pseudo-Matthew, Gospel of, 18, 19, 20; Childhood Gospel of Thomas, 16, 19, 20, 21, 53, 56, 80, 163; Arabic Gospel of the Childhood, 19, 20, 21, 22, 80
Apocryphal Gospels: Gospel of the Hebrews, 171, 174; Gospel of the Ebionites, 23; Gospel of the Marcosians, 3–4
Archelaus, 73, 77
Arendzen, 24
Aretius, 36
Aristotle, 32–34
Artemon, 25
Athanasius, 9, 14, 133
Athenagoras, 152
Augustine, 10, 14, 16, 17, 56, 58, 106, 133, 138, 172
Augustus, Emperor, 77
Augustus, Octavius, 66

Bacon, 40
Baldensperger, 40
Baljon, 44, 101
Bar-Mizvah institution, 76–77
Bardenhewer, 4, 5, 9, 19, 24, 62, 63, 74, 169
Barnabas, Ep. of, 13
Barnes, 47
Barrows, 65
Barth, 67, 94

Bartmann, 48, 49, 109, 137, 141, 145, 184, 185
Basilides, 24
Batiffol, 19
Bauer, Bruno, 43, 65, 107, 116
Bede, 29, 31, 110, 153
Beecher, 47, 131
Beet, 47
Bengel, 47
Berg, van Eysinga, 66
Bernadinus, 137
Beryllus of Bostra, 26
Besser, 47
Beyschlag, 42, 95
Beza, 36
Billiot, 48
Bisping, 48
Blunt, 47, 131
Boardman, 41
Bonaventure, 34, 35, 137
Bornemann, 23, 173
Bossuet, 129
Bourdaloue, 139
Bousset, 40, 61, 86
Bovon, 42
Box, 48, 61, 62, 63, 64, 69, 141, 170, 182
Box and Oesterley, 82
Brandt, 23
Brassac, 48–49
Briggs, 44, 63, 64, 102, 117
Brough, 46, 74, 97, 164
Brown, 42
Bruce, 187, 190, 192
Bruno, 32
Buddha, 66, 67
Buddham, 65
Burkitt, 56, 178
"Business" or "house." For ἐν τοῖς . . . , 56, 57, 98, 99

Cairns, 40
Caius, 25
Cajetan, 35, 36, 79, 131, 139
Calovius, 34
Calvin, 36, 118, 132, 136
Campbell, 61, 123, 132
Candlish, 83
Canisius, 136, 141
Capicelatro, 48
Carmon, 84
Carpenter, 41

239

INDEX

Carpocrates, 23
Carr, 123, 154
Cartwright, 35
Catenae Graecar, 29, 56, 58, 139
Cerinthus, 23-25
Χάρις, meaning of, 152-153
Charles, 82
Christ Child: a God, 14; miraculous power of, 19, 20, 153
Christ: "Son of the Law," 76-77; whether stayed to end of feast, 79; remained behind, 79, 136; among the Doctors, 14, 21, 79, 80, 121ff.
Christ, Virgin Birth, 5, 10, 18, 19, 61, 103, 104, 135, 138, 147, 169, 170, 171, 175, 189, 195: at Feast of Cana, 185; at Nazareth and Capernaum, 177; perfect from the beginning, 15, 16, 33, 196; no growth in consciousness, 20, 97, 112, 134, 135, 195, 196; never suffered ignorance, 15, 16, 32, 103, 104; whether attended school, 3, 20, 74, 75, 161, 162, 163; on God's Fatherhood, 188ff., 192ff.; and His Mother, 186; and the "parents," 110-111, 149, 184; and Samuel, 67-68; and John the Baptist, 153, 169; Genealogy of, 175
Christ's Birth, month of, 76
Christ's, subjection to parents, 143; first recorded saying, historicity of, 70-72: uniqueness of, 71, 72; harmony with later ones, 110-111; not childish, 94; contrast in, 92, 104ff.; reprehension in, 107ff.; morality of, 144ff.; baptism, 7, 23, 40, 43, 171ff., 182, 185; temptation, 175-176; second scene in the Temple, 186; Divinity, 7, 8, 9, 12, 20, 22, 196, 197; preëxistence, 13, 14, 185; real Divine Sonship, 96, 97, 178, 188ff., 195; Divine Sonship in Subapostolic Fathers, 13ff.; real Divine Sonship explains morality of episode, 145ff.; Messianic consciousness, 35, 37, 43, 142, 173; consciousness, as modern problem, 38, 47; Kenosis, 162, 188; knowledge, 14, 15, 32, 33, 155ff., 163, 184; grace, 157ff.; use of "My Father," 97, 193ff.
Christ's Infancy: historicity of narratives, 61ff.; Lucan wording, 62; Semitic colouring, 62-63; circumstances of, 73; political influences, 73-74; social influences, 74-75; religious influences, 75-77; in St. Luke, 169; in St. Matthew, 182

Chrysostom, 14, 16, 17, 26, 99, 110, 133, 148, 149, 186
Clarke, 47, 49
Clemens, 73
Clement, First Epistle of, 13: Second Epistle, 155; of Alexandria, 14, 171
Colarbasus, 24
Conrady, 61-63
Constantinople, Second Council of, 26
Constitutiones Apostolicae, 143
Coponius, 77
Corderius, 4, 37
Coughlan, 48, 160
Cremer, 123
Curci, 48
Cyprian, 174
Cyril, of Alexandria, 4, 8, 9, 12, 15, 16, 24, 53, 56, 58, 97, 106, 133, 159: of Jerusalem, 6, 9, 22

Daab, 39
Dalman, 48, 63, 69, 82, 83, 85, 86, 91, 93, 94, 165, 170, 171, 174, 176, 178, 179, 189, 192, 195, 196
D'Arcy, 48, 106, 109, 174, 176, 194
David, 66
Davis, 45
Deissmann, 155
Denny, 42
δεῖ, in New Testament, 100-101
Dialogus contra Macedonianos, 9, 17, 56, 58
Dickenson, 42, 94
Dickey, 40
Didache, the, 13
Didon, 24
Didymus of Alexandria, 6, 53, 56, 58, 143
Dill, 84
Diognetus, Epistle to, 14
Dionysius the Carthusian, 33
Döderlein, 47, 98, 129
Döllinger, 84
Doren, van, 47, 49, 132
Dorner, 47
Drum, 188
Du Bose, 48, 196
Duchesne, 23
Durand, 61, 63, 65, 73, 137

Ebionites, 7, 9, 23, 25, 26, 61, 171
Ebrard, 46, 134
Edersheim, 44, 73, 74, 75, 76, 78, 79, 80, 117, 123, 134, 143, 163, 187
Ἐκπλήσσομαι, in the New Testament, 127
ἡλικία, meaning of, 155

INDEX

Elkesaites, 23
Ellicott, 47, 80, 129
ἐξίστημι, in the New Testament, 124–125
Ephraim, 14
Epiphanius, 6, 9, 16, 17, 22, 23, 26, 53, 56, 58, 133, 171
Erasmus, 11, 36, 107, 127, 132, 136, 137
Estius, 137
Eusebius, 25–26
Euthymius Zizabenus, 31
Evans, 43
Ewald, 46, 165

Faber, Stapulensis, 36, 139
Fairbain, 41
Fairweather, 86
Farmer, 41, 74, 75, 76, 77, 78, 79, 127, 133, 138, 141, 148, 151, 152, 156
Farquahar, 163
Farrar, 47, 70, 140
Faustus Socinus, 26
Feine, 39
Felder, 48, 49, 96, 118, 145, 170, 173
Feldman, 74, 77
Felton, 128
Field, 140, 155
Fillion, 48, 96, 118, 140
Findlay, 18, 19
Fleetwood, 47
Foote, 47, 49
Foxell, 46
Frederich, 46
Furrer, 43, 70, 97

Galilee, 74
Gamaliel, 80
Garvie, 43
Geikie, 46
Gelpke, 43
Geodfridus, 139
Geometra, 4
George, 64
Gess, 39
Gigot, 48, 65, 101, 135, 139, 141, 175
Gilbert, 43
Gnostics, 19, 24, 25, 26
God's Fatherly relation to man, in Old Testament, 81–82: in Apocryphal books of the Old Testament, 83–84; to special individuals, 83; among the Greeks, 83–84; in New Testament, 188–190
God, Jewish conception of, 81ff.: anthropomorphisms of Old Testament changed, 85; tendency to transcendental view of, 86; names of, 86, 192; subject to the Law, 86
Godet, 42, 43, 64, 95, 134
Gore, 43
Goulburn, 47, 80
Gratiani, 56
Green, 87
Gregory, of Nazianzus, 14–15: of Nyssa, 15; the Great, 14, 110, 133, 184
Grotius, 36
Guignebert, 66
Guinebert, 40

Haecker, 43
Hahn, 47
Hall, Stanley, 46, 47, 93
Hammond, 36
Hamyln, 41
Hanna, 46
Harden, 64
Harnack, 40, 61, 62, 63, 64, 118, 163, 175, 178
Harris, 151
Hartmann, 45
Hase, Karl, 39, 66, 94
Hastings, 48, 109
Hausrath, 66, 80, 128
Hawkins, 62
Haymo of Halberstadt, 30, 137
Heer, 175
Henry, Matt, 129
Heretics, the early, 23, 172
Herford, 86
Hermas, the Pastor of, 14
Herod the Great, 73–74
Hess, 43
Hillel, 80
Hillman, 62
Hippolytus, 23, 25
Hitchcock, 43, 134
Hoffman, 18–19
Hofmeister, 34, 131
Hollmann, 75, 97
Holy Office, condemned propositions, 165, 184
Holtzmann, H., 39, 40, 60, 65, 92, 107, 129, 184
Holtzmann, Oscar, 39, 41, 67, 70, 129
Homer, 84
Homes, 47, 49
Hugo de S. Caro, 35
Hurter, 160

Ignatius, Martyr, 13, 62
Irenaeus, 6

Irenaeus, St., 3, 4, 6, 13, 14, 19, 22, 23, 24, 26, 56, 58, 61, 173, 190
Isaac of Stella, 32

Jacobus, 47, 49
Jacquier, 60
James, St., 71
Jansenius, Yprensis, 35, 37, 79, 140
Jansens, 160
Jeremias, 65, 66
Jerome, 14, 15, 16, 17, 76, 131, 135, 143, 152, 172, 174
Jewish Child: names for, 74; schools for, 74–75; training left to parents, 75; religious training, 75ff.
John Duns Scotus, 33
John of Damascus, 15
John Scotus Erigena, 32
Joseph, only in the place of a Father, 16, 17, 18, 104, 135
Josephus, 66, 67, 73, 74, 154
Joshua ben Gamala, 74
Josias, 66
Jülicher, 60
Justin Martyr, 14, 62, 155, 163, 171
Juvencus, 10, 12, 14, 56, 100

Keil, 46, 102
Keim, 41, 67, 70, 94, 95, 129
Kennedy, 74
Kent, 39, 74, 129
Kilpatrick, 41
Knabenbauer, 48, 125, 132
Knowling, 64
Koran, 19
Krenkel, 66
Kühl, 46
κύριος, applied to the infant Jesus, 170

Lagarde, 63
Lagrange, 48, 63, 80, 129, 137, 141
Lange, 45, 94, 107
à Lapide, Cornelius, 37, 79, 80, 118, 129, 137, 141
LeCanus, 48–49
Leo the Great, 11, 53, 55, 56, 132
Lepicier, 160
Lepin, 48, 49, 173, 180
Lesêtre, 48, 80
Lester, 61
Lightfoot, John, 76, 79, 80, 128, 155
Lobstein, 61, 65
Loisy, 43, 60, 61, 62, 65, 71, 107, 116, 142
Löw, 77
Lucas, 36, 79, 118, 129
Lucianus, 26
Ludolphus of Saxony, 34, 36

Luke, literary dependence, 67, 68
Luke, the author of the Third Gospel as a historian, 60, 61
Luther, 34, 136

Maas, 73, 80, 160
MacDermott, 45
MacEvilly, 48, 49
Machen, 63, 69
Mackintosh, 40, 41, 46
Maclaren, 47, 105
Maclean, 86
MacRory, 60
Magi, 14
Mahaffy, 74
Malan, 45
Malchion, 25
Maldonatus, 34, 36, 80, 129, 137, 141
Mangenot, 48, 63
Marcion, 24, 25, 26, 61
Marcosians, 3, 4, 56, 58, 190
Marcus, 24
Martin, 40, 61, 66, 68, 144
Martineau, 40
Martyr, S. Polycarpi, 152
Mary, Mother of God, 170: handmaid of the dispensation, 8; Luke's authority for Infancy narrative, 64, 71, 72; Luke's authority, 159
Mary's, preserving all, 142; Question, 80, 105ff., 138; motherly point of view, 108; words and action, explanation of, 147ff.
Mason, 103
Matthews, 74
Melanchthon, 34, 36, 131, 136
Melchisedecian heresy, 25
Menochius, 129
Merx, 40
Messiah, the, 83
Meyer, 44, 62, 67, 70, 92, 107, 136, 139
Michaelis, J. C., 34, 37
Michel, 19–21
Miller, H., 40, 66
Milner, 64
Moffatt, 63
Monnier, 42, 43
Montefiore, 41, 66, 71
Moore, 84
Moses, 66
Moulton and Milligan, 155
Muratorian Canon, 61

Natalis, Alexander, 37, 80, 129, 141
Nazareth, 74
Neander, 41, 94
Nebe, 42, 127

INDEX

Nestle, 55, 58
Neumann, 40, 65, 69
Nevin, 47
Nicholas of Lyra, 34
Nicoll, 48, 49
Nilus, 15, 107
Nolloth, 46, 64
Nösgen, 42, 95

Oesterley, 86
Olshausen, 45, 64, 129, 136
Oosterzee, 45
Ophites, 24
Origen, 4, 5, 9, 12, 14, 16, 17, 53, 56, 58, 100, 130, 131, 133, 136, 137, 142, 153, 173, 190
Owen, 47, 94, 196

"Parents" of Christ, 16, 17, 18, 75, 135ff., 146ff.: no negligence on their part, 136; surprised at scene, 137; non-understanding, explanations of, 139ff.; significance of, 140, 142
Pasch, Ritual of, at time of Christ, 78: pilgrims to, 78; fervour at, 78; Psalms sung at, 78
Paterson, 43
Patritius, 129
Paul of Samosata, 25–26
Pauli Praedicatio, 174
Paulus, 43, 116
Paynter, 45
Peabody, 41
Pesch, 48
Pfleiderer, O., 41, 60, 61, 65, 66, 71, 95
Phelan, 47
Philo, 75, 84
Photius, 17, 30, 56, 58, 131, 132
Picard, 48, 129
Piscator, 36
Plato, 84
$\pi\lambda\eta\rho o \acute{u} \mu \epsilon \nu o \nu$, meaning of, 151–152
Plutarch, 66
Plummer, 18, 47, 63, 69, 79, 101, 103, 106, 125, 129, 134, 141, 142, 143, 151, 155, 162
Plumptre, 45, 147
Pohle-Preuss, 48, 157, 160
Polus, 36, 79, 141
Power, 54, 55, 59, 104, 127, 129, 139
de Pressensé, 23, 24
Preuschen, 123, 125
Pricaeus, 98
$\pi\rho o \kappa \acute{o} \pi \tau \omega$, meaning of, 154, 155
Pseudo-Augustinus, 17, 137
Purves, 63, 64

Quirinius, P. Sulpicius, 77

Rabbis, the, 80, 125, 126, 128, 129
Ramsay, vi, 44, 60, 61, 63, 65, 71, 77
Reid, 18, 19
Reinhard, 41, 194
Renan, 64, 65, 144
Resch, 63
Reubelt, 46
Reuss, 43
Réville, 42, 65, 66, 94, 95, 129
Rice, 140
Riddle, 145
Robertson, A. T., 44, 60, 65, 111, 188
Robinson, 46, 103
Ryan, 140
Ryle, 47

Sadler, 47
Salmeron, 36, 80
Samuel, 66, 67, 68
Sanday, 48, 63, 64, 86, 172, 174, 188, 191, 192, 193
Schaefer, 48, 99, 185
Schaff, 47
Schenkel, 39, 40, 66
Schlatter, 43
Schleiermacher, 41, 65, 69, 70, 129
Schmeidel, 60, 61, 65, 66
Schmidt, H., 43, 95, 101
Schmidt, Nat, 40, 70
Schmidt, P. W., 40, 43
Scholia Vetera in Lucam, 29
Schools at time of Christ, 74ff.
Schottgenius, 132
Schulte, 15
Schumacher, 96, 179, 188
Schürer, 40, 74, 75, 76, 80, 128
Schweitzer, 39, 40
Scott, E. F., 44
Seitz, 48
Shammai, 80
Shannahan, 48, 109
Sheldon, 42, 97
Sickenberger, 4, 5
Simeon Metaphrastes, 31, 56, 58, 79, 107, 133, 136, 142
Simon, 74
Smith, D., 49
Smith, 111, 163
Sodon, von, 58
Solomon, 66
Soltan, 61, 65
Sophronius, 17
Spaeth, 40
Stalker, 47, 49, 181, 189, 195
Stapfer, 39, 70, 163

INDEX

Steinmetzer, 61, 67
Steinmeyer, 46, 61, 70, 118, 141
Stella, 35
Stephens, 188
Stewart, 48
Stier, 46, 97, 101, 134
Stoics, Greek, 84
Stokes, 183
Strauss, 43, 65, 66, 116, 129, 136, 139, 142
Streatfeild, 110, 187, 193
Suarez, 136, 138
Suetonius, 66
σύνεσις, in the New Testament, 122
συνίημι, in the New Testament, 121–
Sweet, 46, 61, 63, 64, 71, 149 122
Sylveira, 35, 37, 145
Symmachus, 155

Talmud, Baba Bathra 21a, 74: Aboth V 21, 76; Yoma 82A, 77; Megilla 21A, 128
Targums, 85, 91
Tasker, 19
Temple: part in which Christ was found, 79, 80; episode, silence of other Gospels on, 181; historicity of, 65ff.
Terrien, 48, 141, 146
Tertullian, 10, 24, 25, 56, 58, 62
Theodore, of Mopsuesetia, 26
Theodoret, 9, 13, 15, 25, 26, 56, 58, 106, 107, 133, 160
Theodoret of Cyrus, 8, 9
Theodotus, of Byzantium, 25
Theodotus the banker, 25
Theophylact, 31, 93, 137
Thiriet, 48
Tholuck, 70, 129
Thomas, St., 4, 160, 162, 173
Thomas of Aquin, 33
Thomson, 44
Tirinus, 37
Tischendorf, 9, 17, 53
Titus of Bostra, 5, 56, 93, 103
Toletus, 35, 36
Torrey, 63, 159

Toy, 63, 87
Tractatus de Rebaptismate, 174
Trollope, 129
Tyndal, 121

Usener, 61, 113

Valentinians, 4, 6, 24
Vallings, 47
Veuillott, 48
Victor, 56
Victorinus of Pettau, 24
Vigilius, 15
Vincent, 101, 123
Virgin Birth, 62, 65
Vogels, 17, 58, 69, 137
Völter, 41, 61, 65, 66, 71
Von Sodon, 41
Vonier, 160, 162

Wallis, 44, 108, 144
Ward, 48, 160
Warfield, 126, 127
Weber, 39
Weinel, 40, 62
Weiss, B., 39, 55, 58, 63, 70, 139
Weiss, J., 41, 61, 65, 95
Wellhausen, 40, 61
Wendt, 42, 70, 95, 164
Wernle, 40, 61
Westcott-Hort, 54, 55, 58
Wetstein, 76, 128
Whitefoord, 129
Wicks, 82
Wilkinson, 105, 108, 146, 147
Wisdom, word in the New Testament, 151
Wolf, 80
Wordsworth, J., 57
Wrede, 40
Wright, 63, 64, 141
Wünsche, 80

Zacharias, Chrysopolitanus, 31, 32
Zahn, 63, 139
Zeugma, in Luke, 159
Zimmermann, 62, 69

www.ingramcontent.com/pod-product-compliance
Lightning Source LLC
Chambersburg PA
CBHW071428150426
43191CB00008B/1080